Let Me
Dream Again

Let Me Dream Again

Essays on the Moving Image

Luke McKernan

Sticking Place Books
New York

ISBN 979-8-89976-020-4

Contents

To Marja

Acknowledgments

The idea for this book came from a suggestion made by Ian Christie. He introduced me to Paul Cronin, who quickly accepted it for Sticking Place Books. I am very grateful to both.

Many people have helped in forming the essays in this book, through conversations, online comments and simple friendship. I would particularly like to thank the following for their help and encouragement: Sergio Angelini, for all our good discussions; Neil Brand, for music that understands stories; Dr Libby Damjanovic for suggesting literature on film and memory; Bryony Dixon, for silent film knowledge and image services; David Dunkley Gyimah, for proposing an investigation into the filming of the Windrush story, with additional thanks to Jake Berger and Andrew Martin at BBC Archive and Paul Wilson at the British Library for their generous assistance; David Hendy, for introducing me to Paddy Scannell's work; the late Stephen Herbert, for being the wisest of friends; Pamela Hutchinson, for suggesting something on spoilers; Jeff Jarvis, for sharing his enthusiasm for *Cheers* and his interest in neuroscience; Linda Kaye, for her dedication to the cause of newsreels; Mariann Lewinsky, for the *Zufallshund*; Eden Parker, for explaining video games; William Raban, for his memories of making *Thames Film*; James Scott, for his kind words regarding *Every Picture Tells A Story*; Joe Thompson, for many heartening comments down the years; the late Brian Winston, who so admired Robert Flaherty's quest for the perfect light; John Wyver, for his continual encouragement and enthusiasm.

Thanks also go to the good people at the British Film Institute and the British Library, especially the knowledgeable and obliging reference team in the Newsroom. Historical film research is now unthinkable without the *British Newspaper Archive* (https://www.britishnewspaperarchive.co.uk), a collaboration between the British Library and Findmypast; the *Media History Digital Library* (https://mediahistoryproject.org), created by David Pierce and now managed by the Wisconsin Center for Film and Theater Research; and the *Internet Archive* (https://archive.org). Long may they run.

My most helpful source (and acutest critic) has been Marja Kingma, to whom this book is dedicated.

Some of these essays were previously adapted for publication in print, and my grateful thanks go to the following for permission to republish here: Amsterdam University Press, for 'The Lives of the Characters in Dickensian,' in Ian Christie and Annie van den Oever (eds.), *Stories: Screen Narrative in the Digital Era* (Amsterdam University Press, 2018); the International Buster Keaton Society for 'Just a Brixton Shop Girl,' *The Keaton Chronicle*, vol. 19 issue 3, Summer 2011; *Sight and Sound*, courtesy of The British Film Institute, for 'The Colours of War,' *Sight and Sound*, vol. 28 issue 4, April 2018; the Sir Lenny Henry Centre for Media Diversity for 'Filming Windrush,' *Representology: The Journal of Media and Diversity*, issue 5, Summer 2023.

Permission to republish images has been given by the following: British Film Institute, pp. xvi, xvii, 81, 130; A Guy Named Nyal (https://flic.kr/2pru2bu, CC-BY-SA 2.0), p. 341; Learning on Screen, p. 91; Luke McKernan, pp. 87, 136, 374, 381; Marja Kingma, p. 158; Jason Tester (https://flic.kr/p/tboZZQ, CC BY-ND 2,0), p. 15; Vecteezy.com, p. 355. Public domain images have been accessed from the following: Boston Public Library, pp. 259-264; British Library, pp. 224, 227, 301; Ivan Butler, *Silent Magic* (Columbus, 1987), p. 232; Arthur Calder-Marshall, *The Innocent Eye* (W. H. Allen, 1963), p. 330; Joel Finler, *Silent Cinema* (B. T. Batsford, 1997), p. 336; Wikimedia Commons (CC-BY-SA 4.0), pp. 127, 138, 244, 245, 308. All other images, the majority of which are framegrabs taken from DVD and Blu-Ray discs, are claimed under Fair Use.

Cover image: Anna Karina in *Vivre sa vie* (France 1962).

Introduction

Is this a dream? Then waking would be pain
Oh! do not wake me, do not wake me
Let me dream again!

B. C. Stephenson, 'Let Me Dream Again' (1875)

After four decades of working with moving images, I am still trying to understand what they mean. I have acquired, preserved, documented, promoted, exhibited, researched and written about the medium, but what did it all signify? Certainty over the value of film was what led me to seek a career in archives and libraries that cared for moving images, but as the career progressed, so the questions grew. Not questions of doubt, but rather questions about what were the particular functions and qualities of an undeniably bewitching medium.

Why are we so drawn to the screen? What do moving images tell us? How and why do they work? What do we gain by having them and what would we lose by not having them? What was it that film first brought to society that was so revolutionary? What is the significance of the moving image in the multi-format, hybrid world through which we communicate today? Are films important and, if so, why?

It was to explore such questions that I started to write online. The blog format encouraged a style that differed from traditional academic publishing and suggested a fresh way of thinking. There was an opportunity to be freer, more speculative, definitely more informal, with an imperative to be engaging if you wanted to have people read you and stick with you. I began in 2007 with a blog on silent films, *The Bioscope*, wrote also for various institutional platforms, then in 2012 started an eponymous blog which has covered many subjects, but has always had a particular focus on moving images.

Writing for my personal site, I found myself returning again and again to two interrelated areas of enquiry, which are reflected in the selection of essays for this book: story and form.

Storytelling is fundamental to how we understand the world and our place in it. This is a key conclusion of the exciting recent work in neuroscience which has overturned ideas of comprehension and what it is to be human. We think we apprehend reality, but instead the brain reconstructs 'reality' for us. The world we experience is what Will Storr, in *The Science of Storytelling*, calls 'an act of creation by the storytelling brain.'[1]

Setting aside the small matter of the conclusion of this science, which is that we exist in a meaningless, chaotic void in which our idea of reality is a fiction, the notion of the storytelling brain is a very useful means of understanding why moving images work. They serve a fundamental human need, all the more powerfully for seeming to replicate the function of dreams. This is not simply storytelling as the relaying of standard narratives, but the apprehension of everything we need to feel reassured that we are who we are, and we are where we are. When it comes to stories on film, a televised weather forecast is just as important as *Citizen Kane*.

Some writers on how film narratives work, and how screenwriters might learn from this, have seized on these studies of the brain.[2] Some in film studies have incorporated neuroscience into ideas of how films operate, though not without controversy, as not all accept such 'brain science' as the sole answer to how we see, or appreciate the aesthetics of, moving images.[3] Neuroscience may not explain *how* we see moving images, or not wholly so, but it does go a long way to indicating *why*. There is so much here to excite anyone engaged with moving images, whether fiction (what-

---

[1] Will Storr, *The Science of Storytelling* (London: William Collins, 2019), p. 21.
[2] On neuroscience and screen writers, see Paul Joseph Gulino and Connie Shears (eds.), *The Science of Screenwriting: The Neuroscience Behind Storytelling Strategies* (New York: Bloomsbury Academic, 2018).
[3] Following the publication of Vittorio Gallese and Michele Guerra, *The Empathic Screen: Cinema and Neuroscience* (Oxford: Oxford University Press, 2019), written by a neuroscientist (Gallese) and a film theorist, there was much debate about its conclusions. See David Bordwell, 'Brains, Bodies, and Movies: Ways of thinking about the psychology of cinema,' *Observations on Film Art*, 29 April 2020, https://www.davidbordwell.net/blog/2020/04/29/brains-bodies-and-movies-ways-of-thinking-about-the-psychology-of-cinema and 'Mirror Neurons and Cinema: Further discussion,' *Observations on Film Art*, 16 August 2020, https://www.davidbordwell.net/blog/2020/08/16/mirror-neurons-and-cinema-further-discussion.

ever that might mean) or non-fiction. When neuroscientist David Eagleman writes that 'everything you experience—every sight, sound, smell—rather than being a direct experience, is an electrochemical rendition in a dark theater,' the invitation to understand the brain as a cinema, chemically as well as metaphorically, is compelling.[4]

I am not a neuroscientist, nor a film theorist for that matter. I simply want to grasp why moving images work, how they have the appeal that they have always had, and which made their arrival in the mid-1890s so seismic. At the heart of this lie stories, without which we cannot make sense of the world. Some of the essays reflect this interest directly, some indirectly. Some simply tell stories of their own. But the plain message for me is that moving images only work because of our storytelling brains. Understanding films, of whatever kind, as a source of stories, is vital.

The other theme that informs this book is form. Films are shapeshifters. They are forever reinventing themselves. Technically this has always been the case, as what was shot on negative film needed to be converted to positive film for projection. Technological developments led to different film stocks, different formats, different forms of colour reproduction, different kinds of sound, and finally the discarding of film as a carrier of motion pictures and the universal adoption of digital. Historical films now need to be restored to give them a new life, but restoration is an ambiguous concept. Can films ever remain as they were originally produced and understood, or must they inevitably undergo processes of change to retain meaning? Change in the digital era is in any case inevitable. The digital photographic image itself is inherently manipulable. It is never only what it is, but always what it could be.[5]

Moving images also change their meaning when placed in new contexts. The moment someone first placed one moving image shot, taken at one point in time, alongside another taken at another point of time—i.e. editing—those shots changed their meaning because of the interdependence that was created, triggered by the mind's search for stories. The shot gains new meanings when it is placed alongside

---

[4] David Eagleman, *The Brain: The Story of You* (Edinburgh: Canongate, 2015), pp. 41-42.
[5] See the prescient William J. Mitchell, *The Reconfigured Eye: Visual Truth In The Post-photographic Era* (Cambridge, Mass./MIT Press, 1992); also Ron Burnett, *How Images Think* (Cambridge, Mass.: The MIT Press, 2004), Fred Ritchin, *After Photography* (New York: W. W. Norton & Company, 2009).

another shot, not only in the creation of an intended narrative, but when shots or sequences of shots are incorporated into narratives for which they were not originally designed.

This happens with compilation films or television programmes that employ archive film alongside still images and commentary to illustrate an argument. A contest then arises between context and authenticity. Is that film clip what it once was, or what we now want it to be? If there is no extant film of the *Titanic* at sea and yet we are shown a clip which says that what we are seeing is the *Titanic* heading for an iceberg, is that a lie, or has the clip somehow come to signify what we the viewers want it to signify? Where is the true meaning in any piece of film?

Moving images capture a moment in time, or its appearance, only for time to change and the moving image with it. It is a constant process of rediscovery and loss. Even where we have a fully edited film or television programme, which retains the form in which it was created (dutifully preserved and restored by an archive), it becomes something else for each succeeding generation. Silent films no longer speak to those attuned to a screen world of sound. Monochrome films are rejected by those who can only understand colour. The old simply become older. Of course such obsolescence is true for any cultural artefact, but film's appeal to the heart, its propensity for telling stories, make its fragile nature especially poignant. Film is nothing but a dream that is forever disappearing, even as we return to the screen expecting new dreams to come along.

The title of this book is taken from a British film of 1900. It was made by George Albert Smith, one of the pioneers of editing, and hence the creation of film stories.[6] When Smith made *Let Me Dream Again* he was probably thinking of a popular song of that title from twenty-five years before, with words by B. C. Stephenson and music by Arthur Sullivan. The words suggest the deep compulsion to view that lies at the heart of cinema, but at first sight Smith's film is more of a cheap joke than anything that

---

[6] The British filmmaker Robert Paul, in *Come Along Do!* (UK 1898) and the Frenchman Georges Méliès with *La Lune à un mètre* (*The Astronomer's Dream*) (France 1898) are often credited with the innovation of editing, closely followed by Smith's *A Kiss in the Tunnel* (UK 1899). Frank Gray, *The Brighton School and the Birth of British Film* (Cham: Palgrave Macmillan, 2019), pp. 180-189. However multi-scene editing of non-fiction films preceded that of fiction films. See Stephen Bottomore, 'Shots in the Dark: The Real Origins of Film Editing,' in Thomas Elsaesser and Adam Barker (eds.), *Early Cinema: Space, Frame, Narrative* (London: British Film Institute, 1990), pp. 104-113.

might move us. A man is seen drinking and petting with an agreeable young woman in pierrot costume. The picture dissolves to the same man, possibly older, lying in bed with his complaining wife. He pulls faces indicating that he would far rather return to his dreamworld than face his domestic reality.

Let Me Dream Again – the dream.

Film historians have focussed on the technical innovations of *Let Me Dream Again* rather than its graceless humour. It is an early example of a two-shot narrative. It is possibly the first film to show a dissolve from dream into reality, such as became a staple of film thereafter, though strictly speaking the way the film goes out of focus then back into focus for the second shot is not a true dissolve. It is also interesting for the camera set-up in the second shot, with the couple standing up (or else seated) in front of an upright bed, to give the impression that they are lying down.

But the story alone has its complexities. What is the relationship between the man (played by Tom Green) and the two women? We know that the first shot in the film depicts a dream. According to the entry for the film in the production company's catalogue, he is dreaming of his youth, as it states that at the end of the film he wants to 'dream again of his youthful days and its follies.'[7] But it is

---

[7] 'A scene at a masquerade ball showing a couple having a tête-à-tête helped

not clear if the woman in both shots is meant to be the same person at different stages in life, or if they are two different women, or if the first is a fantasy and not the representation of an actual person at all. The film could have been read differently according to the viewer's experience or prejudices. Or perhaps there is an autobiographical twist involved, given that the younger woman is played by Smith's wife and filmmaking collaborator, Laura Bayley, and the woman in the second shot is played by Tom Green's wife, Nellie. Film scholar Frank Gray has pointed out that *Let Me Dream Again* was produced at the same as Sigmund Freud's key text *The Interpretation of Dreams* and can serve as an illustration of Freud's theory of the wish-fulfilment of dreams.[8] Whatever the scenario, it is a story about the fear of reality matched with the necessity of dreaming. Behind our dreams lie realities, while maybe all of what we think are our realities are only dreams, or stories.

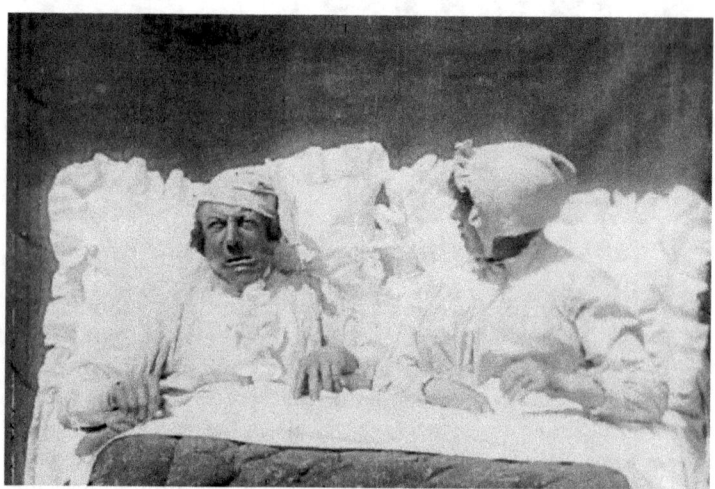

Let Me Dream Again – the reality.

---

on by several bottles. He proves an ardent lover and progresses nicely when the scene gradually changes, dissolving to a view of a bedroom with an old fat couple sleeping peacefully, when the man suddenly starts up in bed (evidently awakening from his dream of which the preceding scene is the subject) and getting a view of the stout Amazon to whom he is linked and with whom he quarrels, reclines on his pillow to dream again of his youthful days and its follies.' Warwick Trading Company catalogue, September 1900, film no. 5730, p. 149, reproduced in John Barnes, *The Beginnings of Cinema in England 1894-1901 — Volume Five: 1900* (Exeter: Exeter University Press, 1997), pp. 198-199.
[8] Gray, *The Brighton School and the Birth of British Film*, p. 200.

There was much copying of good ideas in the early film world, and in 1901 *Let Me Dream Again* was remade by Ferdinand Zecca for the French firm Pathé Frères as *Rêve et réalité* (*Dream and Reality*).[9] The essays in this book are in two sections, Dreams and Realities, acknowledging both Smith and Zecca. Though the majority of the essays in the Dreams section touch on stories, and several of those in Realities on form, there is overlap between the two. The media covered by the essays include film, television, online video, video exhibitions, and video games. They take us from Eadweard Muybridge's sequence photography of the 1880s to the dawn of artificial intelligence in film production, and embrace such topics as memory, literary connections (Charles Dickens, James Joyce, Stevie Smith), spoilers, prequels and sequels, politics, fame, sport (football and the Olympic Games), playing dead, libraries, anarchists, feral children, David Attenborough, *YouTube*, screen shapes and sizes, migration, colourisation, fairy tales, clean shirts, and stray dogs.

The pieces derive from texts that when they were published online were called posts, but in print have magically turned into essays. Perhaps it might be easiest to think of them as entertainments with ideas. The earliest was first published in 2000, the most recent in 2024. When the texts were posts they came with hyperlinks; here they are accompanied by footnotes. Each essay is followed by a short paragraph giving its publication history and some extra information. The essays can be read in any order, but some thought has gone into shaping them as they are. There is a form to the arrangement, and a story to be told.

---

[9] Unlike Smith, Zecca employs a genuine dissolve to link together his two shots, while his older woman is played by a man.

Note

All of the essays in this book were originally published on the websites *Luke McKernan* (https://lukemckernan.com), *The Bioscope* (https://thebioscope.net) or *Moving Image* (http://britishlibrary.typepad.co.uk/movingimage), with the exception of 'Just a Brixton Shop Girl,' originally published online by the International Buster Keaton Society (https://busterkeaton.org). All texts have been amended for publication here, with added footnotes and some additional material.

All film, video and television programme titles are given in the language of the work's primary production country, followed by an English release title where relevant, countries of production and year of production. The titles of film, video and television programmes, books, plays and websites are given in italics; parts of series, episode titles, essays, poems and web pages are given in single quotation marks.

For film, video and television programme credits the *Internet Movie Database* has been used as the primary reference, with cross-referencing to the *AFI Catalog of Feature Films* (https://aficatalog.afi.com), *BFI Collections Search* (https://collections-search.bfi.org.uk/web), and Marrku Salmi (ed.), *National Film Archive: Catalogue of Stills Posters and Designs* (London: British Film Institute, 1982). All running times given are for the original release version of a film, video or television programme, except where specified in the text.

All weblinks cited were active as of 31 May 2025. Long links have been shortened, using *TinyURL* (https://tinyurl.com), for ease of use.

No artificial intelligence was used in the writing of this book.

DREAMS

1.

What Happens Next?

Plots, stories and spoilers

All we ever do is tell stories to one another.

Back in 1999 *Sight and Sound* published a plot summary for *The Blair Witch Project* (USA 1999), as it does for all films released theatrically in the UK. Such plot summaries give the plain details of the plot of the film, as a matter of record, alongside the cast and credit details. Except that on this occasion they did not give the full plot summary. It ended with a row of dots, not giving away what happens in the horror film when the heroine enters a basement with her camera. For this reader it was annoying, because of the lapse in standards for what was meant to be a source for future reference, the magazine apparently kowtowing to the film's publicity machine.[1]

This lapse was—one hopes—a one-off, but it shows how certain films depend on attracting an audience through having some plot twist, or gimmick, which ostensibly becomes the chief reason for going to see it. 'Don't give away the ending—it's the only one we have!' urged publicity for Alfred Hitchcock's *Psycho* (USA 1960). The urge to know what happens next, and the sense of disappointment or even betrayal when some find out the answer before they have seen the film is powerful. The greatest crime a film reviewer can commit is to give away key plot details. Anyone writing about films online feels obliged to preface their comments with the warning that there are 'spoilers' ahead. And my question is, why does this matter?

In his 1927 book *Aspects of the Novel*, E. M. Forster sets out an understanding of how novels operate through seven such aspects: story, people, plot, fantasy, prophecy, pattern and rhythm. He begins with a now famous summary of different people's view of the story:

[1] Charles Taylor, 'The Blair Witch Project,' *Sight and Sound*, vol. 9 issue 11 (November 1999), pp. 38-39.

Let us listen to three voices. If you ask one type of man, 'What does a novel do?' he will reply placidly: 'Well I don't know—it seems a funny sort of question to ask— a novel's a novel—well, I don't know—I suppose it kind of tells a story, so to speak.' He is quite good-tempered and vague, and probably driving a motor-bus at the same time and paying no more attention to literature than it merits. Another man, whom I visualize as on a golf-course, will be aggressive and brisk. He will reply: 'What does a novel do? Why, tell a story, and I've no use for it if it didn't. I like a story. You can take your art, you can take your literature, you can take your music, but give me a good story. And I like a story, mind, and my wife's the same.' And a third man says in a sort of drooping regretful voice, 'Yes—oh, dear, yes—the novel tells a story.' I respect and admire the first speaker. I detest and fear the second. And the third is myself.[2]

Forster acknowledges that the story is the fundamental aspect without which the novel could not exist, defining it as 'a narrative of events arranged in their time sequence' with but one merit, 'that of making the audience want to know what happens next.' It is a primitive desire, he argues, the need to know what lies on the next page, the necessary structure on which the work of art is built, but not the art itself. There has to be a story for there to be meaning, but that is all. He differentiates story from plot, which he defines as 'a narrative of events, the emphasis falling on causality.' He gives this example:

'The king died and then the queen died,' is a story. 'The king died, and then the queen died of grief,' is a plot.[3]

This is useful, and seems reasonable. It shows us why, say, a detective novel may be considered a lower form of art, being driven entirely by the mechanics of what happens next, and tragic drama a higher form, where causality is all. But Forster then suffers an interesting lapse. Having earlier referenced the storytelling of prehistoric man and the means by which Scheherazade stays alive

---

[2] E. M. Forster, *Aspects of the Novel* (Harmondsworth: Penguin Books, 1962), pp. 33-34.
[3] Forster, *Aspects of the Novel*, p. 93.

through storytelling because the sultan always want to know what happens next, he writes:

> Consider the death of the queen. If it is in a story we say 'and then?' If it is in a plot we ask 'why?' That is the fundamental difference between these two aspects of the novel. A plot cannot be told to a gaping audience of cave men or to a tyrannical sultan or to their modern descendant the movie-public. They can only be kept awake by 'and then—and then –' they can only supply curiosity. But a plot demands intelligence and memory also.[4]

This reveals a lazy prejudice against the supposedly unthinking film audience, and it also undermines his argument. The film audience (and the readers of novels) almost never pins its hopes on the primitive mechanics of the story alone. It consigns formulaic genre works to the lowest form of cinema art—the B-movie that is just there to fill up some time in the auditorium. The cinema audience demands plausibility, which is the coming together of character, atmosphere and incident. Plausibility is hand-maiden to causality.

'And then?' and 'Why?' are not separate conditions, but the inseparable key to how we follow narratives. The need to know what happens next drives the urge to turn the page or stick around for the next reel. But we need just as much to be convinced that it is worth doing so, which means ultimately that what we are being offered is grounded in truth. How that truth is expressed may often lie in the artistry that Forster champions, but the essential feature of that artistry must be plausibility—truth to nature, be that in character, situation, description, philosophy or whatever. It is what makes any story worth telling.

Human beings need stories; they define what we are. We need to eat and sleep and socialise, but so do all other animals. Only humans tell stories, and construct their idea of the world through stories. Yuval Noah Harari, in his book *Sapiens*, argues that what has made humans unique and successful as a species is their propensity for imagining things collectively. Human lives are governed by imagined realities—let us call them stories—by belief in concepts such as gods, religion, nations, money, limited liability companies and human rights, which do not objectively exist.[5] They are believed in because to live we need to believe. The

---

[4] Forster, *Aspects of the Novel*, p. 94.
[5] Yuval Noah Harari, *Sapiens* (London: Harvill Secker, 2015), pp. 28-36.

story, a construct which puts a shape to life, which says that there is a beginning, a middle and an end, and says that what holds this thread together is reason or a set of rules which can be predicted to a degree, is fundamental to humans' collective sense of themselves. Without stories we have no idea where we are.

This point can be illustrated by the story of Victor of Aveyron, the feral child captured in 1800, who is the subject of François Truffaut's classic film *L'Enfant sauvage* (*The Wild Child*) (France 1970). Aged around nine when he was caught, after having lived wild in a forest for a number of years, he was cared for and closely observed by French medical student Jean Marc Gaspard Itard. Unable to speak, seemingly indifferent to any kind of human interaction, trapped in a world solely of his own understanding, Victor was—as the philosopher Etienne Bonnot de Condillac, a great influence on Itard, wrote of another feral child—living in a continual present:

> Supposing in order to try every hypothesis, that he had likewise remembered the time when he lived in the forest, it would have been impossible for him to represent it to himself but by the perceptions which he would have re-called to mind. These perceptions could be very few; and as he had not remembrance of those which had preced-ed, followed, or interrupted them, he would never have recollected the succession of the parts of this time [...] In a word, the confused remembrance of his former state would have reduced him to the absurdity of imagining himself to have always existed, though he was as yet in-capable of representing his pretended eternity to himself but as a moment.[6]

Victor had no sense of history, because he had no sense of others by which to measure such a sense of self. Theories of the development of the mind of a child stress the importance of narra-tives as a means for children to create worlds through which they come to understand themselves and human nature. Victor, robbed of a childhood and the company that should nurture it, understood neither.

This helps show how stories define what it is to be human. Not just written stories, but gossip, news, information, instruc-

---

[6] Quoted in Michael Newton, *Savage Girls and Wild Boys: A History of Feral Children* (London: Faber and Faber, 2002), pp. 115-116.

tions, plans, events, games, competitions, and all forms of socialisation. We digest experience and relay it to others as stories, with a beginning, a middle, and end, and a lesson to be learned. Without stories we are just a wild thing, lost in a forest.

Jean March Gaspard Itard (François Truffaut)
and Victor (Jean-Pierre Cargol) in *L'enfant sauvage*.

All of which brings us back to spoilers. When I first thought to write this essay I was minded to defend the use of spoilers, saying that those who are upset when plot points are given away may have a limited appreciation of art. Why things happened the way they did was more important that the plain what, and it was the function of the film or the novel to demonstrate the why, with the story simply being the structural means to achieve this. That is what E. M. Forster was arguing.

But now I am not so sure. There is something about the anticipation of what happens next which is an important aspect of how we determine truth. It is there in the suspense, followed by the satisfaction of understanding. Knowing the 'how' before we appreciate the 'why' diminishes the latter. The two can only work together. Spoilers rob us of experience. I cannot promise that I will not give away plot details, in this book or in any future writings; to do so can look a bit too much like playing the filmmaker's, or novelist's, game for them. But I will try to understand the annoyance a little more.

Originally published as 'What Happens Next?,' 21 September 2015, https://lukemckernan.com/2015/09/21/what-happens-next, and reproduced here with small emendations. On feral children, see Michael Newton, *Savage Girls and Wild Boys: A History of Feral Children* (London: Faber and Faber, 2002). On narrative and children's development, see David Wood, *How Children Think and Learn* (Malden MA/Oxford/ Carlton, Victoria: Blackwell, 1998).

2.

Losing the Plot

Getting film and video stories in the wrong order

Pity *The New York Times'* television critic Mike Hales, who recently reviewed the first few episodes of Amazon's new series *Goliath* (USA 2016-2021). Hales complained of the series having a 'needlessly complicated structure,'

> presumably because the first episode leaves so much unanswered, the next jumps back in time to fill in the history of the case—and when the second episode ends, the story hasn't even caught up to where it started. The narrative juggling has the feel of stretching—of starting with a story suited for an episode of traditional TV or maybe a feature film and extending it to more than nine hours. Final judgment on that will have to wait until all 10 episodes are available.[1]

Four days after his review appeared in print and online a correction was published. The hapless critic had watched the first two episodes in the wrong order. Sadly the original review has now disappeared from the newspaper's website and one which understands *Goliath* in the order its creators intended has taken its place.

Disordered films used to be more common in the days of reels. When films came in a number of cans, rather than as one digital file, then there were opportunities for confusion. The cans would be numbered sequentially, in most cases, but it was possible for a reel to be put in the wrong can, or for two reels to be spliced or printed in the wrong order when making up a double reel. An alert projectionist would pick up on such errors in preparing the films before a screening, but occasional slips were made.

---

[1] Quoted in Jennifer Faull, 'New York Times issues correction as critic slates Amazon's Goliath—but later realises he watched in the wrong order,' *The Drum*, 22 October 2016, https://tinyurl.com/ykvrwab4.

Billy McBride (Billy Bob Thornton) in *Goliath*, season one.

It was fascinating to see a film shown in the wrong order (when you did not know that this was what you were going to see), because — as with Mike Hales — the brain endeavours to rationalise what is put before it. I can remember watching a British 1930s film some years ago at the Museum of London, where reels three and four of the seven-reel feature were shown in the wrong order. Puzzled, but nevertheless determined, the audience did its best to comprehend what was unfolding before it. Characters who had been part of the action were subsequently introduced to us for the first time. Mishaps occurred after their consequences. The dead were seen to walk again.

What was interesting is that we did not think 'this film is in the wrong order'; instead we made the best sense that we could out of what we could see. We excused the absurdities and rationalised the rest, juggling the disordered elements in our heads so that things made sense.

The brain must be doing interesting things in such circumstances. It will be searching for reassurance. We watch such stories in part for their cause and effect, and cause and effect are something that the brain is good at linking up. It sees an action, predicts the consequences based on prior knowledge, then matches that cause with its expected effect. This tells us all is right with our world. But stories are more than just a sequence of causes and effects. They present complex situations within particular landscapes, through

Film reels.

which characters operate. There has been much exciting work done in recent years on now the brain enables us to process the actions and stories which we see on a screen, notably Tim J. Smith's studies into visual cognition using empirical methods such as eye-tracking, and the work by the well-named James Cutting on perceptual and cognitive processing and how these relate film editing and narrative.

But none of this, nor any of the works on memory and mind studies which I have read, quite explain to me how the brain can make sense of a film that is in the wrong order. It is not just about making sense out of (partial) nonsense; it is about finding reassurance in whatever narrative is put before us. So the issue is not just about knowing how films work, but why we need them to work. We need to understand where we are, however confusing the territory may be. It is the same thing when some people feel discomfited by a film when they cannot work out what is going on—the need for sense is not just conservatism, it is vital. This seems to be key to the success of film as an art form—not that it shows us something new each time, but that it continually provides us with the familiar. We keep watching the stories to be certain of things. It is what comes of being sentient creatures, caught in time.

It is this understanding of the purpose of stories that underpins Christopher Booker's book *The Seven Basic Plots: Why We Tell Stories*. For Booker, stories are not something invented each time by authors but instead each conform to archetypal forms grounded in mankind's understanding of itself. As he says, 'the real key to understanding stories lies in seeing how they are ultimately rooted in a level of the unconscious which is collective to all humanity.'[2] Booker's work is contentious, not least in his insistence on the universality of his seven basic plots and some Jungian psychological fancifulness, but the underlying conception seems sound. We need stories, because we think in stories: cause and effect, reward and punishment, beginning and an end.

Films in reels are largely a thing of the past, so Mike Hales' error was rather heartening because it shows that in the digital age we have new ways of mixing up stories. Hales saw a tricky narrative structure because as a critic he was on the look-out for such strategies. What his brain experienced conformed to his expectations, as a critic and as a consumer of stories. He needed to know where he was. We all do.

Originally published as 'Losing the Plot,' 23 October 2016, https://lukemckernan.com/2016/10/23/losing-the-plot, and reproduced here with small emendations. *Goliath* ran for four seasons of eight episodes each between 2016 and 2021.

---

[2] Christopher Booker, *The Seven Basic Plots: Why We Tell Stories* (London/New York: Continuum, 2004), p. 543.

3.

There Was a Third Man

The mystery behind Graham Greene and The Third Man

> Who is the third who walks always beside you?
> When I count, there are only you and I together
> But when I look ahead up the white road
> There is always another one walking beside you...
>
> T. S. Eliot, 'The Waste Land'[1]

The Third Man (UK 1949), directed by Carol Reed, is one of the most satisfying films ever made. From the moment it was released, it was appreciated equally by high-brows and the general public, working as a romantic thriller or as a complex work of art whose depths were as satisfying to explore as it was entertaining to watch. Time has only deepened the appreciation of a film which, through a happy coming together of talent, timing and luck, represents some of the best of what cinema can achieve.

I visited Vienna recently, and took time out to locate several of the famed locations which appear in the film—the Prater fairground with its Ferris wheel, the Zentralfriedhof cemetery, Harry Lime's apartment entrance in Josefplatz, and the doorway in Schreyvogelgasse where Lime (played by Orson Welles) makes his memorable first appearance. In preparation for this pilgrimage, and again afterwards, I watched the film, and tried to get to the heart of what makes it work so well. It seems to lie in the story, or rather in how it does not rely on the story. What I mean by that is that the film has a plot of almost classical perfection, whose ingenuities transfix us throughout, yet what the film does is constantly to elude the specifics of plot. What is going on is not what we see happen, but how the characters stand outside such circumstance even while they are propelled along by it, perhaps helplessly. There

---

[1] T. S. Eliot, 'The Waste Land,' ll. 359-362, in *The Waste Land and Other Poems* (London: Faber and Faber, 1972), p. 41.

Harry Lime (Orson Welles) in the Vienna sewers.

is, moreover, a sense that everyone knows what is going on (albeit their own version of what is going on) except for the storyteller himself, Martins, the man who is trying to piece together the narrative for himself, and for us.

But what is the story? In plain terms it is the tale of an American writer and Czech actress whose loyalties to a friend and lover are severely tested when he is proven to be a black marketeer (with a trail of child victims) and a murderer, all set against an occupied, post-war Vienna. But such synopses are for film encyclopedias. What is the real story of *The Third Man*?

The starting point has to be the title. Why is this film called *The Third Man*? It obviously bothered David O. Selznick, the film's American co-producer, of whom the film's scriptwriter Graham Greene reported—not entirely reliably—that he felt audiences would be puzzled by the title and it should be called something like *Night in Vienna*, a title guaranteed to bring the punters in.[2] The third man is explained early on in the film, when we learn that when Harry Lime's supposedly dead body was taken across the road there were two known people who carried him, but the porter at Lime's apartment block is alone in saying he saw a third

[2] Graham Greene, *Ways of Escape* (London: The Bodley Head, 1980), p. 65.

man ('There was a third man'), to be later murdered because of it. Is that all? Does the title simply point us to a phantom corpse carrier?

There are other third men to be found. One is revealed by Holly Martins (played by Joseph Cotten), the writer of low-brow Westerns, who tells Popescu that he is writing a new novel—meaning that he is in pursuit of the mystery behind Harry Lime's 'death'—and he is to call it *The Third Man*. It certainly helps up to think of *The Third Man* from the perspective of one of Martins' novels. *The Third Man* is perhaps the quintessential British Western film. Martins—author of such works as *The Oklahoma Kid* and *The Lone Rider of Santa Fe*—finds himself living out one of the plots from his imagination, their moral certainties challenged by the complexities of reality. He is the stranger who rides into town, discovers a mystery, clashes with and spurns authority, hunts down the bad guy, and finally gets his man in a final shoot-out. Martins is also Graham Greene's joke on himself—the writer of 'cheap novelettes' in pursuit of his story amid the ruins of Vienna, throwing together one more entertainment for the big screen which could reduce the writer's art down to the barest essentials.

Or perhaps *The Third Man* is a *roman à clef* whose subject is a real 'third man,' namely Kim Philby. Charles Drazin, in his excellent *In Search of the Third Man*, puts forward the thesis that Greene based Harry Lime at least in part on his acquaintance with the British double-agent Philby, who would subsequently be exposed by the press as the 'third man' (that is, third after the exposés of Guy Burgess and Donald Maclean). Philby, with whom Greene worked in British intelligence in Portugal during the Second World War, had lived in Vienna as a young man. There he had worked for the Committee for Aiding Refugees from Fascism and had helped persecuted socialists escape the civil war that broke out of the streets via the city's sewers. He married a young communist, Litzi Friedman, in doing so giving her the protection of his British passport. On his return to London he worked for a news agency gathering information on Eastern and Central Europe and was recruited by Soviet intelligence.[3]

There are interesting echoes here of Lime—living in Vienna, working for a refugee office (in Greene's *The Third Man* novella Lime works for the International Refugee Office), escape via sewers, girlfriend fearing arrest as an illegal alien, the double life.

---

[3] Charles Drazin, *In Search of the Third Man* (London: Methuen, 1999), pp. 144-154.

Drazin also tells us that in Vienna Philby met with one Peter Smolka, who later became *The Times* correspondent in Vienna and interested Greene in his short stories of city life, including one which featured a diluted penicillin racket which Greene then adopted for his film scenario. Drazin speculates that Greene was aware of Philby's double-agent life when they worked together in Portugal, though it was only in the mid-1950s that Philby was openly suspected of being a double agent and hence 'the third man' (this was finally confirmed in 1963). Philby could have watched *The Third Man* and seen his own story, at least metaphorically so, and the sense that Harry Lime represents somebody actual (the specifics of the penicillin racket help suggest it) haunts the film.

Harry Lime in the Ferris wheel cab talking about his victims.

But there is another story of a third man. The 'Who is the third who walks always beside you?' quotation from T. S. Eliot at the top of this essay points to it. Eliot, in his notes to 'The Waste Land,' says that he is referring to an account of the Shackleton Antarctic expedition, when one of the party of explorers 'had the constant delusion that there was *one more member* than could actually be counted.'[4] However, what Eliot is really referring to is the passage in the Gospels where Christ appears, unrecognised, to two disciples on the road to Emmaus. Jesus Christ is the third man.

---

[4] T. S. Eliot, 'Notes on The Waste Land,' in *The Waste Land and Other Poems*, p. 49.

Anna Schmidt (Alida Valli) walks past Holly Martins (Joseph Cotten).

Graham Greene the Roman Catholic habitually wrote about Catholic central figures whose absolute faith is measured against the relativist morals of the unbelievers. Harry Lime is a Catholic—he is given a Roman Catholic burial service (twice) and in Greene's *The Third Man* novella his religion is stated explicitly. In the film Martins reminds him, on the Ferris wheel, that he had religious faith once:

Martins: You used to believe in God.

Lime: Oh, I still do believe in God, old man. I believe in God and Mercy and all that. But the dead are happier dead. They don't miss much here, poor devils.[5]

Greene plays with the paradoxes of faith throughout. When Martins is asked to give a talk to the British Council, the theme chosen for him is 'The Crisis of Faith,' and when the porter tells Martins that Lime is dead he says that he is either in heaven

---

[5] In the novella the exchange is given as, 'You used to be a catholic.' 'Oh, I still *believe*, old man. In God and mercy and all that. I'm not hurting anybody's soul by what I do. The dead are happier dead. They don't miss much here, poor devils.' Graham Greene, *The Third Man and The Fallen Idol* (Harmondsworth: Penguin Books, 1971), p. 106.

(pointing downwards) or hell (pointing upwards). It is a moment of pure Greene mischief.

And then of course Harry Lime is a man who rises from the dead. He is persecuted, betrayed in Judas-like fashion ('What price would you pay?' Martins asks Calloway when he finally agrees to help trap Lime. 'They have a name for faces like that' says Anna, when she learns of this), and executed, before being buried again. The Christ who appears to the two disciples at Emmaus has risen from the dead and crucially is not recognised, until he breaks bread with them. Lime is not recognised for the good that he may represent by any character in the film except Anna.

But Harry Lime is not a good man. He is transparently evil. Although he may have religious faith, to which the film refers only obliquely, he makes no expression of it. He is no one's moral superior. He simply acts for his own selfish ends with no other governing idea in his life that we are made aware of, and nothing virtuous about him at all save possibly some respect (it is hardly love) for Anna, even while he betrays her. Far from being Christ-like he is Lucifer-like; in an echo of the Temptation of Christ, he taunts Holly with his talk of victims by pointing down to the people below them from their Ferris wheel location ('Would you really feel any pity if one of those dots stopped moving forever? If I said you can have twenty thousand pounds for every dot that stops, would you really, old man, tell me to keep my money — or would you calculate how many dots you could afford to spare? Free of income tax, old man, free of income tax').

The most remarkable thing about *The Third Man* is that it makes Harry Lime sympathetic and his end tragic. Holly Martins does the right thing in helping the police capture him, but we do not admire him for it. Anna overlooks the evil he has committed, yet it is her decision to spurn Martins at the end of the film which we instinctively recognise as right. Her faith in Lime, her refusal to betray what she believes in, is revealed as the greater good.

This taps into a deep human feeling, such as religion serves — the yearning for the truth greater than the petty concerns of daily living. He whom Anna believes in is wrong, but her belief is right. This is the story, or at least the underlying moral, which propels *The Third Man*, the story which is in all the protagonists' minds while they negotiate those immediate issues that the film's plot presents to them. Their feet are on the Josefplatz, but their minds are on the road to Emmaus.

Originally published as 'There Was a Third Man,' 27 February 2013, https://lukemckernan.com/2013/02/27/there-was-a-third-man, and reproduced here with small emendations. The website *Location Shots in Vienna of The Third Man* was an excellent guide to the Vienna locations used in the film, with many screengrabs and much ingenious detective work on display. An archived version is available at https://web.archive.org/web/http://axion.physics.ubc.ca/thirdman/thirdman.html.

4.

Memories of a Film

Remembering everything about Moonstruck

The other day I watched *Moonstruck*, the 1987 American film set among the Italian-American community of New York, starring Cher and Nicolas Cage. It is a delightful production, which scarcely puts a foot wrong in any department. I had not seen it some twenty years, but something remarkable occurred. I could remember every single element of the film. It was not just the general tenor, or stand-out scenes such as where Cage and Cher first meet in a bakery and he explains the rage he feels towards his brother, her fiancé. I remembered every scene, every image, every movement of the camera, every word of dialogue. Even the tiniest of features, such as details of costumes, pictures on a wall, or objects in a grocery store—I recalled all of it.

How could this be? I had not seen the film in over two decades, and cannot have given it any thought since then. I have not gone around consciously with every shot and the complete dialogue of *Moonstruck* rolling around in my head. Had you asked me only a week ago what I thought of the film I would have said that I remembered it fondly, that Cher was very good in it and Nicolas Cage too, though he over-acted a bit. But that would have been it. I would not have been able to tell you much of the plot, and if you had asked me who else was in it I would not have been able to say Danny Aiello, or even Olympia Dukakis, who along with Cher won an Academy Award for her performance. So where was *Moonstruck* in my head all that time? How many other films are stored there? And how?

This is quite a common phenomenon for me, and I assume for others. Films that I have not seen in a long time, for which I seem to have little recall, nevertheless come flooding back upon the point of actually seeing them once again. Everything is so familiar, and this is not just at the point of viewing. I not only recognised scenes from *Moonstruck* in their every detail, but I anticipated the scenes coming up as well. I knew what the next line of dialogue was going to be before the actor had said it. When I watched John Mahoney in his fine cameo as a hapless academic who knows nothing about the young women he pursues, I had such a sensation of delight, knowing what he was going to say next and the way in which he was going to say it. Yet a week before I would not have been able to tell you that he was in the film at all.

But this only happens with certain films. Last night I watched *A Midsummer Night's Sex Comedy* (USA 1982), a Woody Allen film I saw just the once when it came out. I remember being rather disappointed with it at the time, but little else, and when it came to watching again I realised I recalled none of it—not the cast (apart from Allen, of course), not the setting, the dialogue, or even its more eye-catching moments which you might expect to have lingered, such as the flying machine invented by Allen's character. But *A Midsummer Night's Sex Comedy* I had seen just the once, when it had made little impression on me (I have to say that I was wrong—it now seems a film of great charm, wit and technical skill).

Moonstruck, in contrast, meant something from the start, and I saw it more than once. I committed it to memory—not consciously, but by repetition and because it held meaning for me.

So *Moonstruck* was in my head while *A Midsummer Night's Sex Comedy* was not. But how many films are in my head? I have seen thousands, many more than once, and I have experienced that total recall, or something close to it, with many films that I have not seen in a long time, but which I could not consciously recall without the trigger of the film itself.

The scientists of memory tell us that there are different kinds of memory systems. We have short-term, or working memory, which is the immediate need system. It manages small amounts of information which may then get passed further along the brain for deeper processing. Long-term memory is the deep-rooted stuff that our mind has elected to keep permanently. This can be sub-divided into explicit (or declarative) and implicit (or procedural) memory, defined as 'knowing what' (memories of facts, figures *etc.*) and 'knowing why' (how to do things, like riding a bicycle, which we have acquired through practice). Declarative memory can be further divided into episodic memory—the memory of partic-ular times, places, contexts—and semantic memory—deriving the common features from different experiences. No memory, however, is exclusive to any one of these systems or procedures: they transfer from one to the other, being stored in different parts of the brain when they do so (including different parts of the brain

Loretta (Cher) and Ronny (Nicolas Cage) in *Moonstruck*.

at the same time, for security purposes—much like any good digital data preservation strategy).

Some argue that long-term memory barely decays over time, so that in principle we could remember everything we have retained, and there is infinite space in which to do so. We could remember everything, if only we had enough time. So I could remember every film there ever was, if only I could impress upon my mind (through repetition) the need to recall, and had many hundreds of years available in which to see all the films that there are, and will be, to see. But our brains deteriorate, and so we lose the capacity to retrieve all we might retrieve.

Moreover, the mind balances that which we may remember with that which, for sanity's sake, we can afford to forget. To be unable to forget anything is a horrible curse, famously analysed in the case of memory prodigy 'S.' (Solomon Shereshevsky), the subject of neuropsychologist A. R. Luria's classic book *The Mind of a Mnemonist*.[1] I did not need to have the whole of *Moonstruck* playing in my head all of the time. I recalled it only when I had need of it, or when it was practical to do so.

So how and why did I remember the film so well? I do not understand enough about the various memory processes and how they operate together, but their relationship to film must be an intricate one. Books on memory give many examples of what we remember and forget, but they seems always to focus on individual

---

[1] A. R. Luria, *The Mind of a Mnemonist: A Little Book About a Vast Memory* (London: Cape, 1969).

Andrew (Woody Allen) and Ariel (Mia Farrow)
in *A Midsummer Night's Sex Comedy*.

aspects, such as faces, words, actions, sounds, specific points in
the past. Films are more complex—they are a reflection of life,
motion in context, all the more powerfully so for being bound up
as stories. Yet I can find little reference to the recall of films in the
literature of memory, at least in their entirety as opposed to single
memorable scenes.[2] An article by Julie Beck for *The Atlantic*, 'Why
We Forget Most of the Books We Read… and the Movies and TV
Shows We Watch' touches on the subject. But her theme is why we
do not remember any book we read or film we see soon after expe-
riencing them, unless we make a particular effort to do so—such
as through repetition. She also argues that memory is changing in
the Internet age, as so much that we might want to recall we do not

---

[2] Archive actuality film has been used for reminiscence therapy, such as the
Yorkshire Film Archive's *Memory Bank* project, https://www.yfanefa.com/
memory_bank. Film has been used in laboratory conditions to study eyewitness memory, including the recreation of crime scenarios. See T. S. Hol-
lins and T. J. Perfect, 'The Confidence–Accuracy Relation in Eyewitness
Event Memory: The Mixed Question Type Effect,' *Legal and Criminolog-
ical Psychology*, vol. 2 issue 2 (September 1997), pp. 205-218, https://doi.
org/10.1111/j.2044-8333.1997.tb00344.x. Psychological research has investigated how music is used to make feature films memorable; see Libby Damjanoivc,
'How Movies Use Music to Manipulate Your Memories.' *The Conversation*, 20
November 2023, https://theconversation.com/how-movies-use-music-to-ma-
nipulate-your-memory-217971.

bother to do so, because we know the information will be some-where. Memory shifts from retention of the substance to retention of the indicators, as though everything were short-term memory nowadays.[3]

Well, maybe so, but this does not tell me why I was able to remember *Moonstruck*. We are closer to an answer when consid-ering a well-attested aspect of autobiographical memory (the facility we have to recall events and experiences from our own lives) known as the 'reminiscence bump.' This is the tendency of adults over the age of thirty-five to experience an increase in the retrieval of memories from between the ages ten to thirty. Films often turn up as a subject in the relevant studies. This makes sense (I was twenty-six when I first saw *Moonstruck*), particularly when some memory scientists argue that this is a period concerned with the 'consolidation of the self.'[4]

But I feel that there is something else also involved. It seems to me that the primary purpose of memory is survival. We retain information that enables us to function, from recognising friend and foe, to knowing what foods are good to eat, to remembering how to open a door. But this core survival function has expanded richly because of the great power of the human brain, combined with the complexities of modern living. I did not, on the face of it, need to recall the plot and dialogue of *Moonstruck* in order to survive—indeed, I had lived in reasonably good health, and without major accident, for twenty years since I last did so.[5]

I retained the film, I think, in part because it made me happy. Its humour and its romance and its characters appealed to me. It confirmed to me things which, in a broad sense, made me feel safe, and hence a survivor. It provided comfort and an affirmation

---

[3] Julie Beck, 'Why We Forget Most of the Books We Read …and the Movies and TV Shows We Watch,' *The Atlantic*, 26 January 2018, https://www.theatlantic.com/science/archive/2018/01/what-was-this-article-about-again/551603.

4 For autobiographical memory, see Helen L. Williams, Martin A. Conway and Gillian Cohen, 'Autobiographical Memory,' in Gillian Cohen and Martin A. Conway (eds.), *Memory in the Real World* [third edition] (Hove/New York: Psychology Press, 2008), pp. 21-90. The reminiscence bump is discussed on p. 59.

[5] There is a branch of the study of memory systems which identifies 'adaptive memory' as that which has evolved to ensure survival. See James S. Nairne, Sarah R. Thompson, Josefa N. S. Pandeirada, 'Adaptive Memory: Survival Pro-cessing Enhances Retention,' *Journal of Experimental Psychology: Learning, Memory, and Cognition*, 33(2), March 2007, pp. 263-273, https://doi.org/10.1037%2F0278-7393.33.2.263.

of the good. I could also speculate that there was an element of professionalism involved. I have been a film archivist and historian for many years, used to looking at films closely, evaluating them, comparing them with other films. I took note of the film because it was noteworthy, though it helped that I saw the film more than once, itself part of a process of identifying value through confirmation. In the same way, I mistakenly did not put the effort into noting *A Midsummer Night's Sex Comedy*, because it seemed to have little to offer compared to other films I was seeing. Now I know, after seeing it again, I will remember it well.

Whether the whole of *Moonstruck* was sitting there in my head, however, I rather doubt. Our memory banks are not giant image stores from which we retrieve the past exactly as we saw it. Memories are profoundly, and biologically, subjective. As psychologist Ulric Neisser puts it, 'Remembering is not like playing back a tape or looking at a picture; it is more like telling a story.'[6] Memories are records of impressions, which change over time and experience. One of my earliest memories is of being discovered at a children's party, reading a book upstairs while everyone else was playing games downstairs. But I remember this incident from my mother's point of view — she comes up the stairs and finds me sitting there. It is not my memory at all, or rather what I now remember of it has been translated through the anecdotes of others and by what the meaning of the memory turned out to be.

In my mind, I had not changed the plot or any other aspect of *Moonstruck*, but there must have been some sort of compression which took place. I could not have remembered every small detail of the costuming or décor, for instance, but something in my mind, upon acknowledging the familiarity of these scenes, decided that those details looked right, so that it was as if I remembered them in full. Perhaps there is some analogy with how digital video compression works: the video files we see on television, on DVD, on streaming sites, and even in cinemas, are all compressed — the term used is lossy — meaning that not all of the visual information recorded in the master file is there. Compression technologies (such as MPEG-2) make a video look like the full thing when it is only partly so, simply to save on file size and so enable more efficient distribution.

So maybe there was, metaphorically speaking, a lossy encoding of *Moonstruck* in my head, at least for those parts which could be

---

[6] Ulric Neisser, 'Memory With a Grain of Salt,' in Harriet Harvey Wood and A. S. Byatt, *Memory: An Anthology* (London: Chatto & Windus, 2008), p. 88.

reconstructed from basic elements, with the power of suggestion doing the rest. That does not explain how I knew what the characters were going to say before they said it, nor might it explain such elements as the looks on the character's faces. By whatever complex combination of processes it occurred, my ability to remember large parts of a film I had not seen in twenty years, and in minute detail, feels extraordinary. The brain is the most astonishing storage system, even if what it stores is subject to all of the vagaries of biological processes.

There are many books, articles and websites on film and memory, nearly all of them on how memory is used as a thematic device, or on film and memory as analogies, seldom on the processes by which film is remembered. There is a gap in our understanding of film that needs filling. The neurologists can tell us the mechanics of *how* we remember films (though I feel they have not told us enough as yet), but we need to think more about the *why*. For me, it all points to something fundamental about the purpose of film, which is to provide assurance and identification of the self. We can live without films, readily enough, but to have them available has proved so useful to us. They enrich our memories. They help us survive.

Originally published as 'Memories of a Film,' 6 January 2019, https://lukemckernan.com/2019/01/06/memories-of-a-film, and reproduced here with some additional text. There is a clear guide to the different forms of memory at https://human-memory.net. Books on memory which were useful in writing this essay are Steven Rose, *The Making of Memory: From Molecules to Mind* (London: Bantam, 1992), Rusiko Bourtchouladze, *Memories Are Made of This: The Biological Building Blocks of Memory* (London: Weidenfeld & Nicolson, 2002) and Gillian Cohen and Martin A. Conway (eds.), *Memory in the Real World* [third edition] (Hove/New York: Psychology Press, 2008).

5.

Give Me A Ring Some Time

The artistry behind the pilot episode of Cheers

I have just finished watching *Cheers*. It must be three or four times now that I have sat through the entire series of the American sit-com—275 half-hour episodes, eleven seasons, originally broadcast over eleven years (1982-1993). It began its re-run in the UK on Channel 4 in the early weekday hours early into the lockdown period, two episodes shown per weekday, and I watched every one without fail. On the last day (26 August 2020), the final episode was followed by the first episode, as Channel 4 began the cycle all over again.

It made for fascinating viewing, to see the end of a story followed by its inception. I will not describe the final episode, for the sake of any reader who has not seen it or seen the whole series—suffice to say that it is unusual in tone, and is so constructed as to be the mirror opposite of the first episode. But that first, pilot episode, entitled 'Give Me a Ring Sometime,' is worth praising and examining, for to describe it is not to give anything away that matters, but merely to open the door.

'Give Me a Ring Sometime' is, to my mind, a perfectly-realised example of narrative art. It is up there with *The Tempest*, *Right Ho Jeeves*, *The Good Soldier*, *The Shop Around the Corner* and *La Nuit Américaine* in which form, language and character are in absolute alignment. It is not that they are necessarily profound—though some are—but that they express such delight in presenting the story that they have to tell.

'Give Me a Ring Sometime' stands out among such company for only being a part of an overall story. It is the pilot episode of what turned out, in time, to be a hugely popular comedy series whose success was based on achieving that ideal state in which the story feels as though it could go on forever. A pilot episode has to introduce its subject, its location and its characters. It has to entice its audience with a formula. It must encapsulate all that the producers hope will follow, establishing a vision. It must tell its own story while promising all other stories that its format can provide. It is a plea and an expression of faith.

When 'Give Me a Ring Sometime' was first aired (30 September 1982, on NBC) the ratings were poor. *Cheers* only picked up momentum after reruns, but that was perhaps the best way in which to experience the pilot. To see some of the series mid-run, to become engrossed in it, and then to encounter how it begins is to be astonished at how much writers, producers and performers saw what was to come. It is though all 275 episodes were conceived of and produced at the same time. All of the necessary elements are there, their purpose understood, their promise certain to be fulfilled. That is what happens with good ideas, sometimes.

The set-up is this. Cheers is a Boston bar run by former base-ball star Sam Malone (played by Ted Danson). We see Malone walking into the main room from a corridor, brushing his hand against the wall and bar, the camera tracking with him to reveal the huge set that will be, they hope, our home as it is theirs. A boy enters with a fake ID suggesting that he is a Vietnam War veteran, but fails to con Malone into serving him a drink. It is the opening gag before the haunting opening credits sequence rolls, rostrum camera shots slowly zooming in over vintage photographs of bar habitués, with the name of the actors with whom we will become so familiar matched up to their past selves. The theme song that must have the strength to last for eleven years and 275 episodes tells us that this is the place where everybody knows your name. This is a home for lost souls.

A couple enter the bar. He is a literature professor who oozes pretension; she is his star-struck teaching assistant. They are about to fly off to Barbados to be married, but it becomes clear that the professor is still in thrall to the wife he has yet to divorce. The woman, Diane Chambers (played by Shelley Long), is left alone at the bar, only gradually realising her true situation.

Other characters appear as a background is laid out: Coach (Nicolas Colasanto), a muddled-headed former baseball coach and now bar-tender; Carla Tortelli (Rhea Perlman), the down-trodden but feisty waitress; and Norm Peterson (George Wendt), an accountant and permanent barfly, Cheers' most loyal customer. Each establishes their character in an instant, so that we feel they have always been there and we have just intruded on any moment. However, this is not a comedy about types, but about verbal inter-action. *Cheers* works by people firing witty lines at one another across the bar, as though it were an arena much as Sam Malone

Diane (Shelley Long) and Sam (Ted Danson) in *Cheers*.

knew from his baseball days. We are still watching the game. This is the world, with a bar at its centre, and while it is refuge it is also somewhere where you have learn to survive, where you have to fit in or you will be rejected. This is the brutal undertone that helps define *Cheers*, a series characterised by the unsettling cruelty which people sometimes inflict on one another. Diane Chambers' failure ever completely to adjust to a world that she wants to welcome her is one of the key elements which will make the series' story so rich.

Another element is her romance with Sam. It is obvious from the start that this will be the primary narrative. He is a plain-speaking, womanising man of the people; she is an uptight blue-stocking, unable to control her academic affectations. They are that most difficult of dramatic propositions, the opposites who attract. But it is there in the immediate realisation each has that they somehow complement one another, in their particular outsider's view of the world. Each will reveal an acute sense of time passing by, as the series progresses, that informs their developing characters. It is exquisite casting, the answer to a producer's dreams (I think wistfully of what Lisa Eichhorn, who was screen-tested, would have made of Diane, but Shelley Long and Ted Danson are an inspired duo). They are the perfect imperfect couple, and on that basis your drama could potentially run forever.

It is not just story, or character, or wit that makes *Cheers* special. An almost unacknowledged feature is its relationship to the everyday, specifically the movement of the everyday. It is there in the background. The bar is filled with people, often twenty or more, just seated at tables, chatting and drinking. They play no part in the narrative, no attention is drawn to them, they are just there. Often people will be seen in the distance, entering the bar and choosing where to sit. In any other drama one might expect them to be a part of the developing action; in *Cheers* they are simply walking into a bar.

This is complemented by the work of the people behind the bar—Sam, Diane, Carla, Coach. They are always doing something. So much time is given to showing them pouring drinks, cleaning glasses, counting change, occupied with the mundane essentials of their working lives, even while firing witty barbs at one another. Inconsequential movement gives the action life. This all plays into the sense of *Cheers* as a place of refuge, where time is steady and the driving forces of the outside world do not intrude. Each episode of *Cheers* has its story within the overall story, an incident driven by a crisis in one or other of the leading character's lives, or the intrusion of an outsider, but *Cheers* is really always fighting against such artificiality. *Cheers* points to a state where nothing happens, where nothing need happen. As the title songs says:

> Making your way in the world today
> Takes everything you've got
> Taking a break from all your worries
> Sure would help a lot
> Wouldn't you like to get away?[1]

Cheers represents the impossible dream in the most believable of settings.

And there is the camerawork. The large set with the long bar in its centre allows for all the variety of multiple locations on a single set. Long shots take in the whole of the bar (with all those people milling about in the back), close shots pick out dramatic points at any end of the bar or in its centre, panning shots sweep from one narrative point to another, while surprise cutaways capture the characters at moments of dramatic tension. All of this is in evidence in 'Give Me a Ring Sometime,' as is the wit of the

---

[1] 'Where Everybody Knows Your Name,' written by Gary Portnoy and Judy Hart-Angelo, and played by Portnoy for the *Cheers* opening credits sequence.

filmic style. This is exemplified by a sublime *Cheers* joke, in which Coach picks up the phone at the bar. Someone is asking for an Ernie Pantuso, so he calls out the name. 'That's you, Coach' says Sam, off screen. 'Speaking,' says Coach, without a break. The timing of the gag (which plays on Coach's befuddledness) is exquisite, but what makes it work is that they do not cut away to Malone for his words, as any other comedy might have done. We only see Coach's mind working to its own logic. The wit in the visuals matches that of the verbals.

'Give Me a Ring Sometime' ends with a necessary compromise. It has to set up the drama more than it needs to resolve its own story. So, somewhat improbably, Sam offers Diane a job as a waitress. 'You like the people here, you *think* that they like you,' he says, pointedly and prophetically. She accepts. It is a mechanical necessity. Yet the episode has the quality of a fairy tale. Carla even refers to Diane as 'Goldilocks,' ostensibly because of her hair, but it is prophetic too. Diane is the abandoned child who must somehow find her home again. She thinks she has found it, but will discover in her moments of crisis that she is still lost in the woods, still seeking refuge.

Eventually Diane Chambers had to leave the series, after five seasons, because Shelley Long wanted to move on, but also because in dramatic terms she could seek no more. She was replaced by Rebecca Howe (played by Kirstie Alley), who brought a new life into the show, but whose crises did not matter. Her dramatic life was one designed for comic situations; there was no fairy tale about it. The gags continued to roll, the wit never dimmed, characters old and new hung on, the bar remained. Fixed things stayed fixed. But, though the ball carried on, Cinderella had fled into the night.

'Give Me a Ring Sometime' is only a pilot. It sets up a situation. Its special quality lies in its anticipation of all that is to come, its almost uncanny apprehension of a particular kind of narrative timelessness. Its genius is to reveal a home for everyone through the hopes and heartache of one who is fated never to call it home.

I have just started watching *Cheers* again. Perhaps this time round she will stay.

Originally published as 'Give Me a Ring Sometime,' 3 September 2020, https://lukemckernan.com/2020/09/03/give-me-a-ring-sometime, and reproduced here with small emendations.

6.

Un Film de Benjamin

The dawn of the artificial intelligence movie

I am aware that I am turning into something of a robot bore. Whatever the human activity, be it work or pleasure, I have become far too prone in conversation to tell people how said activity will be taken over and then transformed by artificial intelligence. And soon—usually I throw in the promise of there being four or five years of human dominance in whatever field it is, before the machines take charge. Telling people how their jobs will be undertaken by robots is a good one. Curator? all you need is a programme that selects, describes, presents and contextualises from existing data. You might want a few human super-curators to oversee the programming of the machine, but the rest of us are history. Most recently I have managed to cause annoyance by speculating on how football will be changed by wiring up the players, changing how fouls are measured, how the game is evaluated and how the fans will follow it. The technology alters not just how the thing is experienced, but how it is understood. In a robot-led world, it is the robots that will make the rules.

And now we have the robot movie, or at least the start of robot filmmaking. *Zone Out* (2018) is a six-and-a-half minute film written, directed, scored and performed by Benjamin, a computer programme. Benjamin was devised in 2016 by British director Oscar Sharp and American artificial intelligence researcher Ross Goodwin, when it, or he, was fed numerous 1980s/90s science fiction scripts. Using a LTSM (long short-term memory) recurrent neural network, Benjamin produced a script which was then acted out by humans, the result being the bizarre but peculiarly haunting *Sunspring* (2016). This was followed by *It's No Game* (2017), a self-spoofing sequel starring David Hasselhoff, with some contributions from William Shakespeare.

Zone Out was produced by feeding Benjamin with science fiction film scripts as before, combined with public domain footage from the feature films *The Brain That Wouldn't Die* (USA

1962) and *The Last Man on Earth* (USA 1964), with the faces from the *Sunspring* actors superimposed on to the faces of the actors in the footage, speaking Benjamin's new dialogue. A score was added from a public domain source. Benjamin was then given two days to produce a short movie.

Benjamin could not entirely produce a film from scratch. He/ it needed some initial prompts in terms of plot set-up, and required some human assistance in matching the archive footage to the new dialogue. Other limitations were caused by constraints on the amount of computing power available (so they could not included synthesized speech, for example).

The results are compelling. Two couples are caught up in emotional scenes, interspersed with scenes in a laboratory. The dialogue is weirdly random: 'Are you sure you need a problem?' 'I'm not certain—I don't remember the loss of a substance.' The aspect ratio alters as different source movies are used. There is a theme of face-swapping in there somewhere, with all of the characters having a disturbing look, as though each has undergone a dubious face transplant. Despite the incoherence, the actions builds up to a persuasive climax, with a female head on the laboratory table laughing with an eerie 'heh, heh, heh' as a monster crashes into the room and strangles one of the scientists. All the while sweet music plays in the background, trying but failing to drown out the alien.

Zone Out has clear links with the *avant garde*. The most obvious parallel is with the work of David Lynch—there is plenty here to make one think of *Eraserhead* (USA 1977), or the red room in *Twin Peaks* (USA 1990-1991). One could posit a connection between Benjamin's re-ordering of found materials into something rich and strange with the cut-up techniques of William S. Burroughs, chiefly literary in execution but which Burroughs transferred to film working with director Anthony Balch. One could argue for a link with the work of musician-performer Laurie Anderson, especially 'O Superman,' whose 'ha-ha-ha-ha' metronomic voice has an echo in *Zone Out*'s closing mirthless laughter.

Is Benjamin an *auteur*? The human beings behind the video speak of wanting to respect 'Benjamin's apparent artistic vision' in prompting its particular construction.[1] What Benjamin has achieved is the absolute quality of a dream world. While a Luis Buñuel or

---

[1] Sam Machkovech, 'This Wild, AI-Generated Film is the Next Step in "Whole-Movie Puppetry,"' *Ars Technica*, 11 June 2018, https://tinyurl.com/mw77wy37.

a David Lynch might create the idea, even the recollection, of a dream state, Benjamin realises this in the process of production. The elements that makes up his/its world are fed into his/its mind. That mind (a neural network) reconfigures this material into something that mirrors reality while at the same time being free of its logical constraints. Such is what goes on while we sleep. Benjamin can make films that other filmmakers can only dream of.

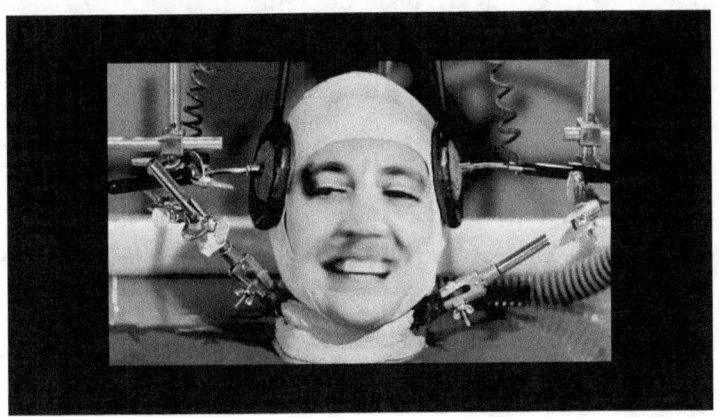

Zone Out (via *The Brain That Wouldn't Die*).

This connects *Zone Out* to work undertaken in 2011 by neuroscientists at the University of California, Berkeley, who scanned the brain activity of volunteers who had been watching films. This neural activity was mapped to an archive of eighteen million one-second video clips taken from *YouTube*, which had not previously been seen by the volunteers. The computer programme then matched the clips to the records it had of the brain activity. The results were a series of beautiful, half-recognisable, half-abstract videos that visualised brain activity in a rather persuasive fashion.[2]

But what was particularly powerful was the thought of *YouTube* itself as a collective memory bank — not just what we have

---

[2] A demonstration video, *Movie Reconstruction from Human Brain Activity*, is available at https://tinyurl.com/ys97vjrc. The project is documented in Shinji Nishimoto, An T. Vu, Thomas Naselaris, Yuval Benjamini, Bin Yu and Jack L. Gallant, 'Reconstructing Visual Experiences from Brain Activity Evoked by Natural Movies,' *Current Biology*, vol. 21 no. 19, 11 October 2011, pp. 1641-1646, https://tinyurl.com/2p8ut9rz. I wrote a report on the project from a silent film perspective, 'Thought Waves,' *The Bioscope*, 27 September 2011, https://thebioscope.net/2011/09/27/thought-waves.

seen, but how we saw it and how it was imprinted in our brains, or echoed that which was imprinted in our brains. Let Benjamin loose on *YouTube*, with multiple scripts to guide him/it, of course, and who knows what stories, or dreams, may come.

To the ordinary sceptic, *Zone Out* is ridiculous, showing the failure of the machine. For the romantic pessimist, it could point to how films could get made, or at least some films, years from now (four or five if you are an optimistic pessimist). As an *Ars Technica* article notes: 'Greater computational efficiency and refined data-parsing tools may very well make this kind of 48-hour computer-crunch of filmmaking a real possibility in the future.'[3]

Somewhere in between lies Benjamin's actual promise, of a kind of film beyond our imagining that nevertheless must come from the products of our imaginations. Androids do not dream of electric sheep. They dream of us.

Originally published as 'Un Film de Benjamin,' 18 June 2018, https://lukemckernan.com/2018/06/18/un-film-de-benjamin, and reproduced here with small emendations. *Zone Out* can be viewed at https://youtu.be/vUgUeFu2Dcw. *Sunspring* is available at https://youtu.be/LY7x2Ihq-jmc and *It's No Game* at https://youtu.be/5qPgG98_CQ8. A.I.-generated films have started to grow in number with the rise of the artificial intelligence chatbot ChatGPT, though they remain at the experimental stage. A twelve-minute film, *The Frost* (2023) made by generative video company Waymark, has every shot created using OpenAI's image-making model DALL-E 2. It has been called the world's first A.I.-generated film, though a human wrote the script. In 2024 a Swiss science fiction feature film, *The Last Screenwriter*, was entirely scripted using ChatGPT except for its human-generated prompt: 'Write a plot for a film where a screenwriter realizes he is less good than artificial intelligence.' *Do Androids Dream of Electric Sheep?* is the title of a Philip K. Dick novel which was adapted into the feature film *Blade Runner* (USA 1982).

---

[3] Machkovech, 'This Wild, AI-Generated Film is the Next Step in "Whole-Movie Puppetry."'

7.

Céline and Julie Go to the Library

Libraries and the filmic imagination in
Céline et Julie vont en bateau

At the British Library they regularly make promotional videos. They are snappy little numbers, designed to show what a bright, inviting and relevant place the Library is. The editing is brisk, the graphics float informatively over the screen, and the music is toe-tapping.

Yet you feel that when any production company is handed a commission to make a promotional film for the British Library that their heart sinks. How on earth does one make an interesting film out of a library? It is nothing but books and manuscripts, shelves upon shelves upon shelves, quaintly amusing staff, and a solemn clientele all of whom are sitting down, reading. There can be little more joy involved in the production of such videos than instructional guides for factory processes, or advertisements for banks.

And yet, what if your filmmaker is a poet? The finest documentary made about a library must be *Tout la mémoire du monde* (*All the Memory in the World*) (France 1956), directed by Alain Resnais. Ostensibly a film informing us about the operations of the Bibliothèque nationale in Paris, in practice it is a disquisition on fear and memory. Over lingering tracking shots of unending, Borgesian corridors of books, the commentary interweaves factual information with thoughts on the human motives behind such a vast undertaking. Humans dread forgetting, so they collect, yet they dread being overwhelmed by the knowledge before them. They strive to catalogue and thereby to gain mastery over that which cannot be controlled, not least because it is never-ending. The books are released from the vaults where all are equal, to the reading rooms where they become personal, and where the readers collectively engage upon an activity which seeks to find an answers to all the questions that there may be, and thereby discover happiness.

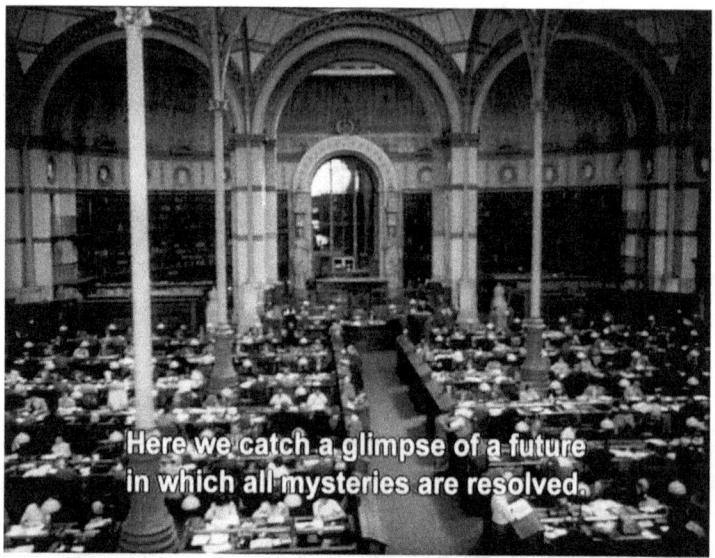

Tout la mémoire du monde.

Perhaps one of the makers of the British Library's promos will go on to make his or her *L'Année dernière à Marienbad* (France 1961)—they may be dreaming so themselves. At any rate they should be encouraged to look out for the British Film Institute's DVD of *Céline et Julie vont en bateau* (*Céline and Julie Go Boating*) (France 1974), made by the late Jacques Rivette, on which Resnais' masterly film is included as an extra.[1]

But what is it doing there, accompanying Rivette's fantastical and very long 1974 film about two women's adventures through Paris, which lead to uncovering and taking part in the stories that lie within a hidden house? It is because *Céline et Julie vont en bateau* is the ultimate library film. Julie (played by Dominique Labourier) is a librarian; Céline (Juliet Berto) a magician. She is not a very good magician, nor does Julie appear to be much of a librarian—she spend her time smoking, dealing out tarot cards and playing with the ink of a book stamper—but it is not the reality but the imagined that counts. Céline and Julie merge into one in any case. The film opens with Julie (reading a book of magic) chasing after Céline when the latter drops something (in imitation of *Alice in Wonderland*); it ends with the same scene but the roles reversed.

---

[1] *Céline and Julie Go Boating*. BFIVD657, British Film Institute, 2006.

Céline (Juliet Berto, right) and Julie (Dominique Labourier)
finally go boating (dressed identically).

They each play the same role in the film-within-a-film. They have interweaving identities. It is a film about the magic underlying the real world, and about how stories all interweave with one another, in a labyrinthine journey through the imagination — much like a library.

The film spends relatively little time in the library where Julie works (they return to it later on to steal some books). Instead it plays upon the idea of the library as a metaphor for the world of stories. *Céline et Julie vont en bateau* — the title alludes to a French term for shaggy dog story, though they do actually go boating towards the end — is about storytelling. It references Lewis Carroll and Henry James (the central film-within-a-film is based on two minor James stories, but there is something about the trapped child theme that reminds one of *What Maisie Knew*). It mimics numerous modes of film genre, or storytelling techniques, as well as specific films — Jean Cocteau's *Orphée* (France 1950), Věra Chytilová's *Sedmikrásky (Daisies)* (Czechoslovakia 1966), Louis Feuillade's *Les Vampires* (France 1915-1916).

Céline et Julie vont en bateau is endlessly fascinating for how it plays with narrative and logic. At just over three hours long it is a challenge for some audiences — when I first saw it at a film society screening many years ago, half the audience had walked out long before the end—especially when it is not always clear what is happening. Céline and Julie's conversations do not always flow logically. Sometimes one seems to give an answer before the other asks the question, while other talk is constructed among seemingly absurdist non sequiturs. Viewing it again recently I found the Jamesian film-within-a-film a bit tedious at times, and felt that the film lost something of its special quality when things in its later stages started to make sense. But a three-hour, semi-improvised film is bound to have its weak points. Other films are nothing but weak. *Céline et Julie vont en bateau* is an adventure through mind and memory, which is what connects it to Resnais' film, and what makes it the perfect library film. It is not the time spent among the books, but the time spent inside them.

Documentarists may have struggled with libraries, but fiction filmmakers have long relied on them. Libraries looms large in *Three Days of the Condor* (USA 1975), *The Name of the Rose* (France/Italy/West Germany 1986), *Citizen Kane* (USA 1941), *Blackmail* (UK 1929), *The Music Man* (USA 1962) (the 'Marion the Librarian' number), *Attack of the Clones* (USA 2002) (looking remarkably like Resnais' Bibliothèque nationale), *The Breakfast Club* (USA 1985) (the library as prison), *All the President's Men* (USA 1976) and any *Harry Potter* film. Librarians themselves are often lazily caricatured. One only has to think of the awful alternative fate envisaged for Donna Reed in *It's a Wonderful Life* (USA 1946): unloved, plain and the town librarian; or the memorably rude librarians played by John Rothman in *Sophie's Choice* (UK/USA 1982) and Judi Dench in *Wetherby* (UK 1985). Just occasionally a librarian gets portrayed sympathetically: Greer Garson in *Adventure* (USA 1946), Peter Sellers in *Only Two Can Play* (UK 1962), Tim Robbins in *The Shawshank Redemption* (USA 1994) and the favourite of many a librarian or archivist, Stephen Poliakoff's television series *Shooting the Past* (UK 1999), where the staff in a photographic library are the defenders of knowledge and humanity in the face of a soulless age.

The movies understand libraries, or at least know how to use them. But Resnais and Rivette understand something more. They understand that libraries are a part of what it is to be human. They collect our hopes and fears, and guide our discoveries. They represent the battle against the fragility of memory. They are the coming together of the prosaic and the magical, so that eventually one cannot tell the one from the other—Céline and Julie.

Originally published as 'Céline and Julie Go to the Library,' 6 February 2016, https://lukemckernan.com/2016/02/06/celine-and-julie-go-to-the-library, and reproduced here with small emendations. The best of the several online lists of libraries in film—all of them created by librarians—is Martin Raish's *Librarians in the Movies*, now only available via the Internet Archive, at https://tinyurl.com/4nrjftrc. It has not been updated since 2011 but remains an ingenious resource.

8.

Eroica

On not caring that much for silent film masterpiece Napoléon

Yesterday I saw the five-and-a-half hour restoration of Abel Gance's *Napoléon* (France 1927), which was shown at the Royal Festival Hall between 13:30 and 21:30 (there were three intervals), with the Philharmonia Orchestra and Carl Davis conducting his music. It is the third time I have seen the film, not counting the DVD of the American version of the restoration with Carmine Coppola's music. However it is now longer than any of us have seen up to now, as the restorer Kevin Brownlow has found more footage since the restoration's original premiere in 1980. To judge from the titles at last night's screening which described a missing section, we lack a sequence where an impoverished Napoleon makes boots for himself out of cardboard. The recent additions to what we now see are mostly sequences in Corsica.

It is not a film that I care for that much. To express dislike for *Napoléon* can be close to heresy in silent film circles, given the heroic story of the film's production and the still more heroic story of its restoration by Kevin Brownlow and David Gill, which is generally argued to have overturned decades of prejudice against silent films and to have ushered in a new appreciation of silent film art, as well as the (expensive) vogue for seeing such films as they were originally presented, with full orchestral accompaniment. But one can be grateful and still be critical at the same time. *Napoléon* is not a good film; it is a very long film with some good things in it.

Abel Gance, its director, originally planned for six films to cover the entirety of Napoleon's life, and this first episode takes us only to Napoleon on the verge of conquering Italy. The remaining five parts never got made, though a German film directed by Lupu Pick from Gance's script for the sixth part, *Napoléon auf St Helena*, was made in 1929. Film history is lettered with bombastic attempts to film the life of Napoleon—Charlie Chaplin and Stanley Kubrick never made theirs, Gance filmed only a sixth of his. The lesson from all three is that the directors maybe saw something of themselves in Napoleon, and what they wanted to film was not so much the man as the idea of absolute vision, absolute control.

Abel Gance's *Napoléon* makes little sense as narrative. It presents episodes—the snowball fight from his childhood, the siege of Toulon, the Terror—rather than a story that grows organically and logically. It offers little in the way of characterisation. The named figures are no more than portrait paintings. Only the excellent Vladimir Roudenko playing the young Napoleon gives us any sense of a rounded character, though this time around I found more to admire in Albért Dieudonné's hypnotic impression of the adult Napoleon. Those scenes that require some interaction of the characters are among the poorest, notably the romance between Napoleon and Josephine (Gina Manès), and the lovelorn Violine (played by Annabella) with her unrequited, quasi-religious worshipping of her hero. Epic events such as the siege of Toulon are rendered incoherent through a lack of narrative skill, while others, such as the orgy sequence, just go on and on to little purpose, or interest.

But it is wrong to expect *Napoléon* to work in terms of story, character, or as conventional cinema at all. It is better to think of it in musical terms, with its themes, impressions, transpositions, recapitulations and codas. Its episodic nature points to symphonic structure; its contrapuntal technique with themes introduced, answered and repeated echoes fugue. Music is fundamental to the film's exhibition, of course—Arthur Honegger wrote the original score, of which only fragments now survive, while Carl Davis' efficient score combines original music with pieces from contemporary French compositions and parts of Beethoven's Third Symphony ('Eroica') which was originally dedicated to Napoleon. However, there is not an exact correlation; rather Gance is playing with images as a composer might play with musical ideas. This is why the film's most powerful sequences are those where images of the past are recapitulated in visionary form—Napoleon's recall of all his encounters with Josephine (an extraordinary rapid montage), a complementary vision of her in multi-superimposition form as Napoleon recalls different aspects of her, and of course in the famous final triptych, which deliver a rapid, ever-changing swirl images of Napoleon's past, present and future.

This musical use of images does not always work. The intercutting between the revolutionary turmoil at the Convention and Napoleon in a boat on a stormy sea, which originally was to have concluded in triptych form, is an overblown irrelevance. The visual correlation is banal and fatuous, reminiscent of D. W. Griffith's weaker 1920s efforts to repeat the cross-cutting bravura of *Intolerance* (USA 1916), described by Terry Ramsaye as 'the first and only film fugue.'[1] Far better is the recurrent use of the eagle motif. This is introduced with what is the film's emotional high point, early on in the childhood sequence when Napoleon's pet eagle returns to him. It is a fundamental weakness of the film that this thematically, emotionally and musically satisfying moment occurs so soon, and is never bettered.

Albért Dieudonné in *Napoléon*.

If you forget story, and character, and dramatic logic, and think of *Napoléon* as a visual symphony, then for the most part it works. There is not a dull nor a false image in the entire work. It reaches apotheosis in those points where it abandons conventional cinematic narrative techniques and delivers the abstract—the nine-image pillow fight, the ghosts of the Revolution revisiting Napoleon at the Convention, the absolute *avant garde* of the concluding triptych. But that is not enough. You have to fill your five-and-a-half hours with more than that, or at least Gance tries to, so the failure of the romantic scenes, for example, is down to poor technique, not to any misunderstanding of what he was trying to do.

---

[1] Terry Ramsaye, *A Million and One Nights: A History of the Motion Picture* (London: Frank Cass, 1964), p. 755.

He wants us to care for Napoleon in the way that he does; and we do not.

In part it is just that I do not like grand film gestures. Big is not better, and the grandiosity of *Napoléon* makes for a great event, but not necessarily great cinema. The cult of the silent cinema restoration with live full orchestra that the 1980 restoration ushered in has led to many ecstatic reviews that suggest that here is the quintessence of cinema, but I beg to differ. Earlier this week at the British Library they screened a ten-minute film, *A Day in the Life of a Coal Miner* (UK 1910), made by Charles Urban's Kineto company, accompanied by the pianist Neil Brand, to an audience of thirty. There was more truth in that documentary film's simple exposition of people, time and place, than in all of *Napoléon*'s strutting bombast—and finer technique too, if we want technique to have purpose. I prefer my films human-sized, and about ordinary humans, not about the heartless visions of world conquerors. Small is beautiful.

Originally published as 'Eroica,' 1 December 2013, https://lukemckernan. com/2013/12/01/eroica, and reproduced here with small emendations. The Royal Festival Hall screening took place on 30 November 2013. The epic story of the production and restoration of *Napoléon* is documented in Kevin Brownlow, *Napoleon: Abel Gance's Classic Film* (London: Photoplay, 2004). *A Day in the Life of a Coal Miner* can be viewed on the *BFI Player*, https://player.bfi.org.uk.

9.

The Scientific Method

Breaking Bad *and a classical era of television*

> Chemistry—well, technically chemistry is the study of matter. But I prefer to see it as the study of change. Now just think about this. Electrons, they change their energy levels. Molecules change their bonds. Elements, they combine and change into compounds. But that's all of life, right? It's just the constant, it's the cycle. Solution, dissolution, just over and over and over. It is growth, then decay, then transformation. It is fascinating. Really.[1]

In the pilot episode of the American television series *Breaking Bad* (USA 2008-2013), the main character, Walter White, an over-qualified high school chemistry teacher, lectures his students on what chemistry is. White's rhapsodic explanation not only pinpoints his profession and his way of thinking, but offers a key to all that we are about to encounter, over sixty-two episodes and two years in the lives of White, his family, and his antagonists. *Breaking Bad* is a drama about change, about solution and dissolution, about both the power and the mutability of bonds, and about the growth, decay and transformation of a person.

I have spent the past month wholly engrossed in watching *Breaking Bad* on Netflix, watching two or three episodes an evening. I have come late to the party, since the series started in 2008, ending with season five in 2013, and long before its finale it had been rightly acclaimed as one of the finest television dramas yet made. It is hard to think of a more intelligently structured piece of television. This essay is an attempt to unpick why it works so well, and what it says about video drama and the art of narrative.

---

[1] 'Pilot,' *Breaking Bad* series one, original transmission date 20 January 2008 (AMC), written and directed by Vince Gilligan, words spoken by Bryan Cranston as Walter White.

Breaking Bad tells the story of Walter White (played by Bryan Cranston), a high school chemistry teacher who discovers he has terminal lung cancer and turns criminal ('breaking bad') by producing the drug methamphetamine, ostensibly to provide for his family. As the series progresses we discover, or White discovers within himself, that he is driven less by an urge to provide than by than a desire to assert himself and think only for himself. We learn that White has seen a fellow chemist with whom he worked closely turn their once shared business into a multi-million dollar concern, while he was bought out at an early stage for a pittance. He has made wrong decisions all his life. He is browbeaten by his family and gently but insistently mocked by his macho brother-in-law Hank Schrader (played by Dean Norris), who works for the Drug Enforcement Agency. Decisions are always being made for him.

The lung cancer should have been the final blow, but instead it becomes the catalyst for extraordinary change, as White discovers first that he is able to produce the best methamphetamine anywhere, then that he possesses a propensity for lying and an ability to think his way out of impossible situations through the application of analytical thinking and practical chemistry. As the series progresses he reveals more and more of a heartless streak that insidiously burrows into audience expectations, as the man we expect to root for instead disgusts, frightens and ultimately bewilders us.

Walter White's transformation has its effects on a wide cast of people—fatally so for quite a number of them. There is his wife Skyler, the supposed moral centre of the drama who gradually becomes compromised herself (played by Anna Gunn); his son Walter Jr. (RJ Mitte), who has cerebral palsy; brother-in-law Hank (the Javert to his Jean Valjean) and Hank's kleptomaniac wife Marie (Betsy Brandt). There is his former pupil and now collaborator in drug production Jesse Pinkman (Aaron Paul), and as the story progresses an extraordinary array of characters, notably among them the elegant fast food proprietor and drug kingpin Gus Fring (Giancarlo Esposito), the crooked, quick-talking lawyer Saul Goodman (Bob Odenkirk), world-weary hitman Mike Ehrmantraut (Jonathan Banks) and corrupt business executive Lydia Rodarte-Quayle (Laura Fraser). Not least among the pleasures of *Breaking Bad* is the matching of compelling names to compelling characters.

Breaking Bad is about many things. It is very obviously and topically about the drugs trade in America, particularly the fears over crystal meth and the traffic in drugs and drug-related crime from Mexico (the action is set in Albuquerque, New Mexico). It is about the attraction and repulsion of family life, prefigured in White's words about 'bonds' (the White family themselves, the violent Salamancas—for whom 'family is all'—the villainous Uncle Jack and his nephew Todd, but also the camaraderie of the DEA agents and Jesse's drug crowd). It is about the anxieties of masculinity, emblematised in the opening shots of the opening episode in which Walter loses his trousers, a recurrent motif thereafter. It is about gun-related violence in America and the travails of living with insufficient medical insurance. It is about father/son, teacher/pupil relationships. It is about business models. It is about class. It is about money versus morality. It is about morality versus survival. It is about cancer. It is about chemistry.

There is a lot of chemistry in *Breaking Bad*. The opening credits feature a criss-crossing of chemical elements, the letters from which are also highlighted in the credit names. Walter White's supreme knowledge of chemistry (we know that in the past his research into crystallography contributed towards some Nobel prize-winning work) allows him to make a fortune and repeatedly to outwit those faced against him. He applies the scientific method to every situation, calculating that for every action there is reaction and a solution. The dehumanising aspect of this is noted early on when we see a flashback to his youth when he lists all the compounds that go to make up the human body in conversation with his then love Gretchen (Jessica Hecht), who will go on to marry the man who made a fortune out of White's knowledge. There seems so little to a human when all you do is add up the chemicals that make up one such being. 'What about the soul?' asks Gretchen, when his numbers do not quite add up to 100%. Meanwhile, intercut with this scene is the ugly reality of White and Pinkman having to dispose of a drug dealer's body that has been insufficiently dissolved with acid. We are more than flesh, more just a collection of elements, surely?

This tension between science and humanism, or maybe between science and art, is exemplified partly by Walter's relationship with his would-be fiction writer wife, but more so by his relationship with Jesse Pinkman. Pinkman is the most uncalculating of people—not a good person, but someone who believes there things that are good. The contrast, and indeed chemistry, between the two is at the core of *Breaking Bad*'s success, and it is hard to believe that the series' creator Vince Gilligan originally considered killing off Pinkman at the end of series one.[2] In Pinkman, flawed as he is, we find a little hope for ourselves; in Walter White we see none.

There are many reasons why *Breaking Bad* is compelling to watch, but what lies at the heart of its success is its control over narrative and time. Everyone who has sung the series' praises says much the same thing about how brilliantly its plot developments evolve, how ingeniously it introduces not so much twists as new vistas. Just as you think that you know where you are and how everyone relates to one another, a new element is introduced which pulls the rug from under your feet. Yet these developments are never gimmicks for their own sake; in every case they simply redefine our perspective. The naturalistic, convincing way in which these plot developments are introduced is another hallmark. *Breaking Bad* has its contrivances, but they are so well hidden that they never jar. An inconsequential action of character in one episode is revealed to have major significance three or four episodes later, forcing us to rethink where we think the story is going.

Such control over narrative over sixty-two episodes and five seasons is all the more remarkable given the uncertain nature of television production. The first season of seven episodes (reduced from nine after a Writers Guild of America strike) had to lay the groundwork for plot developments that might never happen if audiences had rejected it and the networks had not commissioned further seasons. Gilligan was certain about some plot developments, but others emerged as writing progressed as the internal logic of the dramatic situation suggested new directions down which to travel. *Breaking Bad* could have gone in many directions, or could have been any length, even while in its finished state it feels wholly thought through, without padding or irrelevance. It is fully orchestrated drama.

The control over narrative and time is seen at the micro as well as the macro level. Individual episodes are distinguished by the extraordinary amount of action they pack in while never seeming to rush things in any way. Time is played with through flash-backs, and by the regular use of time-lapse photography. Episodes frequently have pre-credit flash-forward sequences, teasing as to the outcome of events, so that we do not think so much what will happen next as how will be get to the point from where we started. Notable examples include the effects of the plane crash that ends

---

[2] Emma Rosenblum, 'The Ascent of Jesse Pinkman,' *New York*, 18 March 2010, https://nymag.com/arts/tv/features/64941.

Walter White (Bryan Cranston) in *Breaking Bad*

season two, or White's return from disappearance under a new identity in season five. It does not matter what happens next: what matters is how we will get there—what matters is the method.

The mastery over the experience of time—something of which Walter White has little left, of course—is there in the different ways in which audiences have been able to watch the series. Those with it from the beginning back in 2008 saw each weekly episode in turn until the end of a season, then had to wait until the next season came along. Those who have found it on DVD, or like me on Netflix, in its full state have the opportunity to watch it in any way that we choose, even in a single sitting should one have the time and the stamina. It works just as well. In effect it is a fifty-hour movie.

Justified comparisons have been drawn between *Breaking Bad* and the works of Charles Dickens. Writers of Dickens' period produced novels in multi-part form in magazines, which only later were collected into volumes, and then single volumes. They had the overarching vision of where their story was to go, yet had to work in an environment where their story was made available to the public and to the market while they were still writing it. They, the story, the characters and the audiences, all grew as a necessary part of the publication model. The process could not be endless (such as a soap opera): there was always a dramatic end in sight. So it is with Vince Gilligan and other writers of multi-season television dramas which lie at the mercy of the audiences and the networks, yet which have a magnificent canvas on which to paint if they get the model right.

There is a Dickensian quality to Gilligan's creation. Walter White is a very different character to Pip, David Copperfield or Nicholas Nickleby, not least in how his actions lead him to the bad rather than Dickens' model of trials-leading-to-redemption, but all show a man asserting himself in the contexts of his time, through a narrative rich in character and incident, incidents which eventually he is the generator of rather than the victim of, as he gains mastery over his domain. There is the same combination of epic sweep and domestic detail. Dickens' understanding of money as the engineer of society is powerfully echoed. There is same use of counterbalancing comic characters (*Breaking Bad* is frequently very funny), from the splendid creation of lawyer Saul Goodman (Micawber-like in comic stature) to the comic chorus of Pinkman's friends Badger and Skinny Pete. It is narrative attuned to, and determined by, the temper of the times. *Breaking Bad* says, as *Great Expectations* once said, that we are living in the most dramatic of times.

The Dickensian analogy does not entirely fit, of course. Charles Dickens operated in a narrative world where good must be rewarded and evil punished. *Breaking Bad* observes moral decisions, but is not determined by them. The bad frequently prosper, the good invariably suffer. Those who live or die do not do so because of some sense of reward, or justice. They die simply because someone points a gun at them and pulls the trigger. Yet it is not a nihilistic drama where unhappy things just happen. Walter White goes to the bad, and we know that it is bad. He and other characters becomes obsessed by their need for money, and this desire is invariably their undoing. We know that there is good, and that there is evil—it is just that life's rewards are not quite allocated in the same way. Stories depend on rewards and punishments for us as readers or viewers to find them satisfying—it is why we choose to experience them in the first place. It is *Breaking Bad*'s notable achievement that it both satisfies our sense of a moral world while showing us the realities of the real one.

I have started watching *Breaking Bad* all over again, and there is just so much else to enjoy. There is the poetic yet naturalistic use of language. Here is Jesse Pinkman saying that reasoning with Tuco Salamanca is a bad idea:

> What is that? Conjecture? Are you basing that on that he's got a normal, healthy brain or something? Did you not see him beat a dude to death for like nothing? And that way, that way he just kept staring at us. Saying,

'You're done.' You're done?! You wanna know what that means? I will tell you what that means! That means exactly how it sounds, yo! Alright, we are witnesses, we are loose ends! Right now, Tuco's thinking, 'Yeah, hey, they cook good meth, but can I trust them?' What happens when he decides 'no'?[3]

There is the inspired use of music, often alt-country bands. There is the casting—everyone is so ordinary, and convincing because they have the peculiar stamp of ordinariness about them. It is a series without star names, Cranston probably the best-known for his role in the comedy series *Malcolm in the Middle* (USA 2000-2006). There is the skilful use of mobile phones to drive the narrative and connect characters—watch *Forbrydelsen* (*The Killing*) (Denmark 2007-2012) for comparison, where the characters' continual use of phones teeters over into absurdity. There is the way White and his wife Skyler try to have amicable conversations only for the suspicion between them to creep in. There is the playful use of significant objects. There is the exceptional cinematography, with any number of surprise camera angles that are wholly appropriate to a drama where we are not too sure where to look or what will happen next, and a sly use of colour coding that could take up a whole essay in itself.

The boxed set television drama, now further invigorated by streaming services such as Netflix, is one of the creative triumphs of our time. Tremendous stories are allowed to unfold, stories of our times rather than times past, stories which take on grand themes that appeal to that which is intelligent in all of us. *24* (USA 2001-2010, 2014), *The Wire* (USA 2002-2008), *House of Cards* (USA 2008-2013), *The West Wing* (USA 1999-2006), *The Bridge* (Denmark/Sweden, 2011-2018), *The Sopranos* (USA 1999-2007)—they transcend the limitations of the movie or the one-off television drama which needs must compact what it wants to tell into a couple of hours. They transcend television itself, finding a new home on disc, tablets or smart TVs that puts the audience in control of what it reads. These multi-part dramas revive the spirit and intent of the nineteenth-century novel and should be considered as co-equal with it, in their art and in their science. We are living in a classical age.

---

[3] 'Seven Thirty-Seven,' *Breaking Bad* series two, original transmission date 8 March 2009 (AMC), written by J. Roberts and directed by Bryan Cranston, words spoken by Aaron Paul as Jesse Pinkman.

Originally published as 'The Scientific Method,' 9 March 2014, https://
lukemckernan.com/2014/03/09/the-scientific-method, and reproduced
here with small emendations. *Breaking Bad* was followed by the prequel
series *Better Call Saul* (USA 2015-2022) and a one-off sequel film, *El
Camino: A Breaking Bad Movie* (USA 2019).

10.

Prequels

Better Call Saul *and the paradoxes of prequels*

The best thing on television just now is *Better Call Saul* (USA 2015-2022), despite some considerable competition. The series is a prequel to *Breaking Bad*, the 2008-2013 series about a high-school chemistry teacher, Walter White, who takes to a life of crime by manufacturing methamphetamine. The crooked lawyer Saul Goodman was one of the particular joys of that series, so there was much delight among the fans when a prequel was announced, which would trace the life of Goodman before he met Walter White, when he was known as Jimmy McGill. This required the actor Bob Odenkirk to play the same character six years before the start of the start of *Breaking Bad*, so effectively playing someone eight years younger than he had been by the end of *Breaking Bad*, in televisual terms (the series embraced two fictional years), or eleven years younger in physical terms.

Make-up, hair dye, and the fresh face of the fifty-four year old Odenkirk have achieved the illusion, while his co-star Jonathan Banks, playing the enforcer Mike Ehrmantraut, has the ageless look of someone was never young in the first place. But for other actors brought in to play their younger selves, often in cameos, the passing of time has not been so easy to disguise. Raymond Cruz, who played the villainous Tuco Salamanca, was patently older when playing younger than he had been when older. And leading character Gus Fring, played by Giancarlo Esposito, bears all the marks of hard experience earned through the passing of time that one might expect in a sequel, but which looks all out of place in a prequel. In no way is this a younger Gus.

Yet that is what we have to accept. We overlook credibility out of gratefulness for the extension of the narrative. Gus Fring is like a robust Brunnhilde in a Wagnerian opera, whose implausibility we must forgive because the voice is right. What matters is not the reality but the story, so long as it is a story in which we need to believe.

Gus Fring (Giancarlo Esposito) in *Better Call Saul.*

We are getting used to this peculiar phenomenon of actors playing the younger versions of established characters. Perhaps the most glaring absurdity has been Anthony Hopkins playing a younger Hannibal Lecter in *Red Dragon* (USA 2002), eleven years after he first portrayed the character in *The Silence of the Lambs* (USA 1991). Make-up and lighting can only do so much. Nothing can be done to disguise the weariness in the eyes. Even in sequels, particularly action franchise films, actors project themselves as still having the energy of their younger selves—Sylvester Stallone, Bruce Willis, Harrison Ford—despite the increasing absurdity of such presumption. We the viewers are being instructed to ignore the passing of time, while being presented with unavoidable evidence to the contrary.

Gus Fring (Giancarlo Esposito) in *Breaking Bad*.

This is one of the defining characteristics of our age—the urge to agelessness. But while those who apply the hair-dye, undergo Botox or plastic surgery, or flex muscles now buried in flab are presumably convinced to a degree of the success of the results, we who view always see differently. And of course, you cannot have a prequel without having the later story first. The prequel is a paradox, always coming afterwards yet trying to persuade you of its prior existence.

But as I watched *Better Call Saul* I found myself equally distracted by and yet indulgent of actors cast against the progress of time. The urge to believe in a story conquers everything. Plausibility defers to credibility. Just as past generations excused cowboy films in which villains were shot without a drop of blood being shed, or corpses still lay breathing, the need to keep the story going blinds me. It is not the suspension of disbelief; it is the sustainment of belief. Without a faith in stories, we are nothing.

We think we are sophisticated viewers, in how we accept meta-narratives, or post-narratives, or whatever you want to call this age of knowing viewing, where we understand the artifice while allowing it credibility. But really we are no different to early cinema audiences, who accepted dramatic codes that later generations find absurd, or Saturday morning cinema children cheering on pudgy heroes whose gunshots never missed. The yearning to believe keeps us young, prequels of our present selves.

Originally published as 'Prequels,' 25 May 2017, https://lukemckernan. com/2017/05/25/prequels, and reproduced here with small emendations. *Better Call Saul* ran 2015-2022 six seasons, with sixty-three episodes, one more than *Breaking Bad*.

11.

Tell It Like It Is

Primary Colors and a love of the political process

There is a scene in *Primary Colors* (USA 1998) that keeps coming back to me as I read about the current presidential race between Hilary Clinton and Donald Trump. Jack Stanton, a Southern governor in pursuit of the Democratic nomination for president, is beset by scandal. His great strength is his empathy with ordinary folk; his great weakness is his libido.

Stanton gives a speech to a crowd of working class Democrats in a shipyard town that has hit hard times. He sets his audience up nicely with some folksy, self-deprecating talk, then launches his big surprise.

> You know what I'm gonna do? I'm gonna do something really outrageous here. I'm gonna tell the truth.

Applause and laughter follow. Stanton's aides look on nervously, wondering what the truth might entail. Stanton goes on:

> OK, here's the truth. No politician can re-open this factory, or bring back the shipyard jobs, or make your union strong again. No politician can make it be the way it used to be. Because we're living in a new world now, a world without economic borders. A guy can push a button in New York and move a billion dollars to Tokyo before you blink an eye. And in that world muscle jobs go where muscle labour is cheap—and that's not here. So if you all want to compete, you're gonna have to exercise a different set of muscles, the ones between your ears.

One Stanton aide murmurs to Henry Burton (the conscience of the film, played by Adrian Lester), 'He's lost them.' Burton replies, 'Fuck them. He's got me,' wide-eyed at Stanton's vision of

Jack Stanton (John Travolta) tells voters the truth.

the new world America will need to face up to, and the strategies needed to do so.

It is not clear whether the audience has taken in the message or not. In the original novel, by Anonymous (subsequently revealed to be journalist Joe Klein) it suggests they have been left deep in thought.[1] Otherwise the scenes in book and film are very similar, indeed *Primary Colors* the film is notable for being almost word-for-word identical to the novel (Elaine May wrote, or perhaps the word should be pruned, the script). Where it differs is in that exchange between the aides, which is only in the film: one worried about the impact, the other lost in the message.

The scene captures a pivotal moment in American life, a call to face up to the fact that the world had changed and that there was no turning back. But did they hear? Stanton wins the nomination, and we must assume that he goes on to become president, because he is so obviously based on Bill Clinton. But does he win on the strength of the argument? The film does not suggest so. Instead it focuses on what it means to speak the truth. Stanton's rival for the nomination is Freddy Picker (played by Larry Hagman), a former Florida governor who joins the race at a late stage when another candidate falls ill.

Picker is the dream politician. He is gently-spoken, without rancour, treats his opponents with courtesy, refuses to engage in negative campaigning. He is an absolutely honest person. He speaks the truth that America wants to hear. Stanton may speak the truth in a common voice, but he is always putting on an act, always calculating. Picker is presented as the absence of calculation. His

---

[1] Anonymous [Joe Klein], *Primary Colors: A Novel of Politics* (London: Chatto & Windus, 1996), pp. 159-163.

is an idealism not of politics but personality. In a cruel twist, we learn that Picker has a sordid past and withdraws from the contest, Stanton proving himself noble if pragmatic in how he lets Picker know what is known about him privately. Stanton goes on to win, but his victory is one of survival, not of message.

You sense that Freddy Picker would storm to victory were he a presidential candidate today, simply for being the antithesis of a politician. But Picker has no political message—at least none that we get to hear about. He simply represents an attitude. In truth he is as calculating as his opponent, indeed he is all calculation, an absolute performer. Stanton is all performance as well, but he has something to say, and believes in what he says.

Primary Colors is a clever film. It sets up Jack Stanton as this wonderful guy, a little rough at the edges but an inspirational force for good, someone we all want to vote for. It then taunts us as we learn of his infidelities, lies, cynicism and cold calculation. Then when we have forgiven him because others have done so, and are still minded to vote for him, it presents us with Freddy Picker and has us wondering what it is that we really want.

The answer is that we want and need politics. *Primary Colors* presents the political process as a courtship: from attraction, to infatuation, to crisis, to acceptance, to understanding, and on to something which might just last. It sets out the dilemma between idealism and realism, asks us what we want of the truth, but ultimately it is a romance. It celebrates the extraordinary drama that is the American primary and presidential election process, and as dispiriting as the current contest has sometimes been, it is still the same story. Whether, after the courtship, we can live with its consequences, we will find out soon.

Originally published as 'Tell It Like It Is,' 27 October 2016, https://lukemckernan.com/2016/10/27/tell-it-like-it-is, and reproduced here with small emendations. *Primary Colors* was directed by Mike Nichols. In the 2016 American presidential election, the Republican Donald Trump defeated the Democrat Hilary Clinton.

12.

The Skull Beneath the Skin

Connecting The Long Good Friday *to* The Duchess of Malfi

The first X-rated film I saw was *The Long Good Friday* (UK 1981).[1] I was nineteen, and a little apprehensive about the promised violence that only someone of the age I had now attained was permitted to see.

The opening scenes of the film were confusing. Money was changing hands, clearly illicitly. The notes were carried in a suitcase from one destination to another. Three men in a remote house were handed the money, only to have men with guns burst in on them as they started to count it. Elsewhere a man was stabbed to death outside a swimming pool. A widow got out of a car and spat on one of two men seated at a pavement cafe, discussing deals. What was going on?

The electronic music, which had quietly racked up the tension, turned to a pounding deep beat as a British Airways Concorde airplane arrived at Heathrow. This is the moment. The music rises to a swaggering earworm of a riff. In comes the face of the man whose fate we are to witness, filling the screen, as the camera tracks his progress. It is simultaneously powerful and mocking, revealing someone at the heart of the dark world to which we have been introduced, who does not yet know how vulnerable he is.

So we meet Harold Shand, London's gangster overlord, played by Bob Hoskins. There can be few better entrances in all of cinema history—certainly you could not hope for better. I was watching the film again recently following the news of the death of Francis Monkman, the progressive rock musician whose inspired score confirmed the film's greatness.[2] There were so many dire British film scores at the time, when cost-cutting meant music via a synthesizer rather than an orchestra. *The Long Good Friday* should

---

[1] The X certificate for films screened in the UK was defined at this time as 'Suitable for those aged 18 and over.' It was replaced in 1982 by the 18 certificate.
[2] Francis Monkman died 12 May 2023, aged seventy-three.

Harold Shand (Bob Hoskins) makes his entrance.

have been another such film, tripped up by economy and poor taste. Instead Monkman came up with music that ideally complemented Shand's rise and fall. We fear him but we laugh at his pretension—nervously, when we think he will not notice us.

I knew at nineteen that here was a great film, an electrifying tale of gangsterdom and hubris, in which all of the required elements fell into place perfectly. It was written by Barrie Keeffe and directed by John Mackenzie. It tells of Harold Shand, a London gangster who has reached the top of his particular tree and now plans to become legitimate (relatively so—he is seeking funding from the American Mafia) by investing in the rebuilding of London Docklands, ready for the 1988 Olympic Games. But at the point when he is about to make the final deal, he is undermined by an adversary whose methods lie outside his understanding.

The film had an easy production history but a difficult distribution one. The power of the script was appreciated by cast and crew, the most significant changes being made, in effect, by Helen Mirren. She demanded that her character Victoria, Shand's girlfriend, be much more than the cardboard moll that had been scripted. Victoria had to be a powerful, capable figure in her own right. By making Victoria Harold's equal in wit and intelligence, the film is hugely enriched. Everyone fears Harold except Victoria; only she can control him; only she has his respect.

The presence of the IRA (Irish Republican Army) in the film caused nervousness among the film's investors. It led to it being shelved for over a year, then almost released in a bowdlerised form on television, until HandMade Films, newly formed by George

Harrison and Denis O'Brien, came to the rescue. They took on the risk and rightly enjoyed the rewards. Its excellence was immediately recognised, and its reputation has continued to grow to where it now viewed as one of the finest British films from any era and a masterpiece of the gangster genre.

Back in 1981 I was in a particularly privileged position, as the previous year I had seen Adrian Noble's production of John Webster's Jacobean tragedy, *The Duchess of Malfi*, at the Royal Exchange Theatre in Manchester. Its lead performers were Bob Hoskins and Helen Mirren, with a strong supporting cast, which included Pete Postlethwaite, Sorcha Cusack, Julian Curry and Mike Gwilym. It too was an electrifying production, images and sounds from which still resonate in my head. The way Hoskins, playing Bosola, uttered the famous words 'We are merely the stars' tennis-balls, struck and bandied / Which way please them' was so comic, so bitter, so true to what we were seeing of figures who had fought against fate and lost.[3] Thrilled beyond measure, I saw the production three times. The Royal Exchange being a theatre-in-the-round, I was able to see the play from a different angle each time.

Therefore, when I saw *The Long Good Friday* a few months later, it was with *The Duchess of Malfi* in mind. I knew these two and could see their world played out again in London's dockland in the 1980s. Where previously it had been a scheming cardinal and duke that condemned them, now it was the IRA. In play and film, they had the same faces, and somehow spoke with the same voice.

The Long Good Friday is often described as being like a Shakespeare tragedy. Shand's arrogance then fall, in the face of powers greater than himself, the goodness (of a kind) mixed with evil, the failure to understand himself until it is too late, the keen study of power relations—these aspects are all recognisably Shakespearean. *Macbeth* would seem to be the closest comparison.

However, it is worthwhile considering the film's affinity with Jacobean drama in general, particularly (though not exclusively) John Webster. There was a school of Jacobean dramatists who shared Shakespeare's stages and who wrote dark tragedies for dark times—Thomas Middleton, Cyril Tourneur, John Marston, John Ford, and pre-eminent among them Webster, for his plays *The White Devil* and *The Duchess of Malfi*. Such tragedies reflected the unease felt at the start of the reign of James I. The dramatists saw

---

[3] John Webster, *The Duchess of Malfi*, in D. C. Gunby (ed.), *John Webster: Three Plays* (Harmondsworth: Penguin Books 1972), Act 5 Scene 4, ll. 53-54.

Bosola (Bob Hoskins) and the Duchess (Helen Mirren)
in *The Duchess of Malfi*.

an unstable state, where morality and value were lost, where the
virtuous life was hard to find and hard to live. It was risky to set
such feelings in a British setting, so they turned to Italy or Spain,
filled with demonic dukes and carnal cardinals, which is what we
find in *The Duchess of Malfi*. But the audience knew where the true
location was.

There is no plot similarity between *The Long Good Friday*
and *The Duchess of Malfi*. The first concerns a London gangster,
Harold Shand, who grows increasingly desperate, and violent,
when he finds members of his entourage being killed by some
unknown party. When one of the corrupt policemen in his pay tells
him that the party responsible is the IRA and that he is getting out
of his depth, Shand does not listen. He tackles them as he would
any ordinary gangster rival, and pays the price for his folly.

The Duchess of Malfi, which is based on an actual historical
case, concerns the fall of the eponymous duchess after she marries
her steward, Antonio, in secret, against the wishes of her brothers,
the Cardinal and Duke, the one a cold and calculating hypocrite,
the other close to mania in his rages. They may want her wealth or,
in the case of the duke, have incestuous desires towards her. At any
rate, she has no right to thoughts of her own. The duke employs
a former servant and galley slave, Bosola, to spy on her, which he

Harold (Bob Hoskins) and Victoria (Helen Mirren)
in *The Long Good Friday*.

does faithfully while increasingly despising them and himself as
the story descends into madness and retributive murder, leaving
none of the main protagonists alive by the end of it.

The lead male and female parts in play and film are different.
Bosola is a servant, Shand a king-like gangland leader. The duchess
is nobility and the title character, Victoria is a supporting role in
someone else's tragedy. They are lovers in the film, not in the play.
But if there is no plot similarity, tonally and thematically there
is plenty shared between the two works. One of the reasons the
film had such a charge to it, for the lucky few who saw the Royal
Exchange Theatre's production, was that it felt so close to the film,
as if Bosola and the duchess had morphed into Harold and Victoria,
either pair transported forward or back in time to the same moral
mayhem, in which no good person can hope to survive.

Harold Shand a good person? Well, not conventionally so,
but he has his idea of what is good, and believes in it. He believes
in order, loyalty, honour. He is resolutely proud of his city and
country. He pities the disadvantaged and bemoans a deteriorating
society. 'Is there no decency in this disgusting world?' he says
when he finds evidence of drug use in the house of someone he
is interrogating—whom he has slashed with a knife to make him
speak. As brutal and criminal as he is, we root for him. He stands
for something.

Bosola is similarly admirable, in spite of himself. He does the
duke's bidding, and continues to do so even when he can see where
it is leading and that the duchess is an innocent victim. But in his

understanding of the evil world into which he has been sucked we see goodness, because he knows what evil is and believes there is goodness somewhere. He is that standard Jacobean character type, the malcontent, one who understands the corruption about him but can only fall victim to it.

Harold Shand is no malcontent, though like those Jacobeans he is disturbed by a changing society and a loss of values. Instead, a closer link between Amalfi and London is religion and retribution. *The Duchess of Malfi* is a play steeped in sin. Its plot-line could be boiled down to 'a fall into a hell-pit.' The duke denies that there is a soul in his fevered desire to bring his sister to despair, while in the final scene the cardinal has these almost calm thoughts about a book he is reading, not knowing they are almost the last words he will utter:

> I am puzzl'd in a question about hell:
> He says, in hell there's one material fire,
> And yet it shall not burn all men alike.
> Lay him by. How tedious is a guilty conscience!
> When I look into the fishponds in my garden,
> Methinks I see a thing, arm'd with a rake
> That seems to strike at me.[4]

The Duchess of Malfi comes out of a world in which religion imbued every aspect of life. *The Long Good Friday* is the product of a secular age, but there is plenty there that Webster's audience might have recognised. Fairly obviously, there is is the fact that it takes place over Good Friday, with a bomb placed outside a Catholic church being one of the film's most striking set pieces. The mass that was being held there was attended by Shand's mother, so it is a reasonable inference that Shand himself was brought up in the Catholic faith. We hear nothing else about this, though script-writer Barrie Keeffe does throw in this cheeky line for Shand:

> Who'd do such a thing, it's outrageous. Outside a
> church... You don't go crucifying people outside a
> church on Good Friday.

But there is plenty going on to puzzle one of his background, even deliberately staged to taunt him. Why does the IRA (peopled by Roman Catholics, one assumes), place a bomb outside a Catholic

---

[4] Webster, *The Duchess of Malfi*, Act 5 Scene 5, ll. 1-7.

church? Why does it effectively crucify a security guard witness by nailing him to a floor? What ironic message are they trying to send? In this drama of retribution, how come the IRA does not meet any retribution of its own? And is not Shand some sort of parody Christ-figure, betrayed by a Judas in his own camp, as he is led by stages, like the Christian stations of the cross, to his own crucifixion?

Another link between play and film is theatricality. *The Long Good Friday* is a remarkably theatrical film. It has scenes, dramatic confrontations, and a series of visual shock moments such as a Jacobean audience would have recognised. It paces itself like a Jacobean tragedy, every action building on the previous one to result in a bloody final act such as Webster would have understood as necessary. It has the unreal reality of the stage. It would work superbly in blank verse.

More than blood-soaked conclusions where half the cast lie on the stage having stabbed one another, there are set pieces in the film which seem almost uncannily Jacobean in their imagination. *The Duchess of Malfi* has a scene in which the duchess is terrorised by a staged group of madmen, before being strangled, and another where the deranged duke could be turning into a wolf ('Pray thee, what's his disease?' 'A very pestilent disease, my lord, They call lycanthropia').[5] The notorious scene in the film where Shand rounds up other London gangster leaders in an abattoir and questions them as they hang upside-down, like pieces of meat, could have come straight out of Webster's imagination. It gets the blend of horror and humour just right. Shand's killing of Jeff (played by Derek Thompson) with a broken bottle has the impulsive rage of a time, so ably captured by Shakespeare, Webster and the rest, when rivals would reach for their swords in an instant, blind to consequences.

With all this said, it has to be pointed out that *The Duchess of Malfi* had no influence on *The Long Good Friday*. Perhaps Barrie Keeffe had some thoughts about Shakespeare, since the film does come across as Shakespeare-like, not least in its concentration on the gaining and loss of power, one of Shakespeare's pre-eminent themes. Webster has no such interest, or rather his skills lay else-where—the loss of souls, perhaps.

But there is something there, beyond Hoskins and Mirren acting in both film and play within a short period, and looking as though one was the extension of the other. *The Long Good*

---

[5] Webster, *The Duchess of Malfi*, Act 5 Scene 2, ll. 5-6.

Friday is a gangster film. It is recognisably one of a genre of films whose tropes are quickly understood by an audience. Genre films adhere to recognised commonalities of style, character and story that appeal to an audience's desire for the familiar. In the gangster film, the gangster lives outside the law and is continually at war with the law. They are defined by their need to have those who enforce such laws, so that they have something to battle against. They have a gang that they must control. They fight to sustain the little world over which, for a time, they have power. They must fail in the end, to satisfy the audience's need for safety. Harold Shand is Ned Kelly, John Dillinger, Clyde Barrow and Ma Barker. His fate has been set out, the moment we see him.

The revenge tragedies of the Jacobean era were a genre too. The audience knew exactly what they were to be offered. They would see noble figures (probably from Italy or Spain, where you would expect to find such goings-on), bound in mutual distrust, transgressing the laws of god and society, damning themselves. There will be an innocent victim. There will be a conflicted inter-mediary. It all ends in a bloodbath which stretches the limits of credulity. The uninteresting good guys get to give the final speech. It is the story, with variations, of *Hamlet* (strictly speaking an Elizabethan drama), of *The Revenger's Tragedy*, *Women Beware Women*, *The Changeling*, *Bussy D'Ambois*, *'Tis Pity She's a Whore* and *The Duchess of Malfi*. Though twentieth-century city crimi-nals and Renaissance courtiers are worlds apart, each are impris-oned in little worlds which they think they can control, only to find that they are unable to escape their downfall. Outside the forces of law and order and undramatic rationality lie waiting. The Duchess and Bosola, and Harold and Victoria, would recognise one another. They are each victims of the predestination of plot.

'Webster was much possessed by death / And saw the skull beneath the skin.' So T. S. Eliot wrote in 'Whispers of Immor-tality.' *The Long Good Friday* is much possessed by death. Every character lives in its shadow, just one stab or explosion away from oblivion. They know that they have transgressed and that their time is short.

Our first and final sights of Harold Shand are of his head. There is the short but telling tracking shot, focussed on a head filled with hopes and apprehension, which introduces him to us in the airport. Then there is his downfall, when he is driven away in a car by the IRA (he sees a despairing Victoria being taken away in a separate car). In a similar but longer tracking shot, the camera

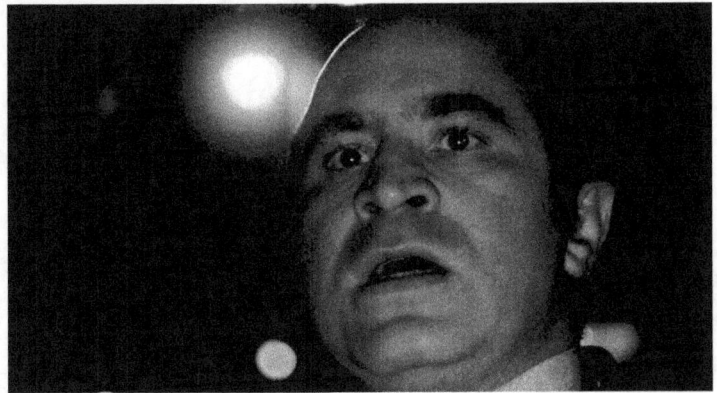

Harold Shand makes his exit.

focusses tightly on his face, as his thoughts turn from rage to calculation to resignation. This will be his last journey. His entrance
and his exit complement one another. In each we look deeply into
the man and see that skull, only thinly hidden beneath the skin.

Originally published as 'The Skull Beneath the Skin,' 16 June 2023, https://
lukemckernan.com/2023/06/16/the-skull-beneath-the-skin, and reproduced here with small emendations. *The Duchess of Malfi* ran at Manchester's Royal Exchange theatre 16 September-18 October 1980. I saw it on 8,
11 and 14 October.

13.

Just a Brixton Shop Girl

The poignant tale of Margaret Leahy, film star competition winner

The first feature film that Buster Keaton directed, *The Three Ages* (USA 1923), is not perhaps as familiar as it should be. A comic history of love in prehistoric, Roman and modern times, it has Keaton fighting his rival, Wallace Beery, over a girl and winning her against the odds each time. Allegedly parodying *Intolerance* (USA 1916), it is really three sketches strung together rather than a true feature, but it is still highly amusing (especially in the Stone Age sequence) and boasts some breathtaking stunts. The actress playing the girl is Margaret Leahy, and it was her only film. While researching the history of a British newsreel, I came across the extraordinary events which led this Brixton shop girl to be Keaton's co-star.

Film star competitions were a particular feature of the silent era; that is, competitions run by newspapers or film magazines for which the prize was to appear in pictures yourself. There were standard beauty competitions where the winner sometimes ended up with a film contract later, there were cinema beauty competitions where the contestants were filmed and then judged by the audience, but competitions that offered directly for the winner to become a film star were something special. In such competitions, newspapers, fan magazines and film companies exploited audience dreams of film stardom with promises of screen tests or parts in forthcoming films. The film companies found this useful publicity for forthcoming productions and may have even hoped to find some future star in this way.

In America, such contests were sufficiently common for them to be made the subject of at least two major feature films. In *The Extra Girl* (USA 1923), Mabel Normand plays a competition winner who finds that her prize of a job in the movies actually means working in the wardrobe department; in *Ella Cinders* (USA 1926), Colleen Moore is a down-trodden Cinderella figure who wins a competition and ends up in Hollywood. Both, needless to say, after some trials and tribulations, find themselves becoming true film stars. The dream for Cinderella could, in any case, some-times come true. By far the best known winner of any film star competition is Clara Bow, who began her career with a bit part as the prize for winning a fan magazine beauty competition. Bow was blessed with a talent significantly lacking in most other film star competition winners, most of whom returned swiftly to obscurity.

In Britain film star competitions sprang up in the immediate post-war period. In 1919 the *Sunday Express* newspaper, in associa-tion with the Stoll Film Company, organised a nation-wide contest, won by Miss Tommy Sinclair, who it was said would be found a 'suitable part in a Stoll production,' though if this were so it was only a bit part. In the same year a more widely publicised contest was organised by the *Daily Mirror* newspaper and the Samuelson film company, won by Miriam Sabbage, whose picture was featured prominently in advertising for the feature film in which she got third billing, *The Bridal Chair* (UK 1919). The trade paper *The Bioscope* in reviewing the film noted accurately that

> it may be questioned whether, from a strictly artistic point of view, prize-winning beauty is in itself a sufficient qual-ification for the creation of a new film star, but there can be no doubt that it is a sound commercial proposition. Everyone will want to see the beautiful Miss Sabbage, and she will be found in 'The Bridal Chair' large as life.[1]

Her on-screen career was to progress no further, but off-screen she went on to have a moderately successful stage career and married a cinematographer.[2]

Pathé held a 'Screen Beauty Competition' in 1920, and in 1921 Gaumont organised a contest they called 'The Golden Apple Challenge,' for which a reported 26,700 contestants entered for a prize of £500 and a promised film contract, with the most promising contestants featured in a 'women-only' serial set in a detective agency. Winifred Nelson, the eventual winner, did get to appear in minor roles in two Gaumont features. Stoll Film Studios returned to beauty competitions in 1925 with its 'Starlings of the Screen' contest. This was won by Sybil Rhoda, who appeared in three subsequent feature films, including a creditable performance in Alfred Hitchcock's *Downhill* (UK 1927). And at the end of the silent era, Molly Lamont became a

---

[1] 'The Bridal Chair,' *The Bioscope*, 10 July 1919, p. 77.
[2] Sabbage's second marriage was to camera operator Harold Bastick, in 1947.

Norma Talmadge (left) and Margaret Leahy, from *Topical Budget*
newsreel held by the BFI National Archive.

minor star in British and American films for twenty years after
winning a competition in 1930 in a South African newspaper.

But minor parts in British feature films were no match for
a starring role in a major Hollywood film, which is what was
offered by the *Daily Sketch* newspaper in 1922, when they organised the grandest and most widely publicised film star competition of them all. The genesis of the idea came from the American
company First National Pictures, with their two leading stars,
the immensely popular Norma and Constance Talmadge. Joseph
Schenck, chairman of First National and Norma Talmadge's
husband, probably proposed the idea, but at the encouragement
of Sir Edward Hulton, a British newspaper owner with interests
in the cinema. Hulton ran a newsreel, the *Topical Budget*, and the
film distributors Film Booking Offices (F.B.O., not to be confused
with the American distributor of the same name), as well as the
popular newspapers the *Daily Sketch* and the *Evening Standard*.
F.B.O. handled major American features in Britain (e.g. *Broken
Blossoms, Blind Husbands*), and the impetus for a competition to
find a British film star probably came from Hulton's contacts and
interests, since the Talmadges might have welcomed, but hardly
needed such a publicity stunt.

The competition was to find a British actress to play second lead in Norma Talmadge's forthcoming film *Within the Law*. Beauty competitions would be organised on a regional basis, with entrants and winners featured regularly in the *Daily Sketch* and the *Topical Budget*. The final one hundred contestants would then be screen-tested and Norma and Constance Talmadge themselves would come to Stoll Film Studios (where the screen tests were to be made) and select the winner. First National would also have the latest Constance Talmadge film, *East is West* (USA 1922), on release that week. The winner would then be taken to Hollywood to appear in *Within the Law*, and groomed as a British film star. It was marvellous publicity for the Talmadges, First National and Hulton; the hapless British film industry would be only too happy to co-operate in creating such a 'star'; and audiences would flock to *Within the Law* and any of the star's subsequent films. Initially at least, it all went perfectly according to plan.

The competition was first announced in the *Daily Sketch* on 11 September 1922. A letter from Norma Talmadge announced that she was looking for a British film star:

> Dear Sir—I have always said those who argue the British girls are not as good film actresses as American girls are wrong. I want to prove that I am right. Will you, with your splendid Daily Sketch, find for me a young girl in England, Ireland, or Scotland—a true, typical British girl, who would like to become a really great heroine of the films?[3]

She was not looking for beauty necessarily, but for talent, an appetite for hard work and character. Hopeful unknowns (no established actresses were wanted) were to send in a photograph and a short description of themselves. Contestants were to apply to one of twenty-one districts nationwide; in Edinburgh, Glasgow, Newcastle, Blackpool, Manchester, Liverpool, York, Leeds, Nottingham, Birmingham, Cardiff, Bristol, Brighton, Norwich, Belfast, Dublin, and for London, Marble Arch, Whitechapel, Holloway, Lewisham and Clapham. Committees were to be set up for each centre, from which the one hundred finalists would be selected for the screen tests. The closing date was 22 October. Although the competition was planned on a grand scale, they must

---

[3] 'Your Opportunity for Film Fame,' *Daily Sketch*, 11 September 1922, p. 7.

still have been overwhelmed by the response; 80,000 would-be British film stars entered.

Norma Talmadge's *Smilin' Through* (USA 1922) was conveniently released at the same time, and for their side of the bargain the Americans certainly got a great deal with very little effort. The success of the promotion and competition owed everything to Hulton's remarkable press campaign, which engrossed the whole country for two months. Every issue of the *Daily Sketch* featured photographs and details of the entrants, accounts of the deliberations of the regional committees (generally composed of the local mayor, mayoress and other dignitaries), and letters of advice from Norma Talmadge, detailing what she was looking for in her British film star, such as this:

> A will to work, tireless energies, temperament, but a character that will prevent her from becoming spoiled by prosperity and success. Sufficient education to enable her to study and fathom the emotions of the characters she is called upon to portray. Ambition, but willingness to profit in the wisdom of others. Her eyes should be large and well shaped. Blue eyes are a detriment, but they may be 'managed' if all other features are good, and if the girl develops a strong personality. The nose should be straight. The lips should be well marked, but the mouth must not be too large. The lower part of the face must not be too heavy, or broad. Teeth are important—and must be regular and good. They show clearly, and in great detail, when the camera catches a smile. She should be under, rather than over, average weight; her ankles must be trim and her wrists neat. Her hands and feet not too large. She must have inherent grace of action—must know how or be capable of learning how, for example, to walk across the room properly in front of the camera. This may become a matter of teaching, but the girl without some inherent grace often finds it most difficult to learn.[4]

Despite such an intimidating list of requirements, the photographs flooded in. With most of them the poses bore strong resemblance to stars of the day, Mary Pickford and Norma Talmadge herself being favoured in particular. The anxious wrote in to

---

[4] 'Film Fame Candidates Chosen,' *Daily Sketch*, 9 October 1922, p. 2.

the *Daily Sketch* with fears about their noses, eye colour, glasses and ankles. Some, of course, appealed to Norma Talmadge directly:

> Dear Miss Talmadge—I read of your splendid offer in the *Daily Sketch*, and writing to ask you to help me. I have always been ambitious to become a kinema actress. Please, will you help me? If only you knew how I pine for a career! Oh, please help me.
>
> I am a typical English girl, and if I am chosen I will work hard to be a credit to England and you, and also strive to surprise America.
>
> My parents have told me that I may go with you if you would take me. They would trust me in your care.
>
> Oh, Miss Talmadge, if you only knew my hoping, wishing, and longing you would not pass me by, I am sure.
>
> My age is sixteen, and ever since I was ten years old the screen has been my hope. I am praying day and night for you to choose me. I am aware that it is selfish of me to ask of you an especial favour, but I know you will forgive. But, please, help me. Please, do help me.
>
> Only Heaven and myself know of the ambitious hope with which I send this letter and my photograph.[5]

On 2 October 1922 Hulton's newsreel *Topical Budget* announced its part in the '*Daily Sketch* film star competition,' and over the following weeks filmed contestants in Brighton, Blackpool, Bournemouth, Bristol, Glasgow, Leeds, London, Manchester, Newcastle and Sunderland. Under titles such as 'Thousands of British girls want to be a film star' and 'Who will be the new British film star?,' items in the newsreel would, typically, show a group of contestants posed together in a woodland setting, then filmed in close-up individually, slowly turning their heads and smiling. The *Daily Sketch* ran articles and featured photographs on those entrants who were lucky enough to appear in the newsreel. Chaos ensued when the Pavilion Cinema in London's Shaftesbury Avenue conducted its own competition to select one of the cleverly named shortlist, the 'Lovely Hundred.' Traffic was held up by the

---

[5] 'Surprise Good Fortune for One Girl,' *Daily Sketch*, 28 September 1922, p. 7.

crowds, and the *Topical Budget* cameraman could only film the entrants by climbing onto the roof of a taxi. Subsequently they were all able to see themselves portrayed on the Pavilion screen. Other cinemas featured photographs of local contestants in their lobbies.

The competition grew as time went on. A Grand Committee was announced which would help narrow the final hundred down to twenty; its members would include Lord Ashfield, Lady Diana Cooper, Sir Gerald Du Maurier, Lionel Tennyson, theatre manager Seymour Hicks and film distributor Sir William Jury. It was then announced that, as an additional prize, five contestants would be invited to appear in Diana Cooper's new feature film *The Virgin Queen* (UK 1923) (the celebrated society beauty experimented with a short film career at this time). It also transpired that at least two current British film actresses had entered their names, or someone had entered their name for them, as Edith Bishop claimed rather weakly had happened to her. They were disqualified.

Norma and Constance Talmadge arrived at Dover on 7 November. By now the 'Lovely Hundred' had been selected and the photographs of all of them printed in the *Daily Sketch*. As had happened when Douglas Fairbanks and Mary Pickford came to Britain in 1920, and Charlie Chaplin in 1921, the country went wild at the sight of Hollywood glamour. The Talmadges were mobbed by crowds on their arrival in London. But although most of the country had greeted the idea of the contest and a real British film star with enthusiasm, there were some dissenting voices. The *Film Renter* viewed the whole affair with some amusement, and having described the Talmadges' arrival at Dover—noting that their entourage included such figures as 'Susie, the mulatto maid' and Esmeralda, Norma Talmadge's pet tortoise—the paper denounced the whole stunt as a 'cheap circus affair' and expressed surprise at Hollywood stooping so low:

> It is astonishing to think that First National should have lent their name to such a stupid piece of buffoonery. Surely the day is past when stars need such cheap methods of publicity, and it is not fair to the Talmadge sisters or to Mr Schenck that they should have been made the victims of circumstances which have certainly made these genuine screen stars look on one or two occasions a little ridiculous.[6]

---

[6] *The Film Renter*, 18 November 2022, p. 4.

The circus rolled on. The Talmadges lunched with the hundred at the Savoy, after which they all went to the fifth 'Victory Ball,' where Lady Hulton gave a speech. The following day the process of filming the screen tests began at Stoll Film Studios, for which First National had brought their own cameramen. Norma Talmadge, it was said, saw to the make-up of each contestant and was reportedly engrossed in her task. The first screenings took place on 10 November, with more filming in the afternoon, followed by final screenings the following day. The Talmadge sisters, Schenck, other representatives of First National, film director Edward José, and members of the Grand Committee all sat and watched the one hundred screen tests at a viewing theatre in Oxford Street and whittled down the entrants to twenty-one. After repeated screenings, they had three finalists. Finally, and after much agonised debate, they had one.

On Tuesday 14 November the *Daily Sketch* had a full front page photograph of the winner. She was Margaret Leahy, an Irish girl aged twenty, who worked in London for a Brixton milliner, and lived in the Marble Arch area. 'A perfect film face,' said Norma Talmadge, adding that she had 'splendid eyes, a supple body, and convincing expressiveness… her features are so perfect, and her character so distinctive!' She had had the greatest difficulty in choosing from her final three, and had almost decided to take the other two, Jean Jay and Irene Coney, to Hollywood as well (Jean Jay would appear in a few British film productions in the mid-1920s and wrote scenarios). But 'Bubbles' Leahy it was, whose face immediately appeared in newspaper advertisements for shampoo and toothbrushes. *Topical Budget* showed Norma Talmadge presenting her with a bouquet, and her appearance at the Marble Arch Pavilion at the premiere of Constance Talmadge's *East Is West*, where she made a speech to the audience and was introduced to the Duke of York (the future King George VI).

The *Daily Sketch* printed her life story, such as it was, and the details of her prize. She would first spend a week touring all the major cities of the country, then sail to America, being paid £100 a week and chaperoned by her mother (also called Margaret), when after suitable training she would appear as Aggie Lynch, second lead in Norma Talmadge's new feature film, *Within the Law*. She would then be given her own starring production. She would be under Norma Talmadge's special guidance, but if she showed a special talent for comedy would be

MISS MARGARET LEAHY.
THE "DAILY SKETCH" GIRL
S. 77-3.   ADOPTED BY MISS NORMA TALMADGE.

Postcard of Margaret Leahy, The "Daily Sketch" Girl.

looked after by Constance Talmadge (Constance's specialism was light comedy, Norma being more of an 'emotional' actress).

So far the competition had been an outstanding success. The Talmadges were the toast of the town, *East is West* was going to be a huge success, the *Daily Sketch* and *Topical Budget* triumphed in the publicity, and Margaret Leahy was proving to be a very popular winner. She went on a rapid tour of the country where she was greeted everywhere by large and enthusiastic crowds. Having said goodbye to the Talmadges at Southampton, her hectic national tour took in Birmingham, Manchester, Leeds, Newcastle, Edinburgh, Glasgow, Liverpool, Cardiff, Bristol, Brighton and Southampton. She reportedly collapsed three times during the week. On 25 November, having been wished farewell by crowds in London, who sang 'Auld Lang Syne' to her, she left for Hollywood on the *Aquitania*.

Everyone was anxious to know how she got on. Postcards of her were put on sale, and the *Daily Sketch* commissioned her to dictate a diary of her experiences (a secretary accompanied her throughout). These touching and observant dispatches show something of the character which Norma Talmadge presumably had seen in her. America knew all about the competition and was just as excited by her imminent arrival. It was said she was to be given the Freedom of New York, and D. W. Griffith and Charlie Chaplin sent her telegrams of congratulations. She arrived on 3 December and lights from skyscrapers flashed out a Morse code message of welcome. Among the huge crowd on the quayside to greet her were the Talmadges, Marion Davies, Anita Stewart and Katherine Macdonald, while Chaplin, Mary Pickford and Lillian Gish were said to have sent representatives to meet her.

The following day she met her director, Frank Lloyd, and went for her first tests at the studios in New York. She was made to walk through a garden setting and tested under different lighting conditions. D. W. Griffith was there, looking on in the company of Joseph Schenck. 'I wonder what he thought of me,' she wrote.[7] Griffith probably exchanged words of concern with Schenck, because they swiftly realised they had a problem on their hands. Margaret Leahy, however attractive, and despite the screen test in Britain, could not act. 'She could not even be coached in the mechanics of walking, standing and sitting down,' says Rudi Blesh, Buster Keaton's biographer.[8] They may have hoped that further

---

[7] 'Our Girl's Week End Letter,' *Daily Sketch*, 9 December 1922, p. 6.
[8] Rudi Blesh, *Keaton* (London: Secker & Warburg, 1967), p. 217.

coaching would cure matters, but already a rumour was allowed to circulate that Miss Leahy would be the star of Keaton's new comedy. This may have been the starring role to follow her second lead, promised as part of her prize, or else Schenck was already preparing for an alternative strategy.

After seeing the sights of New York, Margaret Leahy and her mother travelled with the Talmadges and company by train to Los Angeles. Norma Talmadge appears to have been remarkably attentive to her throughout, partly no doubt because her reputation might depend on it, but also it seems out of genuine concern for her British protégé. Crowds bearing banners greeted her on her arrival in Los Angeles, and Mary Pickford and Charlie Chaplin came to meet her. Soon she was in the studio, with Frank Lloyd trying to turn her into an actress. Her diary ingenuously describes her doing a scene fifteen times.[9] 'They have taken thousands and thousands of feet of film of me,' she wrote, 'Mr Lloyd says he is very proud of me.'[10] Work was then halted until after Christmas.

As Blesh recounts, Frank Lloyd told Schenck that nothing could be done with her; either she went or he did.[11] Clearly she could not be allowed to ruin the film or jeopardise the Talmadge name. Yet equally clearly there would be the likelihood of legal action if they sent her back without having appeared in anything at all, quite apart from the embarrassment that would occur following all the interest aroused on both sides of the Atlantic.

The solution was at hand. Buster Keaton was married to Natalie Talmadge. She was overshadowed by her famous sisters, being simply a secretary at First National. Keaton, having made a number of comedy shorts and appeared in one feature film, *The Saphead* (USA 1920), was about to direct his own, *The Three Ages*. Dominated personally and professionally by the Talmadge clan, Keaton was in no position to object when Joseph Schenck told him that Margaret Leahy would star opposite him in his new film, because 'comic leading ladies don't have to act.'[12] It was also pointed out to him that British interest in Leahy would guarantee him success in that country. The part of Aggie Lynch in *Within the Law* went to American actress Eileen Percy.

In her first diary entry for 1923, Leahy told Britain the good news:

[9] 'Margaret's Film-land Debut,' *Daily Sketch*, 16 December 1922, p. 13.
[10] 'Margaret's Christmas Diary,' *Daily Sketch*, 30 December 1922, p. 4.
[11] Blesh, *Keaton*, p. 217.
[12] Blesh, *Keaton*, p. 218.

Thursday. Tonight, as I write, I am really crying. It seems unbelievable. My telephone bell rang this morning, and the maid said it was New York calling me. It was Mr. Schenck—the first time he has telephoned to me. He talked a moment about little things, and then he said, 'Now, then, Miss Leahy, I am going to tell you something that will surprise you.' And then I learned that I am to be made a star right away. That they think they can trust me with the biggest prize of the year. To play the lead in the big Buster Keaton super-production that all the film fans in America are eagerly waiting for. It really doesn't seem true—but it is. On the signs and in the printing it is to say, 'Mr. Joseph Schenck presents—Margaret Leahy!' Think of it! It is all due to Norma. The secret thing—she didn't tell me a word. But she and Mr. Lloyd, it seems, have been so pleased with me and my film tests that they have decided it would not be necessary for me to play the second part in 'Within the Law' at all. That I can take a star's part right away—with some training of course. Buster Keaton is the most popular comedian in America after Charlie Chaplin. He is to do a great super picture, which is to be one of the biggest productions of the year in America. Every actress in America has been begging for this opportunity—to star with Buster Keaton in this big new film. And Mr. Schenck, the producer, at last decided that I should be the one. 'I am going to show England what we think of its Daily Sketch girl,' Mr. Schenck said. Of course, I cannot write any more now.[13]

Reading between the lines of some of her dispatches, she was clearly afraid of rejection, and relieved not to have been sent home a failure. However, she was still being given the full star treatment by Hollywood, chatting to people she could previously only have dreamt about, and being interviewed by fan magazines. She was given the Freedom of San Francisco. People wrote to her requesting beauty tips. She was reported to have received two hundred proposals of marriage.

This was also the time of the great scandal over the death of the drug-addicted Wallace Reid. Leahy mentions meeting Will Hays, chairman of the Motion Picture Producers and Distributors of America, and the climate of worry which existed. 'There has

---

[13] 'Margaret Gets a Great Surprise,' *Daily Sketch*, 6 January 1923, p. 6.

Margaret Leahy (seated) with Buster Keaton standing next to her on the
Roman set of *The Three Ages*, from family photograph album.

been some trouble here because of a poor fellow, a famous star,
who has broken down. Mr Hays is here about it. I do not know
what it is.'[14] Reid was to die in a sanatorium the following week.
The several references to how well she was being chaperoned were
clearly insisted upon to let Britain know that all was well.

Work began on *The Three Ages*. Her diary faithfully describes
her efforts and failures, how she had to be taught to walk in
a studied manner and not to move too quickly, how she ruined
some scenes, and of Keaton's patience with her. Her observations,
though very much from the point-of-view of a star-struck cinema
fan who had never considered how films were made before, offer
some interesting details of Keaton's working methods:

> It is only preliminary work that we have done so far.
> Mr. Keaton is not quite sure yet about several points in
> the picture. It is to be a super comedy, and several of the
> scenes and incidents are tried out before they are actually
> taken—that is, we do certain scenes two or three ways
> before the camera, then we see them run off in the lit-
> tle projection room, and Mr. Keaton finds things wrong
> with them or gets better ideas, and then we do them over

---

[14] 'Margaret Gets a Great Surprise,' p. 6.

again. When these difficult points are cleared up we will start again, and work the picture right through. There is a scene in which there is a fire—a whole house seems to be burned down, and we have burned it down three times now, and still Mr. Keaton is not satisfied. Of course they do not really burn down an entire house. They build just the front of it. They build it at night, working all night, and then we burn it down in the day time. Mr. Keaton says if he can't get the house to burn down properly he will cut it out of the picture after all.[15]

Margaret Leahy appears from her photographs to have been a little less than ethereal figure, and certainly Norma Talmadge thought so, as Leahy reveals in this entertaining passage:

I have one very important thing to do. It is on my mind day and night. Norma told me in England I would have to take off ten pounds. She watched me all the time and broke me away from eating any sort of candy or sweets, and as soon as we came out here she made me start in earnest to 'reduce.' Think of me 'reducing'—but I find there is hardly a star here who isn't always 'reducing.' We are all so afraid of becoming too heavy. 'Ten pounds off, Margaret' is what Norma even sings out to me when we pass each other in our cars. And 'ten pounds off' it must be if I starve to death.[16]

In this section from her diaries, where she notes again Keaton's habit of improvisation on set, she refers to a director, who is clearly Eddie Cline, Keaton's credited co-director on the picture. We hear of two directors at work, one calling from beside the camera, the other the star on the set, changing gags and other business as he sees fit, while the cameras continue to roll:

Working with Buster Keaton one has to keep one's wits. We rehearse a scene and then the director calls, 'All ready. On the set (that is to say on the stage before the camera). Shoot!' Then we start the scene just as we have rehearsed it. But Mr. Keaton may have a sudden idea right in the midst of the scene and will start doing something entirely

---

[15] 'Margaret's Life as a Star,' *Daily Sketch*, 13 January 1923, pp. 4, 13.
[16] 'Margaret Leahy at Work,' *Daily Sketch*, 20 January 1923, p. 4.

different from what we had rehearsed. If I can 'follow' him, or understand instantly what he is doing and what I should do—then everything is all right. But if I am surprised the least bit and 'caught napping,' then the scene is spoiled. The director shouts 'Off' and the camera stops and we start over again.

I went through one whole day splendidly. Mr. Keaton changed every scene right in the middle of it. For example, in one scene we had rehearsed for him to go slowly out of the door, hat in hand, and turn at the door to wave good-bye to me. I was to stand very straight and solemn—angry with him and indignant. Not noticing him at all as he left. Then, just as he pushed up his hat and started to go out of the door he changed his mind. He threw his hat down and came over to me and grabbed me in his arms and kissed me. I hadn't the least idea he was going to do any such thing. I heard him coming up behind me, but didn't know what it meant. I didn't know what to do—what he had in mind. So I 'took a chance,' as they say here, and just picked up a vase that was on the table and smashed it on the floor—to show how angry I was. The director shouted: 'Good girl—hold it—hold it. Get out, Buster, quick—hold it, Margaret, till he's gone—just that way—there you are—Off.'

I almost fainted with suppressed excitement when the director finished with that 'Off,' which meant the camera stopped and I could sit down. 'Whatever did you do that for?' I asked Mr. Keaton. 'Oh, just had a notion to change the 'business,' he said, 'and you got away with it splendidly.' But another day I hashed every scene we did because he changed so much and I could not catch on quick enough. But he expects this.[17]

Her last diary entry was published in the *Daily Sketch* on 24 February 1923. Work proceeded on the film, with Keaton seeing any number of good scenes ruined and much re-shooting taking place, although he treated her with kindness and tolerance throughout. On 11 June she returned to Britain for the film's premiere, the first major American feature to be premiered in Britain (it was not

---

[17] 'Margaret Leahy at Work,' p. 13.

shown in the USA until September). Enthusiasm for the new British film star had not waned, and again large crowds greeted her on her arrival at Liverpool, though strangely the *Topical Budget* newsreel did not cover her return at all. She then went on to Paris, apparently to film some scenes for her next picture, before arriving in London at Victoria station on 22 June. But she was worried about how her work would be received. She told journalists: 'Please tell everyone *The Three Ages* is my first picture. It is my beginning. I hope I shall improve in my pictures.'[18]

Excitement was as high as when she first won the contest. She made a speech on the 2LO radio service, and then the charity premiere took place on her home ground, at Marble Arch, on 25 June. Princess Alice attended. Leahy, as courageous and honest as ever, gave a rather sad little speech before the show:

> Your Royal Highness, my lords, ladies and gentlemen. I cannot say anything except to thank you from the bottom of my heart for coming tonight to see poor little me, for I am after all, just a Brixton shop girl. You will see tonight my first picture. I am very unhappy now as I look around me. I am very afraid you will think I have not been worthy of you. But I shall work very hard to be better and better as my career goes on, and then, someday, I hope you will greet me here and say I have done well. Then I shall never be unhappy again.[19]

The audience cheered when she first appeared on the screen and warmly applauded the film. It was well made and funny, and as Schenck had guessed, the film was a success, with many people in Britain going to see it purely on the strength of 'that nice English girl who won the contest.' But Leahy was being honest with herself. She is not very good in the film, though thanks to Keaton's hard work she is in no way bad. She is wooden, certainly, but makes some attempt at a performance, and looks attractive enough for Keaton's character's efforts to seem justified. Knowing all that she had been through to get there, the first shots of her, seated alone on a rock in Stone Age dress, looking slightly apprehensive but prepared to do her best, have for us now a special poignancy.

---

[18] 'Margaret Comes Home Today,' *Daily Sketch*, 22 June 1923, p. 2.
[19] 'Margaret's Triumphant and Tumultuous West End Welcome,' *Daily Sketch*, 26 June 1923, p. 2.

The Three Ages was Margaret Leahy's first and last film. There do appear to have been attempts to find her another vehicle—with all that publicity it would have been a waste not to try—with rumours of a British-French co-production and the filming in Paris. She was made one of the Wampas Baby Stars for 1923, the annual list of thirteen potential female film stars chosen by Hollywood publicity and advertising executives. Eleanor Boardman, Evelyn Brent and Laura La Plante were future stars chosen that year alongside her.

But such plans came to nothing, and it appears that Leahy herself decided against a film career. After a short tour promoting the film, she returned to America, declaring that it was nice to see England again but she missed the California skies.[20] What acting qualities Norma Talmadge first saw in her it is hard to determine. But what is incredible is the enthusiasm aroused in Britain for this ready-made film star. What a sad picture it all makes of the national inferiority complex and the dream of Hollywood. Did they really believe that she would be turned into a film star, with a series of films devised to suit her talents? Even the Americans seem to have been taken in by their own magic for a while.

Cinderella did not return to her rags; she went back to California. She married Ernest Victor Vogt in 1924, and settled down. For a while her story was held up as an example of the follies of the film world, but then she was forgotten.[21] We know little of her subsequent life, except that she became an interior decorator at Bullock's department store, while her marriage ended in divorce in 1935. Sadly she came to loathe the movie business and burnt all her scrapbooks, before apparently taking her own life in Los Angeles on 17 February 1967.[22] But something does remain—the newsreels, the newspaper diary, *The Three Ages* itself, and the touching, revealing story of how a Brixton shop girl did manage, for a brief

---

[20] At the end of 1923, a writ was issued by Leahy against the proprietors of the *Daily Sketch* and its sister paper the *Evening Standard*, John Henry Leyford Gates (editor of the *Daily Sketch*), Joseph Schenk and the Talmadges, claiming damages for breach of contract, fraudulent misrepresentation, and conspiracy and libel. Nothing further is reported about this, suggesting that it did not make it to court. 'Action by "Film Girl,"' *Daily News*, 22 December 1923, p. 3.

[21] 'The Up and Down of a Prize Beauty,' *St. Louis Post-Dispatch*, 18 May 1924, pp. 3, 12.

[22] Marion Meade, *Buster Keaton: Cut to the Chase* (New York: HarperCollins, 1995), p. 396. A collection of personal photographs from Leahy's time in America in the early 1920s and an album of newspaper cuttings made by a relative of hers do survive and are now held by Learning on Screen in London (https://learningonscreen.ac.uk).

while, to achieve the dream that eluded millions like her, and win her way to stardom.

Originally published on the busterkeaton.org site in 2000. Revised for *The Keaton Chronicle*, vol. 19 issue 3, Summer 2011, then reproduced on 25 March 2020 as https://lukemckernan.com/2020/03/25/just-a-brixton-shop-girl. This version is based on the 2011 version, with small emendations and some additional material, including notes. I first wrote about Margaret Leahy in my book *Topical Budget: The Great British Newsreel* (London: British Film Institute, 1992). She features alongside other film star competition entrants in Chris O'Rourke, *Acting for the Silent Screen: Film Actors and Aspiration Between the Wars* (London: I. B. Tauris, 2016). She is a character in Julia Parker's novel, *The Stars Shine Bright* (London: Piatkus, 1996).

14.

Beguiled

Filming the life of poet Stevie Smith

I discovered the poet Stevie Smith, as many others probably did, on 19 February 1980, when the film *Stevie* (UK 1978) was first shown on British television—on BBC Two, at 21:00 to be precise. In my memory I hurried out to Whitstable's Pirie & Cavender bookshop the following day and acquired a copy of her selected poems. It cannot have been exactly like that, but that is how I choose to remember it. I have the book still, much worn, not least because I ended up writing my dissertation on Smith five years later when I studied English Literature at the University of Manchester. *Stevie* implanted Stevie in my brain.

> Twas the voice of the Wanderer, I heard her exclaim
> You have weaned me too soon, you must nurse me again
> She taps as she passes at each window pane
> Pray does she not know that she taps in vain?[1]

That name 'Stevie' is a bother. Smith's sometimes playful, whimsical, unpretentious poetry, accompanied as it often was with her childlike drawings, has encouraged a cosy image in which it is too easy for some to address the memory of her by her first name. A collection of her writings was given the cute title *Me Again* because of the lines in the above stanza.[2] It is Stevie again, popping up to say hello. It is an attitude that does not help Smith or her poetry. Away with it, let it go.

> I will never leave you darling
> To be eaten by the starling

---

[1] 'The Wanderer' [extract], in Stevie Smith (ed. Will May), *The Collected Poems and Drawings of Stevie Smith* (London: Faber & Faber, 2015), p. 292.
[2] Jack Barbera and William McBrien, *Me Again: Uncollected Writings of Stevie Smith* (London: Virago, 1981).

For I love you more than ever
In the wet and stormy weather[3]

Smith's poetry is sweet on the surface, colder beneath. Its recurrent themes are childhood, mankind, the natural world, religion and death. In style it ranges between ballad and conversation, nursery rhyme and the lyrical. The seeming artlessness of so much of it is there to trip you up, like a child that floors an unsuspecting adult with a piece of cutting wisdom. Indeed its essential figure, the person from whose perspective we experience the poem, is the child that questions their existence. Never one for coming up with new rhymes when repetition can be more effective, the word 'child' is frequently and tellingly matched by Smith with 'mild,' 'wild' and 'beguiled.' Summing up the comforts and the con-trick of childhood, 'beguiled' occurs again and again in her poetry. It is practically her keyword.

To be so cold and yet not old
Oh what can ail the changeling child?
She has an eye that is too bold
Upon the night. She is beguiled[4]

Stevie the film is sweet on the surface, colder beneath. The film was made in 1978, directed by Robert Enders. It was an adaptation of the 1977 play of the same name by Hugh Leonard, which had been a great success at the Vaudeville Theatre in London, with Glenda Jackson as Smith and Mona Washbourne as her aunt. Both played the same roles in the screen version. The film focusses on Smith's life in suburban Palmers Green with her ageing 'Lion' aunt, rarely leaving their house. There are some short romantic scenes with her 1930s lover Freddie (a peculiarly miscast Alec McCowen) and a commentary of sorts from 'The Man,' played by Trevor Howard, who for the most part is seen in a park, addressing the camera, then joins the action as a long-suffering friend of Smith's who gives her lifts in his car.

It is the antithesis of cinema, the model example of a successful stage play translated to the screen with minimal effort expended in adapting it to the new medium. For *Stevie*, however, this turns out to be the right thing to have done—technically and thematically. Any attempt to have expanded the drama to show the wider life

---

[3] 'The Starling' [extract], in Smith, *Collected Poems*, p. 439.
[4] 'Eulenspiegelei' [extract], in Smith, *Collected Poems*, p. 104.

Aunt (Mona Washourne) and Stevie Smith
(Glenda Jackson) in *Stevie*.

in which Smith engaged, such as her three decades of work as a
private secretary at Newnes Publishing, her attendances at literary
parties, her famed poetry readings, her BBC broadcasts, or wider
exploration of her romantic life (which included the outside possibility of an affair with George Orwell), would have made her
ordinary. Paradoxically, what made her extraordinary was the
constrained life where she felt secure, at 1 Avondale Road, Palmers
Green. It is the film's faithfulness to this denial of the dramatic life
which makes *Stevie* a successful film. It is true to its subject.

Jackson and Washbourne's performances, on stage and on
film, were much acclaimed, and those who knew Smith acknowl-
edged the remarkable way in which Jackson became her. But the
film's finest performer may be Howard. A distinguishing feature
of play and film is the way Smith's poems are dropped into the
dialogue, words half brought up in the conversation, half going on
in the mind as the surface inaction continues. Howard speaks the
verse with a chilly understanding, no more so than when he recites
Smith's most celebrated lines:

> Nobody heard him, the dead man
> But still he lay moaning
> I was much further out than you thought
> And not waving but drowning[5]

---

[5] 'Not Waving But Drowning' [extract], in Smith, *Collected Poems*, p. 347.

Trevor Howard as 'The Man' in *Stevie*.

Howard is the film's anchor, the one who sets the tone and maintains it. It is a voice that reads the poet as well as the poetry. He may never have given a better performance.

There are several feature films about poets, but few good ones. Trying to depict the inspiration and its expression, while conforming to the kind of drama that cinema expects, is not an easy thing to achieve. *A Quiet Passion* (UK 2016), Terence Davies' subtle life of Emily Dickinson, understands the solitude necessary amid the pettiness of ordinary living, to the extent that one can see strong affinities between Dickinson and Smith as people and in their poetry. They share an artistic idiosyncracy. *A Quiet Passion* is, technically, the superior film. But *Stevie* feels truer, because its unaffected style stems from the poetry.

> Donnez à manger aux affamées
> It is a film star who passes this way
> He is looking so nice the women would like
> To have him on a tray
> Donnez à manger aux affamées[6]

Stevie Smith seldom mentions films in her poetry ('The Film Star' may be the only example), though she went to the cinema. Her mention, in 1953, of a quotation from the 1931 German film *Mädchen in Uniform* (*Maidens in Uniform*) suggests not only cine-literacy but that she probably went to London's renowned Academy art-house cinema, where the film had its British

---

[6] 'The Film Star,' in Smith, *Collected Poems*, p. 220.

premiere.[7] One learns so much about a writer through what they leave out of their work, as much as what they include. Cinema was external, not necessary, not the subject of poetry.

> The terrors of the scenery
> The black rocks of the sliding mountain
> Are hidden from the man of family
> Who lives beneath the fountain
> His name is Domesticity
> He's married to an ivy tree
> And the little children laugh and scream
> For they do not know what these things mean[8]

And yet the poetry is cinematic, as most twentieth-century poetry probably has to be. Film, once experienced, must change the attentive eye. It is there in the sheer dramatic verve and suggestion of a poem like 'The Sliding Mountain,' which is symbolic but also works through visual metaphor and depth of scale. It is there in her telling imagery: 'This Englishwoman is so refined / She has no bosom and no behind.'[9] It is there in how such imagery blends with the poems' regular questioning tone, inviting us to look and think.

> Mother, among the dustbins and the manure
> I feel the measure of my humanity, an allure
> As of the presence of God, I am sure
> In the dustbins, in the manure, in the cat at play,
> Is the presence of God, in a sure way
> He moves there. Mother, what do you say?[10]

It is there too in the child's point of view. Cinema is the beguiling medium. It makes us sit down, look up, and puzzle our way through a world it expects us to take on trust. It is a world in which we lose ourselves. Seeking, like a parent, to lull us, instead it opens our eyes, makes us look around, makes us start asking questions. And cinema has no answers, only endings.

> The wood grows darker every day

---

[7] Frances Spalding, *Stevie Smith: A Biography* [revised edition] (Stroud: Sutton Publishing, 2002), p. 184.

[8] 'The Sliding Mountain,' in Smith, *Collected Poems*, p. 252.

[9] 'This Englishwoman,' in Smith, *Collected Poems*, p. 70.

[10] 'Mother, Among the Dustbins' [extract], in Smith, *Collected Poems*, p. 125.

It's not a bad place in a way
But I lost the way
Last Tuesday
Did I love father, mother, home?
Not very much; but now they're gone
I think of them with kindly toleration
Bred inevitably of separation
Really if I could find some food
I should be happy enough in this wood
But darker days and hungrier I must spend
Till hunger and darkness make an end[11]

Originally published as 'Beguiled,' 20 October 2024, https://lukemckernan.com/2024/10/20/beguiled, and reproduced here with small emendations. *Stevie* is a difficult film to find. It was made available on VHS in the UK by Castle Pictures in 1990 but at the time of writing (2025) it has not had a DVD release and is not available on any streaming platform. It was last broadcast on British television in 1981.

---

[11] 'Little Boy Lost' [extract], in Smith, *Collected Poems*, p. 60.

15.

An Almost Perfect Film

The search for perfection in The Shop Around the Corner

There are those touchstone films that you have to see every now and again. Not obsessively, but occasionally—the old friend met once every few years, yet without whom you would not know where you are. You know every scene, every word is familiar to you, but you must see it again. It is not so much that the film matters to you but that you matter to the film. It needs you and your kind to understand it best. Cinema is a two-way phenomenon.

So it was that I watched *The Shop Around the Corner* (USA 1940) for the first time in a while. I have seen the film many times over three decades or more and it was exactly as I remembered it, in content and feeling. It is the most comforting of films. It tells of the romance by accident of Alfred and Klara, employees of a Hungarian general store, played by James Stewart and Margaret Sullavan. Each engages in a correspondence with another they have not met, hoping that the unseen person is the love of their dreams, while battling with the colleague they think is anything but their ideal. If the plot sounds familiar, that is firstly because this premise goes back at least as far as William Shakespeare's *Much Ado About Nothing*, while *The Shop Around the Corner* itself was remade as a film musical with *In the Good Old Summertime* (USA 1949), as a Broadway musical *She Loves Me* (1963) and then as the romantic comedy *You've Got Mail* (USA 1998).

The specific source was a Hungarian play by Miklós László, *Illatszertár*, or *Parfumerie*, which explains the location of *The Shop Around the Corner*. A key element of the film's success is its setting in a middle Europe that is viewed with nostalgia but without false sentiment. The characters have Hungarian names, the books and newspapers that they read have Hungarian text, the currency on the cash register (pengő and fillér) is Hungarian, the shop is Matuschek and Company, a name whose euphonious quality forms a refrain throughout the film. It is a gently realised other world, whose petty details make it our world too.

Its particular quality lies in how it blends fantasy with realism, the romantic with the inevitable. Time and again the film escapes the formulaic by grounding itself in real life. Its mundane setting gives it a special quality, matching the ordinary yet engrossing lives that the majority of us somehow lead. The verbal exchanges ring true because they have the right acerbic quality about them. There is an irregularity to the rhythm of the narrative whose credibility satisfies the viewer. A witty script, from Samuel Raphaelson and an uncredited Ben Hecht, takes wings through direction which is skilfully attuned to how our minds work. We recognise the wit of the style almost ahead of each exposition of that wit. The director Ernst Lubitsch makes us smile at how we are able to see things.

The Shop Around the Corner has seen its reputation grow over the years. In Leslie Halliwell's original *Film Guide* (1977), a reasonable barometer of traditional taste, the film gets a moderate two-star rating (out of four), Halliwell describing it as a 'pleasant period romantic comedy which holds no surprises but is presented with great style.'[1] Latterly, the film's unaffected sweetness, several winning performances, and the ingenuity of its seemingly simple construction, have made it the model film for some. Summing up this feeling, Pauline Kael, in her 1991 collection *5,001 Nights at the Movies*, called the film 'close to perfection.'[2]

But what on earth does close to perfection mean?

For a film to be almost perfect implies that there is such a thing as the perfect film. It must be a film in which all the required elements cohere perfectly, that sustains a sublimity of content and form for the entirety of its duration (which must be the ideal duration for its particular content and form), and that has a particular excellence about it. There will be films of moderate ambition in which all of the elements may combine ideally, but suggest nothing elevated. Excellence is the prerequisite of perfection.

There are reasons, to my mind at least, for thinking *The Shop Around the Corner* to be a little less than perfect. The ousting of the duplicitous Ferencz Vadas (Joseph Schildkraut) from the shop takes too long and is a little clumsily executed. The final gag, in which Alfred raises his trousers for Klara, to show that he is not bow-legged, is a weak piece of comedy unworthy of all that has preceded it. Both of these, this viewer feels, might have been

---

[1] Leslie Halliwell, *Halliwell's Film Guide: A Survey of 8,000 English-Language Movies* (London/New York: Granada Publishing, 1977), p. 683.
[2] *Pauline Kael, 5,001 Nights at the Movies: A Guide from A to Z* (New York: Henry Holt, 1985), p. 531.

Klara (Margaret Sullavan), Hugo Matuschek (Frank Morgan) and
Alfred (James Stewart) in *The Shop Around the Corner.*

emended, making the film—maybe—perfect. Thus the viewer
senses perfection through the imperfections. Any film, any art
work, contains the promise of its own perfection.

Of course others—starting with Leslie Halliwell—do not see
the film as being perfect, or close to perfection, which must mean
that perfection is a subjective concept. Many, if asked to watch the
film now, will reject it simply because it is in black and white and
is acted in a way that no one acts now. Time and taste, however
unkindly, have made the film for the majority to be a period piece,
an object with tarnished values. Subjectivity suggests that the
perfect film is a logical impossibility. It is not an object itself, it is
an aspiration.

This may be what Pauline Kael meant. Every film—and any
other creative work—suggests its own perfection, and because this
is so it can never realise such perfection. The film carries with it its
Platonic ideal; that form in which Valdas is dismissed satisfacto-
rily, and in which Alfred's legs do not feature, and yet nothing is
lost. But others may find the film close to perfection were it only
that other tiny blemishes were amended, so that the perfection of
the film in their view would be different to mine. Yet others may
not see blemishes at all and call the film perfect, and that is that.

Their subjectivity has become objectivity. But logically, because this applies only to them, it cannot be. The perfect film can never be absolutely perfect.

Ironically, or appositely, the film provides the answer to the conundrum. *The Shop Around the Corner* is about finding the perfection in imperfection. Three characters represent facets of this. Although Alfred and Klara would seem to be similar in their quest and their delusion, there is a difference. Alfred's uncertainty about himself makes him realise early on that what he wants is not the impossible but merely the possible. Pirovitch (played by Felix Bressart) questions him about what he is seeking:

> Alfred: I haven't slept for days.
> Porivitch: I'm sure she'll be beautiful.
> Alfred:: Not too beautiful. Oh, what chance would a
> fellow like me...
> Porivitch: What do you want, a homely girl?
> Alfred: No, no. Now, you-you knock on wood for me.
> Just a lovely, average girl. That's... that's all I want.

Alfred wants the complement to his humble self. Klara, however, dreams that her lover will have all of the grace, intelligence and understanding that she wishes for herself. But she betrays herself through her admission that she had originally been attracted to Alfred — 'In those first few weeks, there were moments in the stockroom when you could have swept me off of my feet' — without which admission the film would not resolve itself. Now Alfred can declare his love for Klara, but first he has to dismantle her belief in the imaginary person she thought was her ideal:

> Klara: I'd built up such an illusion about him. I thought
> he was so perfect.
> Alfred: I had to come along and destroy it.

Now they find they complement one another. Each discovers that the person before them is better than the person their dreams had told them they would find. They are almost perfect for each other. So theme and style dovetail: fantasy with realism, the romantic with the inevitable. It is everyone's love story, or should be.

The third character who has sought perfection is the film's linchpin, the shop owner Hugo Matuschek, played by Frank Morgan. This benevolent capitalist, so proud of his shop and so in command of his little world, seems to have the life of his dreams.

But then he discovers his marriage is a sham. A private detective confirms that his wife is having affair with one of his staff, though not the one he has suspected, at which he says:

> Matuschek: Twenty-two years we've been married. Twenty-two years I was proud of my wife. Well, she just didn't want to grow old with me.

Mr and Mrs Matuschek were once Alfred and Klara, and we may be too blinded by the Christmassy setting and the happy conclusion to see the sadness that underlies our story. 'This is my home—this is where I spent most of my life,' says Matuschek of the shop, as he makes his speech at the end to the staff, but the ruefulness of this sentiment escapes all of them. Matuschek thought he knew perfection, and now knows only himself.

The same story, with the same people, learning the same vital lessons about the ideals that they seek, is happening just around the corner—any corner, at any time. This is what makes *The Shop Around the Corner* such a fine, timeless film. But not the perfect film. It knows too much for that.

Originally published as 'An Almost Perfect Film,' 1 April 2023, https://lukemckernan.com/2023/04/11/an-almost-perfect-film, and reproduced here with small emendations. The children's bookshop in *You've Got Mail*, which is run by Meg Ryan's character, is called 'The Shop Around the Corner.'

16.

Pip, Lean and Cinderella

The fairy tale roots of Great Expectations

Plant a pip, and you hope that it will grow. It will, in time, establish roots and shoot upwards, growing in depth while it reaches up to the light. It is how all stories must work. We begin at a point that is presented to us as the beginning, but which we soon learn is some middle point. We come to learn of the past events that got us to this point, as we follow where events will take us. All that is required to germinate the process is the reader, us.

It seems no accident that Charles Dickens named the hero of his great novel, *Great Expectations*, Pip. Philip Pirrip, known only as Pip, is the seed from which the story grows, one where how he climbs towards the sun is rooted in a past from which he needs to learn. Moreover, it is a novel set deeply in the Kent countryside, the fruitful county. Dickens makes no direct mention of the metaphor, but in the vivid opening scene in which Pip encounters the escaped convict, Magwitch, the latter looks upon him as something edible:

> 'You young dog,' said the man, licking his lips, 'what fat cheeks you ha' got.'
>
> I believe they were fat, though I was at that time undersized for my years, and not strong.
>
> 'Darn me if I couldn't eat 'em,' said the man, with a threatening shake of his head, 'and if I han't half a mind to't!'[1]

Making Pip's edible nature all the clearer, he goes on to threaten that his heart and liver could be torn open, roasted and eaten, either by Magwitch or by his still more terrible fellow convict, Compeyson.

---

[1] Charles Dickens, *Great Expectations* (Harmondsworth: Penguin Books, 1965), p. 36.

The Hoo peninsula of north Kent, inspiration for the early scenes in the novel, has its fruit orchards, but Dickens' interest is focussed on its northern edge, where there are few trees, only long stretches of marshlands that fringe the Thames estuary. Pip's view of his surroundings from the churchyard places him as one small being among the elemental things, out of which the seed has somehow to grow:

> … the dark flat wilderness beyond the churchyard, intersected with dikes and mounds and gates, with scattered cattle feeding on it, was the marshes; and that the low leaden line beyond was the river; and that the distant savage lair from which the wind was rushing was the sea; and that the small bundle of shivers growing afraid of it all and beginning to cry, was Pip.[2]

The marshlands of Hoo look much as they must have done in Dickens' time. Little can be built on them; they can only be what they are. There is an unremitting, elemental flatness to the place. Everything feels stripped back, raw. The low fields are intersected by dikes, fences and occasional paths, so there is something to alleviate the sense of absence, but it is all a maze, guiding you nowhere. The skies complement the greyness, streaks of cloud through the morning mist that haunt the mind of the solitary traveller.

The particular quality of flat lands mirrored by grey skies is captured well in the film *Great Expectations* (UK 1946), directed by David Lean. It is remarkable to think of a film production crew coming to this deserted corner of the country, whose busy industry aimed to recreate that sense of a lost place that they would have so effectively disturbed. The production team spent two months in the area, over September to November 1945, before returning to the studio in Denham. They set up location at St Mary's Bay, at the centre of the northern end of Hoo, their equipment being transported there by sea using a landing craft provided by the Admiralty. The production constructed Joe Gargery's forge there (based on a forge building they located at Chalk, at nearby Gravesend) and the Ship Inn, which features in the failed attempt by Pip and Herbert Pocket to engineer Magwitch's escape by a packet-boat. Other Hoo locations used were Colemouth Creek, on the eastern end of the peninsula, and Darnett Ness Island in the Medway estuary, used for the scene where Magwitch wrestles

---

[2] Dickens, *Great Expectations*, pp. 35-36.

Pip (Anthony Wager) emerges out of the mist, in *Great Expectations.*

with Compeyson (known only as Convict in the film's credits) in the mud.

Wandering through the area, one can find locations that clearly feature in the film, though the general featureless of the area means that one bay, dike or flat piece of marshland looks much like another. This generic impression of the marshes is what designer John Bryan and cinematographer Guy Green express so well. It is a land of the fevered imagination, where signposts and a sense of direction have gone, and we find ourselves anchored to nowhere. This is reflected in the skies, which capture the unearthly look of the streaky cloudscapes one may encounter on a cold January, though for the most part they used glass shots—that is, painted skies. The film's opening scenes are a peculiar mixture of location and studio, reducing somewhere to anywhere. The very start of the film has Pip running past gallows along the dike at what is probably St Mary's Bay, actuality on the lower half of the image, artificial mood skies above (in reality the sky had been bright blue). It establishes the thematic visuals from the outset. Here there is no separating the real from the unreal.

It was not an easy shoot. The weather alternated between clear skies with still waters and ideal clouds brought in with the breeze ('too much like a picnic' noted the *Kinematograph Weekly*[3]), to heavy gales with only a few snatches of filming possible. The weather, and with it the variable light, made the matching of shots difficult.

In his biography of David Lean, Kevin Brownlow provides the surprise information that the original cinematographer, Robert Krasker, with whom Lean had worked so successfully on *Brief Encounter*, was fired when Lean saw the initial rushes. The results were 'flat and uninteresting,' 'lacking in "guts"' (Lean's words).[4] They had nothing of the Expressionist look Lean sought, though Krasker would go on to redeem himself emphatically as an Expressionist cinematographer on *The Third Man* (UK 1949). Guy Green was brought it to achieve the effect that Lean needed, guided by Bryan's designs, which was to uncover the hallucinatory effect of the place, not its literal impression. What drove this was not simply the impression of the marshes that Dickens' text gave, but a desire to bring to life the novel's fairy tale premise.

In production notes for the film, cited by Joss Marsh in an essay on Dickens and film, it is stated that the intention was to put 'ordinary human people into a fairy-tale story and background.' Marsh adds that it was 'precisely this doubled effect of the stylized and brutishly real' that the filmmakers set out to achieve, through a mixture of innovative techniques, from forced perspectives learned from 1920s German Expressionist films, to the use of 'cloud glass' (a white backcloth with clouds painted on a sheet of glass projected by arc light onto the cloth) to create the sky effects true to the look required.[5] They sought, and realised, a kind of hyper-reality that suited the elemental qualities of the fairy-tale technique.

Dickens had a deep love of fairy tales from his childhood. Whether he was aware of their influence on his literature, specifically in terms of a conscious knowledge of fairy-tale technique, seems down to conjecture, but the influence is undoubtedly there—not just in narrative form, but in emotional effect and morality, such as could trigger a strong response in his audience. Both Dickens and his readers had within them conceptions of literature moulded by childhood stories that strongly influenced writing and reading respectively.

---

[3] 'Cineguild Ends Location … With a Party,' *Kinematograph Weekly*, 15 November 1945, p. 38.

[4] Kevin Brownlow, *David Lean* (London: Richard Cohen Books, 1996), p. 213.

[5] Joss Marsh, 'Dickens and Film' in John O. Jordan (ed.), *The Cambridge Companion to Charles Dickens* (Cambridge: Cambridge University Press, 2001), p. 213.

Iona and Peter Opie, in *The Classic Fairy Tales*, state that a true fairy tale is not about dreams coming true but of 'reality made evident':

> ...the magic in the tales (if magic is what it is) lies in people and creatures being shown to be what they really are. The beggar woman at the well is really a fairy, the beast in 'Beauty and the Beast' is really a monarch, the frog is a handsome prince, the corpse of Snow White a living princess. Fairy tales are unlike popular romances in that they are seldom the enactments of dream-wishes ... Enchantment, in practice, is the opposite to the golden dream. The wonderful happens, the lover is recognized, the spell of misfortune is broken, when the situation that already exists is utterly accepted, when additional tasks or disappointments are boldly faced, when poverty is seen to be of no consequence, when unfairness is borne without indignation, when the loathsome is loved.[6]

It is not hard to see how *Great Expectations* fits into such an ethical framework. Pip learns that life is not a popular romance, but requires acceptance of its realities before any rewards (his true great expectations). The spell that he casts over himself is only broken by his selfless love for the characters Herbert Pocket, Magwitch and Estella, in each of their own calamities.

Pip alone feels like the starting point to a common feature in fairy tales, the youngest child or orphan. The novel starts with him observing the five lozenge-shaped tombstones of his brothers, all of whom died young ('who gave up trying to get a living, exceedingly early in that universal struggle').[7] His mother and father are dead too, and it is by their tombstone that Pip encounters Magwitch and the seed for the story is sown. More specifically though, numerous commentators have noted the affinity *Great Expectations* has to the story of Cinderella. Claire Tomalin, in *Charles Dickens: A Life*, calls the novel 'not a realistic account of how the world was but a visionary novel, close to ballad or folktale. The orphan boy, with dead parents and siblings in the graveyard in the marsh, has a cruel elder sister who treats him like a male Cinderella.'[8] In his intro-

---

[6] Iona and Peter Opie, *The Classic Fairy Tales* (Frogmore: Granada Publishing, 1980), p. 14.
[7] Dickens, *Great Expectations*, p. 35.
[8] Claire Tomalin, *Charles Dickens: A Life* (London: Viking, 2011), pp. 309-310.

duction to a Penguin English Library edition of the novel, Angus Calder goes further:

> It is a kind of inverted Cinderella, where the ugly sister, Joe and Magwitch, are in the right, the fairy godmother, Miss Havisham, is a witch after all, and the princess, Estella, is a gleaming fake.[9]

But one can see still more to the relationship than this. *Great Expectations* the novel is, structurally, a dual-Cinderella. There are two Cinderella-figures, both of whom confront characters with parallels in the fairy tale, and need to determine their true nature. The first is Pip. As Cinderella comes out of ashes, he comes out of marsh and mist. Like Cinderella he is a drudge, but one who must break out of his drudgery (it is an essential element of the fairy tale, in many of its variants, that Cinderella is not a menial but a princess in disguise, who must be returned to her true nature, for such is the law of things). His two ugly sisters are Joe Gargery, the kindly blacksmith with whom Pip lives, and his ill-tempered wife, Mrs Joe. One is obviously an ugly sister (Mrs Gargery is Pip's sister), and the other one not, but in his snobbishness Pip comes to reject Joe as such too. But there is only the one 'ugly sister,' because what Dickens does repeatedly is to set up two characters, seemingly sharing the same role, and Cinderella must ultimately learn which is which. Joe Gargery is no ugly sister—he is the gentleman Pip wants to be.

Another such pairing is Pip's fairy godmother. He has two— Miss Havisham (false), the reclusive spinster who takes a mysterious interest in Pip, and the convict Magwitch (true). Only after he has been through his ordeal can Pip tell which is which. How fascinating it is to look into the roots of the Cinderella legend, which identify the magical figure who brings about transformation, eventually transformed in Charles Perrault's version into a 'fairy godmother,' as the spirit of the child's dead mother—then to remember that when Pip first encounters Magwitch it is at the graveside of his mother (and father).

Miss Havisham is not the fairy godmother. She is the royal personage who has put on the ball to find a suitor for the prince. Again there are two figures from which Pip has to choose—Estella (Miss Havisham's adopted daughter, whom he meets at Miss Havisham's decaying home, Satis House) or Biddy (who helps out

---

[9] Angus Calder, 'Introduction,' in Dickens, *Great Expectations*, p. 17.

Estella (Valerie Hobson) and Pip (John Mills) in *Great Expectations*.

at the Gargery household when Mrs Joe falls ill). But which is the true and which false? Estella is ostensibly the latter, but can any reader believe that Pip was ever in love with Biddy? Dickens, I think, plays a double-bluff on his readers, in that Estella is Pip's true reward. The happy ending, where Pip and Estella come together, was not Dickens' original choice, but one that he was persuaded to adopt by his writer friend Edward Bulwer-Lytton. In fairy-tale terms Bulwer-Lytton was right (or can be argued to have been right, as few literary critics have agreed). Equally right, therefore, were David Lean and his scriptwriters in choosing that one of the two possible endings (ironically, much like one of Pip's binary choices). Cinderella, having been through her trials, must gain her reward.

The other Cinderella figure is Estella. She too is born into drudgery in Newgate but will come to her own great expectations. She has two fairy godmothers—the same as Pip's, Magwitch and Miss Havisham, with Magwitch the true spirit (or in this case the living actuality) of the lost father. Her ugly sisters are Compeyson and Arthur (his co-conspirator and Miss Havisham's half-brother), though both turn out to be as ugly as the other. Her two princes are Pip and the unspeakable Bentley Drummle. She picks the latter, until Dickens chooses to rescue her and deliver her true reward in Pip.

David Lean (standing centre) and crew filming *Great Expectations* on
Hoo marshland, Magwitch (Finlay Currie) bottom right.

There is nothing to indicate that any of these Cinderella parallels were intended by Dickens. The novel is far too complex and
driven by many narrative and thematic ideas for that. But there is
little denying that there is a fit, because the basic morality on which
he based his novel is that which he had inherited from childhood
fairy tales, which were in turn grounded in understood truths
of life. Cinderella's situation is universal. No matter how interchangeable the characters may be, the plot remains the same. It is
no accident that the tale and the novel are so alike, for they arise
out of the same philosophy.

A story that starts in the graveyard of a church has its Christian implications, likewise Cinderella. The Opies point to the
kinship between the fairy tale and the Christ tale:

> …the prince's admiration of her in her party dress is
> worthless. It is essential he plights himself to her while
> she is a kitchen maid, or the spell can never be broken;
> and in this a curious parallel to the Christ story is appar-
> ent. The man of perfect heart, living in the guise of a poor
> carpenter's son, has to be accepted in his lowly state …
> Had Christ been shown in his full glory, recognition of

his virtues, whether by pauper or by prince, would have been valueless.[10]

Dickens was probably more aware of the Christ parallel than that of Cinderella, but both share the same pattern, again arising out of the same philosophy.

Not all of this is in Lean's film, inevitably. The film's greatest innovation may have been in its faithfulness to the novel's impression on the mind rather than the details of its construction. Many characters and incidents had to be dropped, not simply for reasons of time but because they did not serve the core story. Biddy and Drummle are there, but are incidental—Biddy marries Joe without any suggestion of Pip having feelings for her; Drummle's dreadfulness we have to take on trust. The film also adds to Dickens, most famously in the ending, where Pip encounters Estella at Satis House, in the process of ossifying herself into another Miss Havisham. This triggers his dramatic pulling down of the curtains to let in the light, into which they walk together.

But the fairy tale remains—simplified to its elementals, but no less true. It is impossible that Lean and his collaborators considered a dual Cinderella theme, any more than did Dickens (consciously at least). It is not even certain that they thought of Cinderella. They thought of the fairy-tale method rather than the specifics, a way of placing fundamental human dilemmas through a mixture of reality and fantasy. The morality is consistent as well: *Great Expectations* the film, as with *Great Expectations* the novel, as with the fairy tale both instinctively followed, is about 'reality made evident' and the need to learn what is real, and true. This particular quality the filmmakers sensed in Dickens' novel, and then found the means to realise it in the same locations as inspired the writer. Not just the look of the places, but how they played upon the imagination, how they inspired a particular kind of story.

To live, as this writer does, in the places where Dickens grew up, repeatedly turned them over in his imagination, and then returned to them at the end of this days, is to see story everywhere. It is there in Satis House (a re-imagined Restoration House, still standing in the centre of Rochester); in the coaching inn, the Blue Boar where Pip sets out for London (a re-imagined Royal Victoria and Bull Hotel, which still stands and serves), and where Lean and his crew stayed while filming; in the row of children's graves at Cooling believed to have inspired the novel's opening; in Hoo's

---

[10] Opie and Opie, *The Classic Fairy Tales*, p. 17.

grey skies, flat marshes and deserted St Mary's Bay, offering safe harbour to no one, on the edge of a little world. It all went on, and goes on still. Novel and film, novelist and filmmakers, true and painted skies, location and studio, the real and the visionary, meaning and feeling—and out of the mist a story emerges, ripe for the re-telling.

Originally published as 'Pip, Lean and Cinderella,' 12 January 2022, https://lukemckernan.com/2022/01/12/pip-lean-and-cinderella, and reproduced here with small emendations. The Kent Film Office has information on the Kent locations used for the various film and television versions of *Great Expectations*, including 1946: https://kentfilmoffice.co.uk/filmed-in-kent/tag/great-expectations-film-locations.

17.

Different Trains

Caught on a Train—*film or television?*

I watched *Caught on a Train* (UK 1980) again the other night. It is a work that completed transfixed me when I first saw it, back in 1980, and which I have watched many times since. Made on location, it tells of the train journey across Europe (from Ostend to Linz) taken by Peter (Michael Kitchen), a young, uptight English publishing executive and a grand elderly Austrian lady, Frau Messner (Peggy Ashcroft), used to giving orders. In their journey on a grubby, crowded night train we learn much about a receding old world and a new one thrusting forward. She is rude and demanding, with a seeming blindness to the evils of the Nazi era to which she may have been witness. He is exasperated by her, but in his irritation and impatience we see someone lacking in grace, and ultimately in direction. As she tells him, at the work's conclusion:

> You're a nice boy in many ways [...] You're not really cruel. But you don't care, do you? You may think you do, but you don't really care, about anything. Except success in your work, that's all you have. You don't feel anything else, do you? I wonder what will happen to you.

It is a work entirely harmonious in its construction, where every counterpointing word and image falls true, and where Mike Westbrook's jazz score, by turns melancholy and vibrant, perfectly complements the unsettling tone.

I am calling *Caught on a Train* a 'work,' because the moment that you admit that it is a television programme, different rules apply. It was originally broadcast on BBC One on 31 October 1980, in the *Playhouse* slot, though many commentators have remarked upon its cinematic qualities, some saying that they see it as being as much a film as television.

But read the DVD blurb, or watch the featurette that comes with it, and you will see that this is television, because the writer is everywhere and the director is nowhere.[1] *Caught on a Train* is a Stephen Poliakoff 'play,' and it is Poliakoff who speaks throughout the featurette, and whose work it is recognised to be. Of course this is true — *Caught on Train* was his conception, based on his own experiences, he wrote the words, and has becomes an auteur among programme makers, to the extent of frequently directing his own scripts (*Close My Eyes, Shooting the Past, The Lost Prince, Joe's Palace*).

Peter (Michael Kitchen) in *Caught on a Train.*

Yet *Caught on the Train* had a director, and I was watching it again because Peter Duffell, the man in question, died on 12 December 2017, aged ninety-five. He was a director of astute style, much of whose work seems to be marked with a quiet, wry observation. His films included the portmanteau horror film *The House That Dripped Blood* (UK 1971) the underrated Graham Greene adaptation *England Made Me* (UK 1973), which Greene so admired that he wanted Duffell to film *The Honorary Consul* — which sadly did not happen; and the charming *Experience Preferred But Not Essential* (UK 1982), originally made for Channel 4 but shown theatrically in the USA and elsewhere.

---

[1] *Caught on a Train*, BBCDVD 1325, BBC Worldwide (2004).

His greatest work, however, was *Caught on Train*, which is as much a director's piece as it is a writer's. It takes its tone from the above-mentioned Mike Westbrook score (Duffell was a keen jazz fan, and was presumably instrumental in signing up Westbrook), which both establishes a mood while creating a form of ironic commentary. The people, and the Europe, that we see, are travelling nowhere. There is some progress in this post-war world, but it is expressed in cold architecture, cold businessmen and a cold light. It tries to maintain some elements of the past, but the dream of gracious train travel from another age has been rudely replaced by the crowded train with seatless youngsters crammed into the corridors, much as Frau Messner points out that the restaurant car table is a plastic fake, not the true wood of the past. The train is a metaphor for a conflicted, paradoxical society, in which the illusion of privilege is crumbling, with its reservations, dining cards and first-class travel, as the hordes amass, all too visible, biding their time.

The unease is in part a reflection of the political nervousness of the period. It is the time of the Baader-Meinhof gang, with jumpy police stopping trains to check for potential terrorists and finding Peter's arrogance suspicious. Belgian youths on the train taunt Peter, then get into a bloody fight with broken bottles. Young rough sleepers huddle at night on Frankfurt station ('They are probably all from good families,' says Frau Messner). Peter's assumptions are challenged further by the character of Lorraine (played by Wendy Raebeck), an American tourist to whom he is attracted but who offers a withering dismissal of Britain and Europe, from which she cannot wait to escape. Things are falling apart.

Yet the train keeps going. *Caught on a Train* follows the well-worn path of the journey narrative. The main characters find out more about themselves, or reveal more about themselves, as we progress. However, it is never so simplistic as to make a clear statement on the world, or Europe, or even an Englishman lost in Europe (Peter's discomfiture looks all the more pointed in these days of Brexit). It sets a particular mood, not so much of unanswered questions as of answers to which the words have yet to be found. Where Peter will go at the end of his journey we cannot say. All we know is that Frau Messner and her world are leaving. They are, in the end, on different trains.

Thus, though this is a work justly acclaimed for its dialogue, in which every word tells (heightened by two outstanding performances from actors relishing what has been offered to them), it is as much about things seen as heard. There are the claustrophobic train carriage settings, whose effect is accentuated by continual cross-cutting between Ashcroft and Kitchen—only at the end of the film do we have a shot of the two of them addressing one another face to face. The claustrophobia has filmic roots. There are resonances of Alfred Hitchcock's *The Lady Vanishes* (UK 1938), the classic train journey across an uneasy Europe, but also Hitchcock's *The 39 Steps* (UK 1935), with Kitchen's persecution by the German police echoing Robert Donat's experiences as Richard Hannay. Peggy Ashcroft, of course, featured in Hitchcock's 1935 film.

Frau Messner (Peggy Ashcroft) in *Caught on a Train*.

One only escapes this visual tension in the sequences at railway stations, or when the train is seen hurtling by through a landscape that could be anywhere, and where the sun never shines. *Caught on a Train* is a hymn to grey skies.

To bind all this together required filmmaking of great skill but effacing manner. A more heavy-handed, symbolic approach would not have worked at all. It would have had a deleterious effect on the dialogue. Peter Duffell, a director of quiet efficiency, understated intelligence and a particular affinity with his actors, was the ideal candidate. His great achievement was to create a work that transcended form. *Caught on a Train* sometimes gets called a television play, but it does not look like television, nor feel like a play. There is too much opening out for that. Yet it is not a film either—despite its look and metaphorical sense, it suggests more than the cinema prefers to show, while the final statements from Kitchen and Ashcroft, though memorable, have the patness of theatre about them. *Caught on a Train* could in fact work well as a radio play, with the punctuating images replaced by sounds. Or it could work, with just a few intertitles, as a silent movie, where everything we need to understand is there in the faces and the locations.

It is not a play, or a television programme, or a film. It is *sui generis*, the optimum expression of its subject, and that is the key to its greatness.

If you watch the featurette on the DVD of *Caught on a Train*, you will see a lot of Stephen Poliakoff being interviewed. You will not see Peter Duffell. He is not even mentioned. Nor are Tony Pierce-Roberts and John Else, the photographers whose images of poetic drabness so effectively establish the mood; nor Mike Westbrook, without whose deft score it is hard to imagine *Caught on a Train* at all.

Caught on a Train is a product of the genius of Stephen Poliakoff. But it was the late Peter Duffell who realised such inspiration on screen, who made the work exceptional, by thinking beyond the boundaries of form. Perhaps future screen histories and reference works could do a little more to recognise such artistry.

Originally published as 'Different Trains,' 1 January 2018, https://lukemckernan.com/2018/01/01/different-trains, and reproduced here with small emendations.

18.

75%

Video games and worlds of our own choosing

At the start of the exhibition at the Victoria & Albert Museum, *Videogames: Design/Play/Disrupt*, you are told that 25% of the people on the planet play video games. I am one of the 75%. I do not play video games; indeed, I do not think I have played a video game of any kind since *Pong*, the minimalist tennis-like arcade game, in the mid-1970s. I have seen many a game being played by others, and briefly have pushed the same buttons or waved the same joystick to see what the technology did, but only out of passing curiosity. There was no appeal, nor much understanding on my part as to what that appeal might be. So what was I, as a representative of the excluded 75%, to get out of an exhibition on video games?

A great deal, it turned out. It is an excellent exhibition: in its presentation, layout, understanding of its subject and appreciation of its audience. It makes particularly good use of space, with no wasted corners, and a keen sense of the dramatic—midway through the exhibition there is a grand *coup de théâtre* when you walk into a hall-like space with a huge display screen towering above you, the audience clinging to the edges of the room for the finest view. There is a startling use of a long screen showing up to five life-size interviewees against a background. Four are frozen at any one point, while one speaks (with subtitles). The debates were compelling, the viewers transfixed. There was so much active technology on display—invariably a nightmare for exhibition organisers, yet everything was working.

The exhibition's theme is the design and culture of the contemporary videogame. So it is not a history of the video game, and many of the most celebrated titles—i.e. the ones that even this stubborn denier has heard of—are absent: *Halo, Grand Theft Auto, World of Warcraft, Tomb Raider*. Instead it presents examples of cutting edge design and critical ideas, showing how the creative minds behind the phenomenon are continually challenging what

Journey.

they do. The more they establish themselves, the more they wish to break free, particularly beyond the confines of story. That was the exhibition's primary theme for me: the compulsion towards, yet the equal reaction against, conformity, especially narrative conformity.

It helps to be accompanied by someone acquainted with this world, and I was fortunate in having a sixteen-year-old with me, who knew not only every game but had a strong interest in design as well. It is a world that excites the intelligence, if the intelligence is there to be excited.

Not knowing my way around this landscape, I looked for reference points outside it. The dreamy landscapes of *Journey*, designed as an exploration of an endless landscape beyond the narrow confines of narrative, reminded me strongly of the space fantasy album covers designed by Roger Dean, *de rigueur* for any 1970s progressive rock band. The storyboards looked comfortingly like those of a film, while the creators of the assorted games often identified films as reference points—*Das Cabinet des Dr. Caligari* (Germany 1919), a television production of *Death of a Salesman* (USA 1985), somewhat surprisingly.

Film comparisons seem the most pertinent. It is not just the much-cherished cinematic qualities (to be called 'cinematic' in this world is a badge of honour); video games share with film a universality that truly transcends borders. Film was the medium that succeeded everywhere, with the same product. There was, and remains, a particularity to that product, because it was American

Das Cabinet des Dr. Caligari.

film that became pervasive, not films of any kind from any territory appealing to any audience. So it was, and remains, culturally idealist and culturally imperialist at the same time. Video games likewise are played by everyone (or 25% of us) and most of those playing are playing the same games, often with others across the world at the same time. And likewise there is domination of American companies and culture to some degree, but also of the English language. There is a compelling section in the exhibition where we learn that you cannot code powerful games in Arabic. English is the very lifeblood of the video games industry.

It is an interesting exercise, trying to understand other people's stories. Much of the problem I have had with video games is that the narratives seem so unsatisfying. Everything appears to be a quest or a shoot-em-up. It is relentlessly linear, wearingly narrow. Characterisation never rises above the crudely simple. Atmosphere is everything, human interaction is minimal. There is nothing to be learned from such stories. They are just games.

But of course such an argument ignores the major component of the narrative, which is the gamer. It is we who make the story. Traditionally stories present us with a credible world in which an adventure takes place and a lesson is learned. We may identify with one or more of the characters involved, but fundamentally we are witnesses. We encounter impossible worlds in which everything comes together and make sense (which is why they are impossible), for our entertainment and instruction. In video games we inhabit impossible worlds which only make sense because we are moving through them. It is not really a shift from the passive to the active. Rather, it is a shift from the illusion of community (everyone shares in these stories, most visibly in a cinema) to the illusion of individuality. We move through worlds of our own choosing.

That must mean, ultimately, a fundamental shift in how stories operate for us. We escape into these worlds, but they are worlds from which there is no escape. We are constantly on guard, not simply because that monster is lurking around the corner, or because that sinister figure heading towards us is carrying a weapon, but because if we are not there then there is no story. It is pure solipsism. Without us, the world ceases to exist. Who can say what a psychic burden that may place on us in the long run?

I admired the skill and creativity on display at the V&A. I saw something of the video game's appeal. But I think I am happier staying with the 75%.

Originally published as '75%,' 6 February 2019, https://lukemckernan.com/2019/02/06/75, and reproduced here with small emendations. *Videogames: Design/Play/Disrupt* ran at the Victoria and Albert Museum in London between 8 September 2018 and 24 February 2019.

19.

First Film Dogs

Stray dogs and the cinema of distractions

David Bordwell recently posted yet another jaw-droppingly good piece on his *Observations on Film Art* blog, whose consistently high quality makes the rest of the competition look like mere gossip-mongers. This post, entitled 'Gradations of Emphasis, Starring Glenn Ford,' examines widescreen cinema (you will have to read it to find out what the title means).[1] But there was one aspect of it that caught my eye, something captured drifting across the screen, that reminded me of one of the odder alleyways of early film down which I like to wander sometimes.

In his survey of lateral staging in film—that is, action happening within the frame, literally coming in from the sides—Bordwell looks at early film strategies, and reproduces frames from the Lumières' *Le Faux cul-de-jatte* (France 1897), in which a fake amputee begs in the street. He describes the action, until one frame, where a stray dog enters the action from the right. He writes of this, 'The cop comes to the beggar, partially blocking the dog, who takes care of other business. (Not everything in this movie is staged.)' What interests Bordwell is the staged action. What interests me is the dog. Let me explain...

It was when I was presenting a series of programmes at London's National Film Theatre on Victorian cinema (that is, films made before 1901), in 1994, that I first noticed a peculiar phenomenon. As I introduced each short film in the compilation, and pointed out those points of central interest which I had recorded in my notes, I started to notice that the audience's attention was being frequently drawn away from the supposed subject of the film. Instead they were detecting action to the edge of the frame, or crossing the frame, interrupting the subject or courageously ignoring

---

[1] David Bordwell, 'Gradation of Emphasis, Starring Glenn Ford,' *Observations on Film Art*, 13 November 2008, https://www.davidbordwell.net/blog/2008/11/13/gradation-of-emphasis-starring-glenn-ford.

A dog joins in the action in *Washing the Sweep*.

it, creating a vital counter-narrative. In short, their attention was irresistibly drawn to stray dogs.

This was a surprising phenomenon, which I exploited at the time for some simple humour, but on mature reflection it seemed that here was a hitherto wholly ignored yet clearly important facet of early cinema, a theme overlooked yet superabundantly obvious once pointed out to the idle observer. The number of stray dogs in early films is considerable, as anyone familiar with the period will readily acknowledge, and their distracting and engrossing qualities seemed to be in urgent need of analysis. Why were stray dogs accepted in early film dramas? What were they doing there? Where did they come from? Were there more such dogs in British films than other countries'? What could their presence tell us about early film practice? How could one construct an overarching vision of early cinema that encompasses the animal and the accidental? Why were there no stray cats? Why, ultimately, were the audience looking in the wrong direction? Were the original audiences similarly distracted? In what sense could it said that such canine interruptions were directed, and by what agency? I resolved to write a paper that would answer these nagging enquiries. It would be called 'First Film Dogs.'

I began first by collating the necessary data, and working on a critical theory which would most usefully and succinctly describe the phenomenon. The examples were easy to find: the exuberant Jack Russell which joins in the punishing of a sweep who wanders into a garden and dirties the laundry in James Williamson's *Washing the Sweep* (UK 1898); the stray dogs wandering over the parade ground amid the marching soldiers in the Boer War actuality *Lord Roberts Hoisting the Union Jack at Pretoria* (UK 1900), upsetting the solemnity of the situation; dogs wandering casually onto the studio set of early Pathé films; the dog that takes position centre frame in film of a genuine mining tragedy funeral in the middle of the BFI's print of Pathé mining drama *Au Pays Noir* (France 1905); actualities such as *Funeral of the World's Greatest Monarch* (UK 1910), where King Edward VII's own dog takes part in the procession, and is then accompanied by a passing stray (such thematic complexity!); the efforts of Monarch the Lifeboat Dog to contribute to a life-saving re-enactment performed on the beach in *Launch of the Worthing Lifeboat* (UK 1899).

Monarch's contribution to an actuality which in fact incorporates a dramatic element illustrated the next stage of the theme, where the cinema progressively encroached upon the freedom of the dog, containing the dog within the frame, from Edison's *Laura Comstock's Bag-Punching Dog* (USA 1901) (though one must watch the film to see how the dog, Mannie, keeps trying to leap out of the frame only to be drawn back into it);[2] to the passing dogs that enthusiastically take part in early chase films; to the triumph/defeat of Hepworth's *Rescued by Rover* (UK 1905), where the dog's natural motion is contained entirely within the cinematic narrative. Did the sequel to that film, *The Dog Outwits the Kidnapper* (UK 1908), where Rover gets to drive a car, indicate canine empowerment or slavery? What price the freedom of early cinematic form, when all that results from it in the end is Rin Tin Tin and Lassie?

The critical theory at this stage consisted mostly of a series of such questions, without a key, but I began to work on the concept of 'canine space.' There was more going on in these early films than first appeared. There was a central performance, or news event, which the original catalogues declared to be the subject matter, but this could not necessarily be what the audience saw, nor was such a dictate bound to be obeyed by those appearing in these films. Anyone familiar with early films will know of the puzzled glances from passers-by that characterise street scenes, of the distracting matter

---

[2] See https://www.youtube.com/watch?v=9rr7CG9kAnA.

The Dog Outwits the Kidnapper, with Rover
(played by Blair) at the wheel.

which suggests that the camera operator was not in full command of the subject. In such circumstances, dogs run free. What adds to the fascination, reinforcing one's belief in the essentially liberated nature of early films, is that stray dogs can be found in studio films of the period. The drama is enacted, the comedy routine performed, and in the background a dog watches, or wanders past, or joins in if it so desires, and this is accepted as part of the total action. 'Canine space' is therefore that other space, that world onto which the camera has intruded.

I never did write the paper. It was intended as a spoof of early film studies, but I could not quite get the humour right. I was scheduled to speak on the topic at a British silent film festival, but in the end got up and apologised to the audience and said that the paper was beyond me. But I gave them enough of the argument that it probably affected the rest of the festival, as people starting spotting stray animals in every film, and ever since I have had people send me images or information on roving animals which they have spotted in some silent or other. A chord was touched.

It is not a phenomenon entirely restricted to the early cinema, but it is a noticeable characteristic of early film which could make one think about the special free nature of film at that time. A cinema where dogs run free is a cinema that has not yet been pinned down, one that lets us look at the edges. You could call it

the cinema of distractions. You could theorise about it seriously—
there is perhaps some parallel with Roland Barthes' concept of the
'punctum,' the oddity in a photograph that should not really be
there but which draws your attention away from what the photograph is ostensibly trying to convey.[3]

Maybe I will write the paper one day. Maybe it is the sort
of paper that is not meant to be written. Maybe we are always
going to be looking at the centre, while at the edges, or wandering
across the frame, another kind of story passes by, always eluding
us even though it may for a moment catch our eye. I don't know.
Try asking a dog.

Originally published as 'First Film Dogs,' 14 November 2008, https://
thebioscope.net/2008/11/14/first-film-dogs, and reproduced here with
small emendations. 'Cinema of distractions' is a reference to 'the cinema of attractions,' a standard term in early film studies, coined by Tom
Gunning. The ideas in this tongue-in-cheek piece were taken up by some
film scholars, among them Frank Kessler and Mariann Lewinsky, the latter programming some early films featuring stray dogs at the Il Cinema
Ritrovato festival in Bologna in 2009. She also came up with the inspired
critical term *Zufallshund*, the accidental or unintentional dog. Years later,
Pao-Chen Tang published a prize-winning essay, 'Of Dogs and Hot Dogs:
distractions in early cinema,' in *Early Popular Visual Culture*, February
2017 issue. It is an entirely serious and intelligent study of some of the
themes suggested above. It even uses the phrase 'cinema of distractions.'
There is no indication that the author was aware of the *Bioscope* post.

---

[3] Roland Barthes, *Camera Lucida* (London: Vintage, 1993), pp. 26-27.

20.

The Round Window

A history of the circular screen

Lucifer (Belgium/Mexico 2014), directed by the Belgian filmmaker Gust Van den Berghe, is a remarkable work of art. Loosely based on the 1654 Dutch play of the same title by Joost van den Vondel, it tells of the visitation of the Devil to a present-day Mexican village, bringing sin and sorrow in his wake. This leads to the loss — or perhaps the regaining — of paradise (the play was once believed to have been an influence on Milton's *Paradise Lost*, though this argument has been discredited). The film, which is the third in a trilogy of religious-themed works from the director, mixes the worldly with the otherworldly in an extraordinarily effective way.[1] It is beautiful to look at and to listen to, hauntingly performed by local amateurs, and often deliciously funny.

But what is most remarkable about the film is its circular frame. Until its final shot, showing a return to the everyday, the film's screen shape is a circle. Abandoning over a century of rectangular film framing, *Lucifer* shows its world in the round. Everything is framed according to the demands of the circle, which includes not only how the images are composed, but how the performers are seen to interact, even the sound design. The technique has been named Tondoscope by the director (from tondo, the Renaissance term for a circular work of art), and at key points involved filming into a conical mirror to capture action in 360 degrees.

This is no gimmick. The aesthetic choice is designed to reflect a faith-based view of the world, in which that faith is all-encompassing. Specifically it reflects that holistic world picture which was fundamental to the sixteenth century's understanding of itself, but which started to fall apart in the seventeenth century (in which Vondel's play was written). In such a world the cosmic overrides

---

[1] The earlier films are *En waar de sterre bleef stille staan* (*Little Baby Jesus of Flandr*) (Belgium 2010) and *Blue Bird* (France/Belgium 2011).

1904 British postcard showing a lecturer
at a film show pointing to a circular screen

the earthly, as the assumed perfection of creation finds its logical expression in the perfect shape of a circle.

Gust Van den Berghe cites examples from the history of art where the images is circular, including works by Bosch and Pieter Brueghel. He also references Dauguerrotype portraits and pre-cinema optical devices, such as the Praxinoscope and the magic lantern, whose images were frequently circular projections. He writes:

> These magic lanterns hold the true legacy of pre-cinema in them, as they were used in variety theaters with live piano music and sing-alongs, right before they were replaced by silent films. As the first of all these registered and reproduced images came in a circular form, one might say that this is their native shape as they pass through any lens or aperture hole, based on the construction of the human eye. It is only when man applies a masking to it that they get a constrained quadrilateral geometrical figure, for example 1:1, 4:3, 16:9, 2,35:1 …[2]

Other circular images existed—images seen through microscopes and telescopes, kaleidoscopes. So there was a rational aesthetic choice and a clear pre-cinema history of circular images upon which to draw, but what about circular cinema? Has it always been the squares and rectangles of 1:1, 4:3, 16:9, 2.35:1 and so on?

Well yes, but with a qualified no. In the first years of cinema there was confusion among some artists illustrating the phenomenon as to what they were actually seeing. Still thinking of how magic lantern projections often worked, on occasion some depicted film shows as though they also employed circular projection. There were no circular film projections, but some imagined that they existed.

But there might have been circular film projections, had things turned out differently. Some of the earliest film experiments, when successive image capture was being perfected but playback had yet to be worked out, featured round images. British inventor and political agitator Wordsworth Donisthorpe, very probably inspired by Kodak's early (1888) circular snapshot picture format, took a proto-film of London's Trafalgar Square in 1890,

---

[2] Gust Van den Berghe, 'What is Tondoscope' and 'Where Did the Idea of Tondoscope Arise From,' n. d., archived versions at https://web.archive.org/web/20150312175329/http://www.tondoscope.com/Site/Welcome.html.

ten frames of which survive. W. K.-L. Dickson, working in the Edison laboratories in early 1891, produced some strips of film with circular images, and in July 1894 Charles Francis Jenkins published some successive circular images with his Phantascope camera, showing a man shot-putting. The rules of how a film should look were not yet set, though soon enough Dickson's use of a 4:3 frame on 35mm film would set an industry standard.

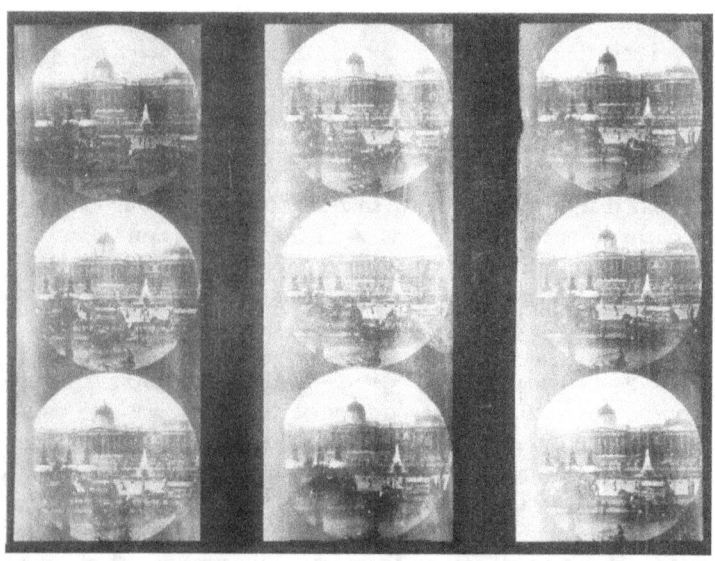

Nine surviving circular frames from Wordsworth Donisthorpe and William Carr Crofts' 1890 Kinesigraph film of Trafalgar Square, London.

Circular projection could occur within the frame. With his mind still grounded to a degree in magic lantern practice, the British filmmaker George Albert Smith made *Santa Claus* (UK 1898), in which a child in its bedroom sees Santa arriving on the roof of the house via a circular moving image in a corner of the frame. It is film in the round, albeit contained within a larger rectangle.

Thereafter film has, for the most part stayed horizontally rectangular. Vignettes and iris-out effects have been employed which change the screen image to a circle for a brief period, circular projections are used within the main rectangular screen shape for eye-catching effect—consider the gun barrel-view opening to the title sequence for *Dr. No* (UK 1962), for example—and circular films have been used in some video installations, but until now, there seems to have been no attempt at a sustained piece of film shaped as a circle until 2014 and *Lucifer*.

But why are films (horizontally) rectangular? It seems an obvious aesthetic choice, but that is because we are familiar with it. Of course for film it is an inheritance from earlier art forms, ranging from paintings to poster to magic lantern projections. The screens that accommodated the new art form of cinema had been constructed to suit prior forms, which were in turn so shaped through long-held cultural conventions.

The rectangular picture dates back to Renaissance times. Edmund Burke Feldman, in his *Varieties of Visual Experience*, states:

> The rectangular canvas is one of many possible shapes. But it dominates all others mainly because of the Renaissance convention that a picture is a window opened on the world and then painted by an artist. The convention has been so thoroughly absorbed by our culture that we are hardly aware of it, but it crops up in popular architecture as the 'picture window.' The design of a wall around a scenic or pictorial opening is a strange reversal of history, because pictorial imagery has usually been *subordinated* to architecture—in mosaics, stained glass, murals, and large-scale tapestries. Painting tends to 'obey' externally determined formats.[3]

As with paintings, so with the motion picture screen, though it is important to note the change the Renaissance brought about in the art object as a fixture in itself, rather than something to fill a space (as in those mosaics and murals). Art moved from wall to window. That window on the world—a concept introduced by Leon Baptista Alberti in his 1435 theoretical work *De Pictura*— generally presents the viewer with a horizon, with human figures placed within that picture, whose positioning creates the inherent dramatic interest. It usefully emulates how we comprehend what lies before us, how we scan the visual display for information. By such means do we understand where we are.

Film shape has therefore remained rectangular because of the art tradition that preceded it. The precise dimensions of those rectangles have changed, firstly because different interests wanted to promote a unique product, and then assorted wide-

---

[3] Edmund Burke Feldman, *Varieties of Visual Experience: Basic Edition* (Englewood Cliffs, NJ/New York: Prentice-Hall/Harry N. Abrams, 1967), p. 321.

screen variants were created to present film as a spectacular that could not be replicated on traditional television sets (it is worth noting that early television sets had curved or even entirely round screens because of how the cathode rays were bombarded at the screen, but the original image composition was rectangular — Academy ratio — so the viewer simply lost some of the full image). Nowadays such battles have settled down, and 16:9 is the aspect ratio of choice for home screens, and 1.85:1 in cinemas.

But our windows on the world are changing. The rise of videos shot on mobile phones has led to the rise of vertical videos — portrait rather than landscape. First viewed as an amateurish error, these are starting to be accepted as a viable aesthetic alternative. *YouTube* now allows for vertical video on its Android app and serious compositions are being produced with the 'new' ratio.

So why not round cinema? Gust Van den Berghe's thoughts on filming in Tondoscope shows how what was originally a cosmological, historically informed aesthetic choice, brought about changes in how the pictures were composed and how we read these in projection:

> What comes to mind, is that if Tondoscope had the means of having a solid or holographic nature, it would probably be a ball or a sphere. This, because at the same time it will yield a very naturalistic and unhindered look on a scene, and also portray this scene as an event that happens in a bubble. Every scene that takes place that way becomes a happening that has its individual importance in time and space. A personage finding itself in this circular frame is regarded as isolated and has his world to himself, and accordingly, if one would circularly frame more people together, for a moment, they share experiences or a world.
>
> This results in the effect that when we film in Tondo-scope, and there is a scene where multiple personages partake, whenever a single person is framed, this person ends up extra isolated from the group when these shots are combined or intercut with other shots containing more than one personage, who then share more with each other than that one. The inter-human relationships seem emphasized by circling them. In general, in Tondoscope, the circle emphasizes every emotional relation between the personages and throws out a direct line to the viewer.[4]

[4] Berghe, 'What is Tondoscope.'

Lucifer.

Whether this is absolutely so, only the viewer can decide. There are distractions that come with the circular video. Although the image is shown in the round, it is still presented to us on horizontal rectangular screens, because that is how our cinemas and home screens are constructed. There is a large amount of extraneous black space for our eyes to manage. We see not only the circle but the void that surrounds it. Moreover, our eyes are trained to read cinema in landscape format. We yearn to scan the horizon. We may fight against what *Lucifer* forces us to see.

Yet *Lucifer* probably wins the battle. The skill involved in its production, and the alignment of subject matter and technique, make us look in a changed way, with a changed understanding. It arranges things differently, and we as viewers must appreciate that. Whether *Lucifer* is a one-off, or if there will be other circular films, it is hard to say. Van den Berghe may have claimed the format as his own, but there is enough in that suggestion of a distinctive way of portraying inter-human relationships and a directness to the viewer to indicate that others may want to explore the possibilities. Artworks have long since broken out of their frames to find shapes determined by the imagination rather than by architecture. Films can follow. Our windows are changing.

Originally published as 'The Round Window,' 18 October 2015, https://lukemckernan.com/2015/10/18/the-round-window, and reproduced here with small emendations. In 2016 a partly circular feature film appeared, *I Am Not Pan Jinlian* (*I Am Not Madame Bovary*) (China 2016). A circular frame is used for rural scenes; city scenes are square-shaped.

21.

Kane and Kong

Citizen Kane, King Kong *and the tragic dimension*

Have you seen the pterodactyls in *Citizen Kane* (USA 1941)? They are there, in Orson Welles' classic film drama of a newspaper magnate's rise and fall, supposedly in the background of the beach picnic scene towards the end of the film. As the camera tracks through the party guests, following Kane's butler Raymond (played by Paul Stewart), just before we enter the Kanes' tent, there in the background are silhouettes of flapping bird-like creatures, seen briefly flying through the trees, perhaps unexpected members of the famed Kane menagerie.

Many lovers of obscure film trivia hold that they are back-projected images of a jungle with pterodactyls taken from another film, *Song of Kong* (USA 1933). Doubt has been cast on this, as no shot from the 1933 film matches that in *Kane*, but *Citizen Kane*, *Song of Kong* and *King Kong* (USA 1933), of which *Song of Kong* was a quickie sequel, shared the same background artist, Mario Larrinaga.[1] So we can keep on speculating. Whatever the truth might be, viewing the sequence while watching *Citizen Kane* the other day, for the umpteenth time, made me think of *King Kong*, Merian C. Cooper and Ernest B. Schoedsack's equally classic film drama of the capture and escape of a giant ape. What might be the greater connection between *King Kong* and *Citizen Kane*? Might they be, in some peculiar way, the same film?

Let us consider first the obvious connections.

Both films tell a story of a larger-than-life figure who comes crashing down to earth.

Both are among the most iconic of all films, films whose primary images are an essential part of any visual overview of film history.

---

[1] There is a good analysis of the pterodactyls and the work of matte artist Mario Larringa by David Cairns, 'Son of Kane,' *Shadowplay*, 21 September 2011, https://dcairns.wordpress.com/2011/09/21/son-of-kane.

Both films were made by RKO Radio Pictures and can be argued as being the twin major highlights of the studio's output, produced at either end of a golden decade of Hollywood film production.

Both films were signature productions of producers whose towering presence might be read into the subject matter of either film. *King Kong* was one of the last films green-lighted by David O. Selznick, during his brilliant short run as Head of Production at RKO. Eight years on, *Citizen Kane* was overseen by RKO president George Schaefer, who would find its director Orson Welles too great a monster to overcome, being fired by his own company after the failure of Welles' second feature, *The Magnificent Ambersons* (USA 1942). Equally, Kong might be Meriam C. Cooper, co-director and co-producer of *King Kong*, who took over from Selznick as RKO's production head, while Kane is Welles, the *wunderkind* who looks into the crystal ball and foresees his inevitable downfall.

The titles of both films make prominent use of the letter K. There is something about K, as there is with Q, X and Z, those unusual, arresting letters that writers and filmmakers have used to denote the commanding and otherworldly. K points to a German-American inheritance (the Katzenjammer Kids comic strip), to brutal passions (the Ku Klux Klan), to Kings—a letter that stands high on two legs, with arms stretched out over us: like Kane, like Kong.

Both films could be titled, or subtitled, 'Beauty and the Beast.' Carl Denham (played by Robert Armstrong), the explorer-filmmaker in *King Kong*, revels in the phrase that will sell his story. King Kong is brought down, literally, by his love for Ann Darrow (Fay Wray). At the end of the film, after Kong has been shot down from the top of the Empire State Building by warplanes, a policeman says, 'Gee, what a sight. Well, the airplanes got him.' Denham corrects him: 'Oh no, it wasn't the airplanes—it was Beauty killed the Beast.' *Citizen Kane* is no less the story of greatness felled by beauty, Kane (played by Orson Welles) having the world in his hands, a step or two away from the presidency, only to be humbled by his love for Susan Alexander (Dorothy Comingore). He loses power in pursuit of that he feels he must possess. It is Susan, not the trivial red herring of 'Rosebud' which underlies *Citizen Kane*, that is the thing Kane 'couldn't get or lost,' as the reporter Thompson (William Alland) says near the end of the film.

Charles Foster Kane (Orson Welles) in *Citizen Kane*.

Digging deeper, both films have a tragic dimension and structure. They tell of a heroic figure whose underlying flaw leads to a terrible fall. We, the humble audience, recognise these powerful things while being unable to know fully what brings about the end of one whose greatness makes them not as others are. Of course, the protagonists are very different in the roles that they play. Kane is, in part, the engineer of his own destiny. Kong (animated by Willis O'Brien) is all victim—he has no inner tragic flaw. But tragedy, as defined by Aristotle, is about the arousing of pity and fear.[2] It is what the audience feels that makes for tragedy. We see both brought down through what they cannot help but be. Kong and Kane are different but complementary tragic figures.

Although *Citizen Kane* is a far more complex film structurally than the linear *King Kong*, both can be viewed as following a classical tragic drama format. The five-act structure that the Jacobean dramatists learned from Seneca can be found first in *King Kong*, the succession of settings mirroring the development of the tragedy. Using Gustav Freytag's pyramidal shaping of Western dramatic structure,[3] we have:

---

[2] Aristotle, *On the Art of Poetry*, in *Classical Literary Criticism* (Harmondsworth: Penguin Books, 1965), p. 39.

[3] There is an explanation of nineteenth-century German writer Gustav Freytag's

King Kong.

Exposition—Denham plans a secret voyage to an island, discovering the actress he needs in Ann Darrow's New York waif.

Complication—The filmmakers travel from the known to the unknown, landing at Skull Island, where Ann is kidnapped by the native inhabitants.

Climax—Denham and the ship's crew head into the island to rescue Ann from Kong. Most die, but first mate Driscoll (Bruce Cabot) saves her and Kong, enraged that Ann has been taken from him, is captured.

Fall—Kong is presented in chains before an incredulous Broadway audience, then breaks free when he thinks Ann is threatened.

Catastrophe—Kong, having climbed to the top of the Empire State Building while carrying Ann, sets her down before planes shoot him and he falls to earth.

Citizen Kane, with its deconstruction of linear narrative, is the polar opposite of *King Kong* as cinematic experience. Nevertheless, when we look back on the tale that has been told, what has unfolded breaks down in similar fashion:

'Pyramid' concept of the five stages in any tragedy in John Yorke, *Into The Woods: How Stories Work and Why We Tell Them* (New York: The Overlook Press), pp. 36–37.

Exposition—Thanks to a mining deed held by his mother, the young Charles Foster Kane inherits a fortune and is brought up by guardians.

Rise—Kane spends lavishly, then decides to concentrate his attentions on running a newspaper. He becomes famous, influential and ambitious.

Climax—Kane believes himself to be unstoppable. But while running for the governorship of New York, Kane starts an affair with Susan Alexander, which is exposed by his opponent, leading to the end of his political ambitions.

Fall—Kane tries but fails to turn Alexander into an opera star, unable to understand the limits of his power.

Catastrophe—Susan leaves Kane. He retreats from the world at his palace, Xanadu, obsessed with collecting, dying surrounded by things but alone.

What engineers their fall is similar for both Kong and Kane. Each is brought down through the media. Firstly, each film is structured around the production of a film. Denham is a Paul J. Rainey-like figure, filming wildlife in exotic locations with the aim of making exciting films for audiences to view from the safety of their cinema seats.[4] The trip to Skull Island will be his greatest adventure, Ann his petrified heroine. He goes on to make Kong a theatrical exhibit, but this scarcely matters (indeed it could be that showing Kong on stage is a stunt designed to raise publicity for the film he has made).

Citizen Kane is framed by the making of a newsreel in the manner of *The March of Time*, the American radio news series (USA 1931-1945) and cinema newsreel (USA 1935-1951). Thompson, the reporter, is sent to find out more about Charles Foster Kane, because the newsreel we see at the start of the film tells us nothing about motivation. That Thompson, ostensibly working for a news-film company, has no camera with him and would appear to be preparing a magazine profile, is one of *Citizen Kane*'s unexplained oddities, but this petty matter is not important. The feature film that unfolds is the newsreel promised to us by his quest.

Both *Kong* and *Kane* become the films that their fictional progenitors dreamed that they might be.

---

[4] Paul J. Rainey was an American businessman and big game hunter. A feature-length documentary about his African expedition, *Paul J. Rainey's African Hunt* (USA 1912), was a huge success in its day and inspired many similar expedition films, including those of *King Kong*'s filmmakers Cooper and Schoedsack.

The role played by the media in each film is therefore established at the start, self-reflexively determining their shape and
outcome. Film is but one medium, and by 'media' we should understand all those mechanisms by which stories of the great are trans-
mitted to the small. In *King Kong*, there is literally a trigger moment,
when Kong is chained in front of the Broadway audience. The flash
of the press photographers' cameras Kong interprets as an attack
on Ann, causing him to break free and run amok through the city.
Kane's flash moment is when the 'love nest' story is broken in the
newspapers, leading to defeats in the polls and his decline as a figure
with credible power. His fall is longer in duration than Kong's, but
at the end it is the press and their cameras that pore over the 'loot of
the world' that he has left behind him.

King Kong and *Citizen Kane* are products of their time. Each
were creations of the period between the two world wars, when
people looked for solutions to the crises that civilisation apparently
faced, by raising up new kinds of king. Figures rose up with all-encompassing ideologies: dictators, demagogues, egotists, supermen,
Übermenschen. They saw the death of God and the fall of kings
brought about by the First World War. They positioned themselves in the gap that they believed was there for them to fill. The
media came to their aid, allowing for messages to be mass-circu-
lated. The cinema provided the perfect realisation of their dreams,
with its captive audience and the hypnotic figure on the screen,
towering over them all, loved and feared and everlasting.

They missed the point, however. The audience was not the
passive mass that they imagined it to be. It was looking for stories.
It too had drawn lessons from the fall of kings. It knew that there
had to be a rise and fall, a lesson to be learned, and then the curtain
would close until it was time for the next show. The supermen did
not own the story; the audience did. Some in that audience believed
such stories for a while, of course, but they were just stories and
all stories must have an end. The time of kings was past. The real,
underlying story was that power was drifting to the masses, to the
people in those cinema seats, whom the media were there to serve.
It is that change in power relations which brings down both Kong
and Kane. They grew too big for their democratic times. It was
not beauty who killed the beast; it was we the people who pulled
it down.

King Kong and *Citizen Kane* are both about the fall of
monsters. As William Shakespeare might have pointed out, both

tell sad stories of the death of kings.[5] That we pity Kong but not Kane (has anyone ever felt sorry for Charles Foster Kane, even when we think about the loss of his childhood?), may make *King Kong* the greater film. It is pure myth, the emblematic story of our times.

Originally published as 'Kane and Kong,' 31 October 2021, https://lukem-ckernan.com/2021/10/31/kane-and-kong, and reproduced here with small emendations.

---

[5] William Shakespeare, *Richard II*, Stanley Wells and Gary Taylor (eds.), *The Oxford Shakespeare: The Complete Works* (Oxford: Oxford University Press, 2005), Act 2, Scene 3, l. 152.

22.

A Death in the Comedy

Death, grief and Upstart Crow

Two things that it may not seem wise to introduce into a television comedy are religion and death. The final episode in the most recent series of the BBC's *Upstart Crow* (UK 2016-2020) gave us both, and it was the appearance of the latter that felt so extraordinary. When can someone die in a comedy, and what does that say about comedy itself?

Upstart Crow is a sitcom based around the life of William Shakespeare, which makes some attempt at acknowledging the historical figures and facts that relate to Shakespeare's life, as well as following the production of the plays in a roughly chronological sequence (each episode usually revolves around the experiences in Shakespeare's life which then inspire him to produce a play). First produced in 2016, marking the four-hundredth anniversary of Shakespeare's death, the series is written by Ben Elton, and has obvious echoes of the television series he wrote with Richard Curtis, *Blackadder II* (UK 1986). Both are set in the Elizabethan era, both feature a central male character with a circle of acolytes on whose company they rely, both are the victim of malign characters of higher station than theirs.

However, *Upstart Crow* is a lesser, because lighter, work than *Blackadder II* (or its successor series). It has none of the latter's savagery, nor satiric bite. Edmund Blackadder, as played by Rowan Atkinson, is a malcontent, a figure common in Elizabethan (strictly speaking, Jacobean) theatre, who rails against the society that must exclude him.[1] William Shakespeare, as played by David Mitchell, is a petit bourgeois, as worried about his commute from Stratford to London as he may be about the state of things, whose moments of genius are as much of a surprise to him as they are to his associates. *Upstart Crow* mocks modern living through

---

[1] See Luke McKernan, 'The Malcontent,' 4 May 2016, https://lukemckernan.com/2014/04/05/the-malcontent.

the absurdities of Elizabethan conditions, but there is no strong governing idea behind it.

Its chief virtue is the figure of Shakespeare. Mitchell gives us possibly the most convincing screen portrayal yet of the play-wright, indeed probably the only one. His Shakespeare is moderate in everything except his muse. He fusses over petty matters, he worries constantly about himself, he cheats but only in small things, he is defensive without strong argument, and he lives for home life. Yet at the same time he thinks poetically, with stubborn determination. The programme understands that elevated ideas have their home on the page, offset by life's essential ordinariness.

Shakespeare also provides *Upstart Crow* with its best lines. A paradoxical feature of the series is that jokes are continually made at the expense of Shakespeare's reputation, characters complaining at how dull, improbable or convoluted his work can be, yet at the same time it revels in quoting from the plays in a manner that can only silence all criticism. Time and again, beautiful words halt action and argument:

> Grief fills the room up of my absent child,
> Lies in his bed, walks up and down with me,
> Puts on his pretty looks, repeats his words,
> Remembers me of all his gracious parts,
> Stuffs out his vacant garments with his form:
> Then have I reason to be fond of grief?[2]

Constance's lines from *King John* on the death of her son Arthur come at the end of episode six of the third season of *Upstart Crow*, entitled 'Go On and I Will Follow.'[3] The action had been proceeding in expected fashion, with some fine laughs generated by a satire on awards ceremonies. Early on, however, there had been an odd introduction of seriousness at Shakespeare's home, where the family is preparing for his son's Hamnet's confirmation, and there is disagreement between Shakespeare and his wife Anne (played by Liza Tarbuck) over religious faith. Shakespeare will have none of it, and leaves in anticipation of acclaim at the award ceremony rather than attend the religious ceremony. He returns,

---

[2] William Shakespeare, *King John*, in Stanley Wells and Gary Taylor (eds.), *The Oxford Shakespeare: The Complete Works* (Oxford: Oxford University Press, 2005), Act 3, Scene 4, ll. 93-98.
[3] 'Go On and I Will Follow,' *Upstart Crow*, season 3 episode 6, tx. 3 October 2018 (BBC Two).

Anne Hathaway (Liza Tarbuck) and William Shakespeare
(David Mitchell) in *Upstart Crow*, 'Go On and I Will Follow.'

empty-handed, and complaining of his coach travel as usual, but the audience laughter has gone. The family sits in silence, waiting for him to stop. Then he is told that his son has died.

The family's reaction is more resignation than devastation. It is a time when many children die; they must be grateful that their two daughters are still living. The elder daughter Susanna, played by Helen Monks, asks her father if he believes, as they do, in an afterlife in which they will meet Hamnet again, but he cannot. The programme ends with Shakespeare and Anne seated at home. Earlier episodes end with the two of them contemplating recent events with ironic humour. In this episode, they are silent, while we hear Mitchell's voice reciting the words from *King John*. The end titles then remind us that Hamnet was a real person, giving us his dates—February 1585 to August 1596. Time falls away, and every viewer understands the Shakespeares' pain.

Deaths are rarities in comedies. The obvious precedent is in Elton's and Curtis' *Blackadder Goes Forth* (UK 1989), set during the First World War, where the leading players go over the top in the final episode, facing certain slaughter. Other television comedy deaths have come about through the death of an actor—Nicholas Colasanto, who played Coach in *Cheers* (USA 1982-1993), died towards the end of series three, his absence through ill-health and then his passing being written into the scripts. Death features in black comedies and sketch shows, of course, but death as an unforced element in a comedy series does seem exceptional.

So what is comedy, and how can anyone die in it? Of course, comedy sets out to amuse and to generate laughter, but what lies at the root of it? Aristotle, in *On the Art of Poetry*, saw comedy as it contrasted with the higher dramatic form, tragedy: 'Comedy aims at representing men as worse than they are nowadays, tragedy as better.'[4] Comedy, for Aristotle, was something chiefly concerned with the affairs of 'the worse types of men; worse, however, not in the sense that it embraces any and every kind of badness, but in the sense that the ridiculous is a species of ugliness or badness.'[5] It was good, because it brought about pleasure. George Meredith, in a once-famous essay on comedy, argues that comedy concerns a social group, whereas tragedy is concerned with the fate of the individual, and that comedy is a mark of civilisation:

> The laughter of Comedy is impersonal and of unrivalled politeness, nearer a smile; often no more than a smile. It laughs through the mind, for the mind directs it; and it might be called the humour of the mind. One excellent test of the civilization of a country ... I take to be the flourishing of the Comic idea and Comedy; and the test of true Comedy is that it shall awaken thoughtful laughter.[6]

For comedy to work, the laughter must be thoughtful, must trigger thought. The action generates a recognition of ourselves, of how we survive despite and because of our follies. Comedy brings about understanding through a recognition of the social self. The tragic victim is someone set apart from the rest of us, whose fate we can never fully comprehend. The comic figure is one of us, the audience looking in on itself. Whether the comedy is satirical, farcical or sentimental will affect how we view its subjects, but we still recognise them as our neighbours, and ourselves.

Of course, in modern times the classical idea of comedy has fallen away. Comedies can be absurd, brutal, cruel, nihilistic even. They may challenge the idea of laughter itself, when we find

---

[4] Aristotle, *On the Art of Poetry*, in *Classical Literary Criticism* (Harmondsworth: Penguin Books, 1965), p. 33.
[5] Aristotle, *On the Art of Poetry*, p. 37.
[6] George Meredith, 'An Essay on Comedy and Uses of the Comic Spirit,' *The New Quarterly Magazine* (April 1877), pp. 1-40.

ourselves in a world that is no laughing matter. Comedy, in its traditional sense, suggests a compliance with societal norms, even when it may hold these up to ridicule. It needs an acceptance of normality to thrive.

Death is a part of normality, but it cannot be funny—it destroys the illusion of continuity on which comedy depends. This is particularly so in a comedy series that trades on a warmth of feeling towards its characters. We stick with a long-running comedy series not just because it makes us laugh but because of our recognition of the characters. Their world makes our world understandable, and tolerable.

The purpose of comedy might therefore be said to be not to make us laugh but to make us realise that we are not alone. The function of stories is, at root, to instruct us in how to survive in the world. This is the conclusion of John Yorke's fine study of narrative form, *Into the Woods*, which argues that stories fulfil our need to see order imposed, saving us from the arbitrary nature of existence.[7] Different genres then must supply different forms of that lesson. A thriller or horror film ultimately reassures us that we are safe. A tragic drama confirms that our own decisions have been, on the whole, wise. A comedy tells us that we belong. Laughter is not its purpose, but the outcome.

Other forms of drama perform a similar, affirmative societal function (soap operas, for example). The distinguishing feature of comedy is that it makes us laugh. So it is that the death of Hamnet (not a major figure in the drama, it must be noted) can belong in a comedy for its social function, but is disturbing because it cannot generate laughter. It is not a trick that the series could pull off twice. Notably, despite the series' efforts at acknowledging history, the character of Christopher Marlowe is not murdered, as he was in reality. Instead he fakes his death and thereafter goes into hiding, before re-emerging as his identical twin, Kurt.

Upstart Crow achieved the coup because it had established sufficient trust with its audience, and because it had formed a particular relationship to historical reality. Its underlying intention has been to make Shakespeare meaningful to a modern audience, not through performance but through character. Ironically, it is through performance that Shakespeare has been shown to have greatest meaning after all. His words again and again have trumped all satire throughout the series, being the only words possible at

---

[7] John Yorke, *Into the Woods: How Stories Work and Why We Tell Them* (New York: The Overlook Press), pp. 36-37.

the end of 'Go On and I Will Follow,' when the laughter had to stop.

Originally published as 'A Death in the Comedy,' 6 October 2018, https://lukemckernan.com/2018/10/06/a-death-in-the-comedy, and reproduced here with small emendations. *Upstart Crow* ran for three series, twenty-one episodes in total (including three specials). It did not feature every single Shakespeare play, some of which featured in more than one episode. A stage version, *The Upstart Crow*, also written by Ben Elton, opened in London in 2020.

23.

Scorsese on the Phone

Looking at The Irishman *on the small screen*

Martin Scorsese has been inveighing against modern cinema trends.[1] He cannot see the dramatic value in all these films based on superhero comic characters, and indeed it is puzzling how such thin content can have been stretched so far and yet remain popular. He has also said that he does not want us to see his new film *The Irishman* (USA 2019) on our phones, but rather on a cinema screen—a big cinema screen—because that is where films are meant to be. So I decided to watch it on my phone.

I had not watched a feature film on a phone before now. It is not that easy a thing to do. Though we may seem to have our eyes fixed on our phones for much of our waking hours, the engagement is bitty, a checking-in on things or following gobbets of entertainment, rather than prolonged engagement requiring time and concentration—*The Irishman* is three-and-a-half hours long. Maybe on a train or plane, but in the daily round of things our journeys tend not to last as long as does a feature film. So we may see such films in bits, maybe starting on the phone on a journey home, then finishing off the film via the same platform (in the case of *The Irishman*, Netflix) but on another device with a larger screen later. To watch an entire feature film on a phone therefore requires time and effort.

The effort is exacerbated by the size of the phone. Even the largest of smartphones will fit in the hand, which requires particular positioning for the duration of a feature. You may position a tablet on the back of the train seat in front of you, as I frequently see others do on the daily commute, but a phone needs to be closer—maybe propped up on a table or shelf, but really you need greater closeness for the film to register. You need to judge scale,

---

[1] Martin Scorsese's comments cited in this essay come from an interview on the *Popcorn with Peter Travers* ABC television show, tx. 22 November 2019, https://tinyurl.com/4cu3hkkd.

Watching *The Irishman* on a cracked phone.

between eye and screen, much as one may do when selecting a cinema seat or positioning a chair for optimum television viewing. To watch *The Irishman*, I had to hold the phone in my hand, practically pinioned. It felt like I had this precious object, a film, and could not move because of it. But as far as eye-in-relation-to-screen was concerned, I was satisfied. There was an added personal touch in that I had dropped the phone recently and the screen was cracked. It was something I could look through without trouble, but it was not an effect one would normally experience in a cinema. Perhaps it formed some sort of commentary on the film's theme of broken lives, as former mob hitman Frank Sheeran (played by Robert de Niro) looks back on his many years in organised crime, through to the nursing home where life has left him.

Of course, I needed earphones. The sound from the phone's speaker would have been absurdly tinny, so I was not only pinned (on my sofa) with screen in my hand held still at a fixed distance, but—lacking wireless earphones—I was wired to the device in order to experience credible sound. Rapid movement was out of the question, simply reaching for a drink a matter of intricate co-ordination. All I could do was lie there, carefully ordered, looking down on the screen in my hand.

So what of the film experience as opposed to the physical experience? On the face of it, I missed very little from any other kind of screen; though I have only seen the film on the one screen, so cannot compare absolutely. Every detail, every nuance was there to be relished. It packed in every punch. Losing myself in the screen, scale became redundant. Experience overcame circumstance. That experience was everything that the filmmaker ought to have hoped for. I was taken out of time and space into the time and space that he had conjured up for me. Size had nothing to do with it.

It is—which helps—a very fine film. To my mind, it is the best thing Scorsese has done in decades, aided greatly by Steve Zaillian's uncannily well-judged script. It starts as a study in the exercise of power, only to reveal its subject as being the inexorability of time. The final half hour or so, when Frank Sheeran battles with the infirmities and the absurdities of old age (those absurdities including the criminal causes to which he devoted his life and the loyalty he retains towards those who are now all dead), is greatly moving. This is a film about the ageing process, in which we see actors come to the end of their performing lives (De Niro, Joe Pesci, Al Pacino), reanimated as their supposed younger selves with cine-trickery that at first seems absurd, then settles into acceptable, then is revealed as a comment on cinema itself, its ultimate failure to cheat time, and on us.

Cinema cannot sustain the illusion. Time must eventually run out on it. So one could argue that watching *The Irishman* on a phone is not an indication of failure, but a logical outcome of Scorsese's intentions, even a necessity. This is where film ends up. Scorsese says that he makes his films for the big screen:

> In the past 20 years I have made film for television, in terms of screen size, and for theatre. Never for a phone. I wish I could. I don't know how.

But he does know how. He has. He has by making the physical screen irrelevant, forgettable. Yes, traditional cinema gives us scale and with that maybe a sense of awe (though the average multiplex screen these days rather diminishes cinema's former awe-inducing capacity). But I think that is mostly just sentiment. Cinema only works because it is in our heads.

And maybe there is something else that, deep down, bothers Scorsese. In cinema we look up, in thrall to the big screen, subservient in our way. Television we see on a level, medium and recipient in equal control of the other. With a phone, we look down. We are in charge. It is not the pictures that got small, it is Scorsese.

Originally published as 'Scorsese on the Phone,' 4 December 2019, https://lukemckernan.com/2019/12/04/scorsese-on-the-phone, and reproduced here with small emendations. This writer was not alone in not following Scorsese's instruction. John Gay, on the same day, wrote an article, 'Sorry, Martin Scorsese—I Watched "The Irishman" on My Phone,' for the *Wall Street Journal*. It should be pointed out that Scorsese does say using an iPad might just be permissible.

24.

Alice—Random But Cool

Learning from early films going viral

It has been fascinating to watch what has been happening to the British Film Institute's latest online video release of *Alice in Wonderland* (UK 1903).[1] Restored and issued to coincide with the release in the UK of Tim Burton's new feature film *Alice in Wonderland* (USA 2010), made for Disney, the film has enjoyed a remarkable reception. In just a week from its publication on *YouTube* on 25 February 2010 it had attracted 123,564 hits on that platform and had been embedded on numerous other websites. Blogs commented on it, websites reviewed it. The link has been passed on goodness knows how many times via Twitter, and again and again the reaction from all kinds of people has been positive about the film. The line that keeps on being repeated is that the film is superior to Burton's bloated effort, but there is more enough evidence of genuine appreciation for what could be achieved in 1903. Here are some sample comments:

> Random but cool: silent Alice in Wonderland film from 1903
>
> Wow…just…wow
>
> You can totally see the kids staring at the camera as they walk by and when they ran, probably half of them lost their hats. Hilarious! Love it!
>
> This kind of creeps me out …in an awesome way
>
> Why is the speed normal not sped up like in old movies?
>
> I can do almost the same on my iPhone!

---

[1] *Alice in Wonderland* (1903) - Lewis Carroll | BFI National Archive, https://tinyurl.com/yc2fzrwu.

I bet if my great great grandpa saw this back in the day he'd be like 'woooow the effects are amazing!' :)

Cool! Does anyone know how the film got so ruined? I haven't had any luck searching on google :(

this is fake!

Sorry, but how could this be fake? Just wondering...
It's clear that people were brilliant with movie making before it had really even begun...

The thing was that back then people just kind of assumed film would last forever, because it was only 8 years old and they had no real idea of what time would do to it, and therefore didn't really take many precautions to keep it in a safe environment or to keep it clear of dirt or water and stuff

This dissolving effect would have been monumental in 1903. Amazing that we are watching a movie over 100 years old, sharing some of the exact same film techniques as ourselves, and it is STILL better than Tim Burton's version

Looks a little bit like a hoax

Nah, it's uploaded by BFI it won't be a hoax

100 years from now they will be blown away by how fake Avatar looks ;o)

Way too much cgi for me

wow ...we have come a long way

im accually scared of this

The special effects are better here than they are in some of today's movies! I would love to have been there when they were filming that :)

lol the Cheshire cat is just a random cat

Its amazing to see this after over 100 years and see how

far we've come! Its sad to think that everyone in this video is dead by now though :(but I love this video so much :D

Yeah, I was thinking that too, life is so precious and so short[1]

I read this as meaning that the general audience of 2010 is more than capable of appreciating the creative strengths of early cinema. There is delight at its invention alongside amusement at its quaintness. There is genuine appreciation of its proto-special effects with an understanding of how they fit into an ongoing history of film fantasy.

How different from the ways such films were disseminated and received only a few years ago. *Alice in Wonderland* has been preserved for many years in the BFI National Archive, where I used to work. The common ways in which we were able to present such films to an audience were at very occasional screenings at the National Film Theatre in London as part of early cinema programmes, attended by a couple of dozen people if you were lucky, or at festivals and exchange screenings with other film archives and institutes. Sometimes we just viewed the films by ourselves and bemoaned the fact that so few people could see them, or might ever want to see them. Only we understood their true value—or so we believed. VHS and DVD came along to help spread the message, but it was always a tough proposition to sell a compilation of early films. What one seldom had the opportunity to do was to show such films individually.

Now look where we are. *Alice* may well have garnered more views in the first week than it received on the entirety of its original release in 1903. Moreover it is being seen by such a wide range of people. It has been taken out of its specialist field into general appreciation. This is what *YouTube* does, and what other film archives need to take note of. It establishes a common platform that is so much better for these films than the specialist ones that we have created for them in retrospectives, festivals and niche DVD releases.

---

[1] These comments are selected from those posted on *YouTube* and social media sites in the first few weeks of the publication of the restored version of *Alice in Wonderland*. The phrase 'random but cool' comes from the celebrity gossip site *Oh No They Didn't!*, 3 March 2010, https://ohnotheydidnt.livejournal.com/44627605.html

Schoolchildren dressed as playing cards in *Alice in Wonderland*.

When these films are shown to the aficionados or those deemed to know best how to appreciate them, we learn little about them that is new. They are constrained by their select surroundings. Make them available among the skateboarding cats, comic skits, rants and ravings, music videos and television clips that make up *YouTube*'s mad mix—all of them short films, just like early cinema—and they are given new life through new audiences. The reactions will be wild at times, there will be plenty of misinterpretation or ignorance of "proper" film history, but the positives far outweigh the petty negatives. The positives are that the film is available to all, that it will be placed in contexts that we as curators or custodians might never think of, that it is exchangeable and shareable as information, that it belongs to today as much as yesterday. Meanwhile, the viewing figures keep rising.

For the record, *Alice in Wonderland* was produced in Britain by Cecil Hepworth, whose studies were in Walton-on-Thames outside London. Denis Gifford, in his *British Film Catalogue*, credits the direction to Hepworth and his regular director at this period, Percy Stow.[2] Mabel (May) Clark, who had joined Hepworth as a film cutter, plays Alice; Hepworth himself plays a

---

[2] Denis Gifford, *The British Film Catalogue 1895-1985* (New York/Oxford: Facts on File, 1986), cat. no. 00651.

frog, his wife Margaret plays the White Rabbit and the Queen of Hearts, while future director of Irish films Norman Whitten plays the Mad Hatter and a fish, while cinematographer Geoffrey Faithfull and his brother Stanley are two of the playing cards. The film was originally 800 feet or twelve minutes in length, though it was divided up into sixteen scenes which could be bought separately. Eight minutes survive today, in a somewhat ragged state. It was the longest British film yet made.

Alice was made with close attention to Tenniel's original illustrations, though it was bold enough to include its own additions to the narrative, giving Alice a magic fan (Tim Burton adds the Jabberwock to his version of the tale, which seems a somewhat greater liberty to take). Its special effects, achieved using optical printing and some ingenious use of scenery, allow us to see Alice grow large and small with impressive effectiveness. But perhaps the most delightful element is the procession of playing cards (filmed at the Mount Felix estate at Walton), which seems to have involved the participation of a local school. The narrative makes no sense when viewed with cold logic, but then neither does Lewis Carroll's original. In short it is random—but cool. Now go tell someone about it.

Originally published as 'Alice—Random But Cool,' 3 March 2010, https://thebioscope.net/2010/03/03/alice-random-but-cool, and reproduced here with small emendations. The text was extended for a talk entitled 'Film Archives Online—Random but Cool,' which I gave at the European Film Gateway symposium, *Film Archives and Their Users in the 'Second Century'—Risks and Benefits of the Transition to Digital*, Bologna, Italy, 30 June 2011. The text of the talk is available at https://tinyurl.com/59zy52u3. The restored film remains on *YouTube*, and as of May 2025 it had gained 2.8 million views.

25

The Lives of the Characters

The soap imagination of Tony Jordan's Dickensian

Christmas Eve, sometime in the 1840s. In a warren of London streets, a number of people are facing crises in their lives. Amelia and Arthur Havisham have attended their father's funeral and have returned to their home, Satis House. Outside, the moneylender Jacob Marley scowls at the cheerful Mrs Gamp, then sends a boy with a message to Fagin. He runs past Mr and Mrs Bumble as he does so. Elsewhere Marley's business, Ebeneezer Scrooge, passes by the Old Curiosity Shop, which has a notice saying it is closed owing to illness. Inside a dangerously ill Little Nell is tended to by her grandfather and a bibulous Mrs Gamp. At Scrooge and Marley's office their assistant learns that there has been a deduction in his wages, but prompt payment of a loan is still expected of him. Sensing that he must move quickly to gain a financial advantage, Scrooge asks for the Old Curiosity Shop account. At Satis House, Amelia is comforted by her good friend Honoria Barbary, whose hapless father is facing financial ruin. Arthur Havisham starts to plot against his sister with an accomplice, Compeyson. In his den Fagin tells the prostitute Nancy that she has an appointment with Jacob Marley that evening. She shivers with fear …

The opening episode of the British television series *Dickensian* (UK 2015-2016) boldly and brilliantly introduced viewers to the back stories of characters from Charles Dickens' novels. These stories then unfolded and intertwined over the series. The roots of *Great Expectations*, *Bleak House*, *Oliver Twist*, *A Christmas Carol*, *The Old Curiosity Shop* and others were imagined as having come from a single narrative source, a journey by suggestion into the mind of Charles Dickens, reinventing his *oeuvre* as a Balzacian *Comédie Humaine*, with interlocking characters across the different novels, revealing a fully realised alternative world. The figure that initially pulls all these characters and their personal stories together is Jacob Marley. By the end of the first episode we see that almost everyone has good reason to wish him dead, and then his body is found lying in an alley. The mystery of who killed him must then be investigated by, of course, Inspector Bucket, the detective from *Bleak House*.

Dickensian was the invention of British television scriptwriter, Tony Jordan, creator or co-creator of such popular series as *Hustle* (UK 2004-2012) and *Life on Mars* (UK 2006-2007), best known as the lead writer over nearly three decades of the BBC soap opera *EastEnders* (UK 1985-). Jordan writes that his interest in Charles Dickens as source material began when he was invited to present an episode of the BBC series *The Secret Life of Books* (UK 2014-2016), on *Great Expectations*.[1] The programme explored Dickens' art through the eyes of an expert soap opera writer: the serial nature of publication, the use of cliff-hangers, the interwoven personal stories, and the high appeal to a mass audience. Inspired by a sense of affinity, Jordan then set about writing *Dickensian*, a twenty-part series of thirty-minute episodes produced by his own Red Planet Pictures.

The connection between Dickens and soap opera has been made on many occasions. Jordan set out to prove his case, but rather than adapt any one of Dickens' works, he would appropriate them all. In the world of *Dickensian*, Fagin (*Oliver Twist*) rubs shoulders with Scrooge (*A Christmas Carol*), Inspector Bucket (*Bleak House*) crosses with Bob Cratchit (*A Christmas Carol*), a fawning Mr Bumble (*Oliver Twist*) plays host to Gradgrind (*Hard Times*), Amelia Havisham (*Great Expectations*, though her first name is Jordan's invention) is best friends with Honoria Barbary (*Bleak House*). The three main narratives are the Marley murder, the Barbary bankruptcy, and the false wooing of Miss Havisham. However, several smaller stories unfold: the Bumbles' hapless attempts at social advancement, a romance between Peter Cratchit (*A Christmas Carol*) and Little Nell (*The Old Curiosity Shop*), Sikes freeing Nancy from Fagin's control (all three from *Oliver Twist*). And there are many wry references to other parts of the Dickens canon: the orders for an unseen Mr Pickwick (*The Pickwick Papers*) being taken at the Three Cripples pub (*Oliver Twist*), Honoria working at Mantalini's dressmakers (as featured in *Nicholas Nickleby*), Uriah Heep named as Jaggers' secretary (combining *David Copperfield* with *Great Expectations*),

---

[1] Tony Jordan, 'I turned down the chance to research Charles Dickens for a TV series nine times… then I found a kindred spirit,' *The Independent*, 27 August 2014, https://tinyurl.com/4xkpwzk7'; *Great Expectations—The Secret Life of Books*, episode one, tx. 5 September 2014 (BBC Four).

Oliver Twist asking for more. It begins with the starting point of *A Christmas Carol* ('Marley was dead: to begin with. There is no doubt whatever about that'). It ends at the point where *Great Expectations* could begin, the jilted bride asserting that, from this point onwards, time for her would stand still.

What could have been merely a clever intellectual exercise revealed itself to be an original and logical entertainment. You could see the delight in the actors' eyes at the quality of the writing and the piquancy of the situations in which they found themselves. It is possible that twenty episodes was too long, with the series' structural logic torn between the endless unfolding of a soap opera, and the expected conclusion of a time-limited narrative, the difference between what Robert C. Allen in his studies of soap opera form defines as open and closed serials (the various narratives are all resolved by the time of the final episode, featuring Amelia Havisham's disastrous wedding day).[2] At its weakest *Dickensian* overplayed the obvious (in particular the Miss Havisham strand). At its best it was, to this viewer's eyes, as good a television drama as there has ever been.

In particular episode sixteen, in which Honoria Barbary (played by Sophie Rundle) gives birth, aided only by her embittered sister Frances (Alexandra Moen), was among the best thirty minutes of televised drama that this writer has ever seen. While previous episodes had criss-crossed over the series' different story strands, in the usual soap opera manner, this episode concentrated on the one story alone with remorseless intensity and extraordinary effect, from the panic leading up to the birth to the shock of the dilemma Frances puts herself in at the end of the episode (the outcome of which would be known only to those had read *Bleak House*). In writing, pacing, performance, lighting, decorative detail, and use of our knowledge of the characters' pasts to create tension and force climax, this was a programme to hold up as the best of what the medium can achieve. It was also a convincing argument for why literature belongs on the screen.

It can often seem that we are growing bored of the classics, and must mangle with them to sustain our jaded appetites. Sequels and prequels, modernisations, parodies, and revered characters battling with the living dead—as with *Pride and Prejudice and Zombies* (UK/USA 2016)—seem to express an ennui, an admission that no

---

[2] Robert C. Allen, introduction to Robert C. Allen (ed.), *To Be Continued...: Soap Operas Around the World* (London: Routledge, 1995), pp. 17-24.

one has the patience to read novels any more, or else frustration at some great novelists not having written more than they did.

On its announcement, *Dickensian* sounded as though it was going to be yet another example of this syndrome, a desperate stirring of the ingredients to try and come up with something new to lay on the table. Instead, it showed that there was life in these characters beyond that set down on the page by Charles Dickens—and that re-imagining of the classics is not sacrilege, but can be insightful, and even necessary, when it is done well. It showed how characters on the page remain in our minds because they live convincing lives. Those lives can be sustained in other forms, where there is enough imagination and belief. Indeed, to sustain those convincing lives, it may be as important to re-imagine such stories as to read them. If we can no longer read past works as those in the past did, because we are different people (different in outlook, different in sense of time), but if those works' status as art must endure, then re-imagining becomes an essential part of how we continue to tell them. Which does not mean *Little Dorrit* and the undead—it means getting inside the mind of the author and plucking out something new along with the familiar. This is exactly what Tony Jordan and his team did: they re-energised the mind of Charles Dickens.

Dickensian was an artistic success, but its fortunes with audiences were mixed. The first two episodes were broadcast on BBC One, separated by an hour, on 26 December 2015. The timing was completely appropriate, but thereafter the series suffered from erratic scheduling. The slots of episodes seemed to change hour and day each week, making it difficult for an audience to acquire a habit for the programme in the manner of a soap opera, which had clearly been the producers' intention.[3] This seems to have been caused partly by uncertainty on the part of the BBC as to how best to present the series, but also to some degree a consequence of waning audience interest early on. The first two episodes attracted an audience of five million and 4.3 million respectively (excluding

---

[3] The original broadcast dates (all BBC One) were: Episode 1: tx. 26 December 2015; 2: tx. 26 December 2015; 3: tx. 27 December 2015; 4: tx. 27 December 2015; 5: tx. 1 January 2016; 6: tx. 6 January 2016; 7: tx. 7 January 2016; 8: tx. 13 January 2016; 9: tx. 14 January 2016; 10: tx. 21 January 2016; 11: tx. 22 January 2016; 12: tx. 27 January 2016; 13: tx. 28 January 2016; 14: tx. 4 February 2017; 15: tx. 5 February 2017; 16: tx. 11 February 2016; 17: tx. 12 February 2016; 18: tx. 18 February 2016; 19: tx. 19 February 2016; 20: tx. 21 February 2016.

Frances (Alexandra Moen, left) and Honoria (Sophie Rundle),
in *Dickensian*, episode 16.

later catch-up figures), but dropped steadily thereafter, down to
two million by the time of the twentieth episode.[4]

Every effort had been made to give the series a broad appeal.
The production values were high, with a reported ten million
pounds being spent, including the construction of a large single-set
boasting twenty-seven two-storey buildings and a ninety-metre
cobbled street that placed the Dickensian characters in close prox-
imity to one another.[5] The cast was particularly strong: Stephen
Rea (Inspector Bucket), Tuppence Middleton (Miss Havisham),
Anton Lesser (Fagin), Caroline Quentin (Mrs Bumble), Pauline
Collins (Mrs Gamp), Omid Djalili (Mr Venus) and Peter Firth
(Jacob Marley) among them. The faces were as familiar as the characters.

Yet something, beyond the troublesome scheduling, did not
quite work. Critics were for the most part generous with their
praise, admiring the wit of the conception and the style of its realisation. Still, some felt a nagging sense of an uncertainty of purpose,
perhaps best expressed by Ben Dowell in *Radio Times*:

---

[4] 'Festive ratings highlights: Sherlock, Dickensian & Fungus,' *Broadcast*,
4 January 2016, http://www.broadcastnow.co.uk/ratings/festive-ratings-high-
lights-sherlock-dickensian-and-fungus/5098483.article; Jane Martinson, 'BBC
axes Dickensian after one series,' *The Guardian*, 21 April 2016, https://www.
theguardian.com/media/2016/apr/21/bbc-axes-dickensian-after-one-series.
[5] Ian Burrell, '"Dickensian" is the BBC's biggest Christmas offering: When
Fagin met Scrooge,' *The Independent*, 1 December 2015, http://www.inde-
pendent.co.uk/arts-entertainment/tv/features/dickensian-is-the-bbcs-biggest-
christmas-offering-when-fagin-met-scrooge-a6756276.html.

[T]he first and most obvious question to ask is this: they may have the same names and look like they are described in the books but who are these people? Can they really be said to be Dickens characters? The great Victorian novelist invented these richly drawn characters to fit into the novels he wrote. He was a storyteller, first and foremost, someone who wrote episodic narratives driven by the unstoppable force of his ingeniously-crafted plots. He populated his books with amazing characters, of course, but tearing them away from their stories is to essentially denude them of their essential life and being [...] If I am quite honest I couldn't see the point of this exercise which failed to teach us anything new about any of Dickens' characters, or allowed them to develop in any meaningful way.[6]

For Dowell, the problem was that *Dickensian* was not Dickens. The characters existed within the fictions that had been originally created for them. They did not have, or could not have, exterior lives. The exercise was clever, but added nothing to Dickens' expression of those people, whose reason for being existed solely within his pages.

This is an understandable line of argument, but to my mind it is fundamentally false. A writer does not own the characters that they create, nor the works in which such characters may be found. Of course in a legal sense such ownership may exist. Charles Dickens raged against the American 'pirates' who republished or adapted his original creations, in the absence of any international copyright legislation (such as was first introduced in 1886 with the Berne Convention). Copyright law identifies particular rights of ownership that lie with the originator of a creative work, but it is a different matter when one considers how people read. Ownership of the play of a creative work upon the imagination lies with any individual reader (or viewer), and more than stories, we feel that we own the characters. If the author has imbued any life in them at all, then our imaginations must flesh out what is presented to us on the printed page. We want to know what will happen to them; we want to know from where they came. They lead convincing lives.

---

[6] Ben Dowell, 'Soapy and Silly — what the Dickens is the BBC up to in its latest drama series Dickensian?,' *Radio Times*, 26 December 2015, https://tinyurl.com/3fzszytc.

This is the sentimental tendency against which L. C. Knights famously railed in his essay *How Many Children Had Lady Macbeth?*[7] A great work of fiction, Knights argued, is not driven by the personal but by the thematic. Characters exist inasmuch as they support the governing ideas. Speculation on their lives beyond that which was the express purpose of the artist is fatuous, as critical enquiry.

But that does not stop the reader from such speculation, nor the writer who might want to capitalise upon such enthusiasm. Tony Jordan expressed just such an enthusiasm when he considered Miss Havisham:

> I have always been fascinated by the character of Miss Havisham—this mad woman in a wedding dress and veil, sitting at the table, jilted on the day of her wedding, an event she found so traumatic that she never took off her wedding dress. We've all seen that image and we all know it, so I was interested in how she got to be that woman. What was she like as a young woman and in love? Did she laugh? Who was she? What did she care about? So I decided that was one of the first stories I wanted to tell, it was exciting because nobody had ever seen the young Miss Havisham before—it was then that I knew I had something.[8]

Prequels and sequels to the classics, from Mary Cowden Clarke's 1850-1852 series *The Girlhood of Shakespeare's Heroines*, to Jean Rhys' *Wide Sargasso Sea* (a prequel to *Jane Eyre*), to the mini-industry that is the Jane Austen sequel novel (such as Emma Tennant's *Pemberley: or Pride and Prejudice Continued*), all betray the urge to extend our belief. The film industry is sustained by sequels and prequels that recapitulate narrative elements and particular characters that a mass audience will pay to see once again.

The digital era has created a thirst for the extension of narrative and character, and the means by which to achieve this. Fan fiction, in which the fans of a creative work publish their own stories developed out of the original characters or settings. Some

---

[7] L. C. Knights, *How Many Children Had Lady Macbeth?: an essay in the theory and practice of Shakespeare criticism* (Cambridge: Gordon Fraser, 1933).
[8] 'Interview with Tony Jordan,' *BBC Media Centre*, 9 December 2015, http://www.bbc.co.uk/mediacentre/mediapacks/dickensian/tony.

authors have embraced this development of their imaginative originals (J. K. Rowling); others have reacted angrily against it (Anne Rice, George R. R. Martin). Either way, the evidence is clear. Stories and characters have lives of their own. We appropriate them through our affection. Once you have asked how many children Lady Macbeth had, someone will want to know the answer — and someone will set out to provide that answer. Lady Macbeth's other life matters.

Various commentators have suggested a link between *Dickensian* and fan fiction, though Tony Jordan denies any connection. However, the fundamental motivation was the same. Jordan says that 'it had to be about taking ownership of the characters, after all Dickens never wrote a scene between Scrooge and Fagin, or between a young Miss Havisham and Martha Cratchit, but I had to do just that.'[9] This derives, fundamentally, from the sense of entitlement that the sharing of content over the Internet has engendered. It is not just about the assertion of a post-copyright age where former boundaries no longer apply. It is about a release of the imagination created by opportunity. The age of the copy is producing stories that must exist because they are copies.

Dickens himself was said to have appropriated characters, turning people that he met into figures on a page. It is a common accusation, but except for certain *romans à clef*, it is a misleading one. Peter Ackroyd writes of this tendency:

> Dickens used certain salient characteristics of the people whom he met or knew, but there are very few instances when he simply transcribed what he had seen and heard into the page. The novelist's art is not of that kind: Dickens perceived a striking characteristic, or mood, or piece of behaviour, and then in his imagination proceeded to elaborate upon it until the 'character' bears only a passing resemblance to the real person. In his fiction Dickens entered a world of words which has its own procedures and connections, so that the original 'being' of any individual is subsumed into something much larger and generally much more conclusive.[10]

---

[9] 'Creating Dickensian,' *BBC Writers Room* blog, 22 December 2015, https://tinyurl.com/mk3ssm9m.
[10] Peter Ackroyd, *Dickens* (London: Sinclair-Stevenson, 1990), p. 119.

As with Dickens and real life, so it was with Tony Jordan and Dickens. Salient characteristics have been appropriated to build a fresh creative work. *Dickensian* is not Dickens; it is Dickensian. It takes ownership of the characters and settings to make sense of them in a world of the new writer's invention.

In an essay on *The Mystery of Edwin Drood*, V. S. Pritchett considers the meaning of the word 'Dickensian' in relation to style and characters. Arguing that much of what is understood as Dickensian in style is an inheritance from Laurence Sterne, Tobias Smollett and Samuel Richardson, Pritchett looks instead at Dickens' people:

> [T]he distinguishing quality of Dickens' people is that they are solitaries. They are people caught living in a world of their own. They soliloquise in it. They do not talk to one another; they talk to themselves. The pressure of society has created fits of twitching in mind and speech, and fantasies in the soul [...] In how many of that famous congress of 'characters' — Micawber, Barkis, Moddles, Jingle, Mrs Gamp or Miss Twitterton: take them at random — and in how many of the straight personages, like Jasper and Neville Landless in *Edwin Drood*, are we chiefly made aware of the individual's obliviousness of any existence but his own?[11]

For Pritchett, Dickens' characters are 'all out of touch and out of hearing of each other, each conducting its own inner monologue,' a disassociation he identifies as having its roots in 'the fright of childhood.' Quite the opposite is the case with *Dickensian*. In this world, which is the world of the soap opera, existence is defined by the individuals' relations to others. They form an organic piece, no element of which has meaning except in how it impacts on the fate of the other elements. The rapid cutting from story element to story element reinforces the sense of characters bound together by an overarching narrative whose direction, indeed existence, they do not sense — for the most part. Soap operas are sustained dramatically by the idea of the community that they portray, even if Tony Jordan's *EastEnders* regularly challenges the idea of community as something still valid in modern times; characters, particularly in the early years of *EastEnders*, would speak of better, more

[11] V. S. Pritchett, 'Edwin Drood,' in *The Pritchett Century: The Selected Writings of V. S. Pritchett* (London: Chatto & Windus, 1998), pp. 473-474.

communal times in the past—maybe as far back as the 1840s.[12] If there is a childhood root in this to complement that identified in Dickens by Pritchett, then it is the urge to belong. But this lies not in the writer but the readership, which yearns to own what it sees.

There are moments when a realisation of community and shared destiny are made apparent. Particularly these come when Nancy (played by Bethany Muir) sings at the Three Cripples, on occasions where many of the leading characters have gathered in that same place (a pub, the Queen Vic, is the communal centrepiece of *EastEnders*). This occurs at the end of episode ten and especially at the end of the final episode, where her rendition of the aria 'I Dreamt I Dwelt in Marble Halls' touches every heart within, the camera panning from face to face, as each sets aside private troubles and finds themselves caught up in the collective sentiment. Beyond, but at the same time, Miss Havisham weeps at the table with her wedding feast; Arthur Havisham, his selfish plans in ruins, prepares to commit suicide; the ghostly voice of Marley is heard by Scrooge; and Oliver Twist is taken in by the Artful Dodger. No one, we learn, can exist alone.

The fatal flaw of *Dickensian* was that it could not escape its cleverness. It wanted to tell a set of good stories, through engrossing characters, in a particularly televisual form. It did so, most successfully, but all the while it was inviting the viewer to see how ingeniously the pieces of the puzzle had been put together. There was an expectation, at least to a degree, that the viewer would be familiar with the novels, so that they would recognise the people involved and have a sense of their fate. Prequels can only be read with an understanding that their conclusion must be to arrive at the starting point of a story with which we are familiar. But despite countless film and television adaptations, and the familiarity of certain characters, the mass audience's grasp of why these characters were coming together in the way that they did was probably not all that Jordan might have hoped for.

Paradoxically, what hampered *Dickensian* was its allegiance to Dickens. No matter how widely the writer's imagination might range, the ending could only be to return to Dickens. The ownership conferred by originality never goes away. So it was that, despite good reviews and a fervent body of fans, *Dickensian* was not re-commissioned by the BBC. This is a great loss, because there was every promise of Jordan's creation seeking out endings

---

[12] Christine Geraghty, 'Social Issues and Realist Soaps: A study of British soaps in the 1980/1990s,' in Allen, *To Be Continued...*, p. 70.

beyond what were Dickens' starting points. Jordan had story-lined sixty episodes, pointing out that Dickens had created over 2,000 characters and so far he had only used around twenty-five.[13] A work of art lies unmade, maybe several such works of art. It is as tragic as a burnt manuscript, a what-might-have-been that could still be reality if only someone was braver, and the schedulers more consistent. In some alternative universe *Dickensian* series two and three can be seen, bringing delight at their ingenuity and pleasure at how they extend the art of a great novelist through characters that are owned by all of us. But not in this one.

Originally published as 'Dickensian,' 22 April 2016, https://lukemcker-nan.com/2016/04/22/dickensian, then extended for publication as 'The Lives of the Characters in Dickensian,' in Ian Christie and Annie van den Oever (eds.), *Stories: Screen Narrative in the Digital Era* (Amsterdam University Press, 2018). The above derives from the extended version, with some small changes.

---

[13] Burrell, '"Dickensian" is the BBC's biggest Christmas offering.'

26.

Simple Twist of Fate

Bob Dylan's Masked and Anonymous

It is curious how a fine work of art immediately catches the eye. You walk through a gallery, and there is that picture at the far end whose ideal resolution of form and feeling stops all else except its contemplation. You pick up a book at random and on opening at any page a phrase is there telling you instantly that this is a skilled work through and through. Any part of the whole reveals the whole.

So it was in channel-hopping that I saw just thirty seconds of *Masked and Anonymous* (USA, 2004), starring Bob Dylan. It was being screened to mark the man's eightieth birthday. It was immediately clear that here was a remarkable film. It was there in the framing, in the very balance of things.

I knew of the film but had never seen it. It had been thoroughly trashed by the critics on release, only to gain grudging appreciation in time, but despite being a long-time follower of Dylan's I had not sought it out. Now I did, watching the following night on catch-up. And as those thirty seconds had promised, it was indeed a good film, demonstrating astute judgment from the start that was sustained throughout. Any part of the whole revealed the whole.

Masked and Anonymous is as good as any American film of the past two decades, and a good deal better than most. It is, I think, the best film with which Dylan has been associated. It is not a film for the mass audience, certainly, hovering as it does between sense and confusion, indifferent to story, hallucinatory in effect. It is set in a future yet present American society that is falling apart. The country has turned into banana republic, governed by an ailing dictator, descending into civil war. A televised benefit concert for the victims of the war is being organised by promoter Uncle Sweetheart (played by John Goodman), who needs money to pay off hoodlums. Frustratingly for him, Paul McCartney, Billy Joel and Sting are not available. The only star he can book is has-been Jack Fate, the son (we eventually learn) of the dictator, who is released from prison for the show. Fate (played by Dylan) rehearses with his band Simple Twist of Fate (played by Dylan's touring band of the time), as plot and society start to crumble. The dictator dies, the concert takes place. Fate is taken away by troops for a murder he did not commit. Sitting in the back of a van, handcuffed, he thinks aloud:

> I was always a singer and maybe no more than that. Sometimes it's not enough to know the meaning of things, sometimes we have to know what things don't mean as well. Like, what does it mean to not know what the person you love is capable of? Things fall apart …

The film is both conceited and wry, a homage to Dylan while mocking the very idea of such worship. Fate is continually told that he is past it, and there is a great gag when a set list is proposed for him including 'Street Fighting Man,' 'Eve of Destruction' and 'Kick out the Jams.' 'You can do all those,' Uncle Sweetheart assures him. This knowingness inevitably limits its appeal, since anyone who does not recognise the references, or does not care that much for Dylan, will be indifferent if not repulsed by such apparent self-indulgence. But beneath the play with the idea of Dylan/Fate is a serious exposition of the abiding theme of Dylan's music and outlook, from the 1990s onwards, of the world gone wrong. *World Gone Wrong*, comprising covers of traditional songs that map out the thesis, was released in 1993. *Masked and Anonymous*, with its portrayal of corruption and disintegration, where people play at roles that they sense no longer make sense, where money and power have failed, and only song can crystallise some sort of truth, feels like the perfect exposition of Dylan's prevailing view of things.

The film has two particular qualities. One is the nature of the narrative. Director Larry Charles, now best known as a director of Sacha Baron Cohen films, wanted the film to have 'the interior landscape of a great Bob Dylan song—rich with vivid imagery, poetic language and the dance of reality and illusion.'[1] Dylan has consistently come up with songs characterised by a mysterious story and odd characters whose precise connection with one another is never clear, maybe not even to themselves. Songs such as 'Lily Rosemary and the Jack of Hearts,' 'Isis' or 'Tin Angel' are films of the mind,

---

[1] 'Masked and Anonymous—About the Production,' *Sony Pictures Classics*, https://www.sonyclassics.com/masked/about-the-production.html.

working to their own interior logic but which could never actually work on screen in reality—or so it has been argued. *Masked and Anonymous* is like the Dylan song that finally solved the problem.

The other quality is Dylan's presence. As prior dramatic film appearances have demonstrated—*Pat Garrett & Billy the Kid* (USA 1973), *Renaldo & Clara* (USA 1978), *Hearts of Fire* (USA 1978)—Bob Dylan cannot act, but has an extraordinary screen presence nonetheless. He both belongs and yet does not belong on the screen, serving as a comment on the absurdity of human pretension. Why are we acting in this story? But what else can we do? In *Masked and Anonymous*, however, he comes close to acting quite well. Not well enough so that anyone else would cast him for being anything other than himself, but credible within the bounds of a film which revolves around someone who is a reflection of him.

Jack Fate (Bob Dylan) and Tom Friend (Jeff Bridges)
in *Masked and Anonymous*.

Renaldo & Clara tried the same thing, but that was directed by Dylan, who likes film but has not the first idea how to direct one. Larry Charles does, working from a script by himself and 'Sergei Petrov,' a pseudonym for Dylan, who it seems supplied the rough ideas and characters, jotted down on scraps of hotel stationery, which Charles was able to transmute into something filmic. The film is built around the strangeness of Dylan's presence. The starry cast—Goodman, Jeff Bridges, Jessica Lange, Angela Bassett, Luke Wilson, Penélope Cruz, Val Kilmer, Bruce Dern, Ed Harris, Mickey Rourke—put heart and soul into their mysterious roles, yet each finds their scenes stolen by the man who does not act, or who is good at acting someone who does not act. Maybe the only exception is Giovanni Ribisi, whose short scene as a troubled soldier travelling on a bus with Fate, about to meet with fate, is singularly haunting. But Jack Fate leaves him to his death, and travels on.

The film has plenty that is wrong with it. The female characters are inconsequential, with the exception of Jessica Lange, as TV producer Nina Veronica. Jeff Bridges' boorish journalist, asking questions about music and motivation to which he does not really want answers, feels like a tired 'Ballad of a Thin Man' satire, or Dylan's fierce assault on an interviewer in the documentary *Dont Look Back* (USA 1967), while his climactic fight with Fate is unnecessary and too absurd (you really cannot imagine Dylan flooring anyone with a punch). The film was shot cheaply and, though richly textured, has a washed-out look that feels almost as though it were shot on video. The famous names, mostly working for union rates, helped secure the funding but look awkward alongside the wordless poor and down-and-outs whose presence feels more true to the kinds of world Dylan conjures up, ones where the sham of borders is exposed.

But it has far more that is good about it. As noted, every composition confirms the excellence of the whole. The film is particularly good at framing Dylan/Fate and his band, with striking use of a wide-angle lens and dynamic positioning of the musicians. The dialogue is compelling even when the sense is unclear—the starry performers must have signed up not just for the chance to be on set with Dylan but because they were given interesting things to say, and interesting situations in which to say them. For a serious, quite obscure film, it is also lot of fun. Uncle Sweetheart invites supporting acts for the show into his cabin: Dally the Rubber Girl, Eddie Quicksand with Milo, the Great El Mundo with Ellen the Fortune Teller, Abraham Lincoln, Pope John Paul II and Mahatma Gandhi. Only in a Dylan song… Nina Veronica asks if anyone will recognise the songs. 'All of his songs are recognisable, even when they're not recognisable' replies Sweetheart, mocking Dylan's notorious mangling of his back catalogue in concert.

And of course, there is the music—some terrific live contributions from Dylan and band ('Down in the Flood,' 'Cold Irons Bound,' 'Drifter's Escape,' 'I'll Remember You,' the traditional songs 'Diamond Joe' and 'Dixie'), but significantly some imaginative cover versions on the soundtrack. We hear Italian hip-hop band Articolo 39 mixing up 'Like a Rolling Stone,' Turkish singer

Sertab Erener's plaintive take on 'One More Cup of Coffee,' Japanese rockers Magokoro Brothers enthusiastically ripping into 'My Back Pages.' It is Dylan's music as world music, the cover as important as the so-called original.

The influence of film on Bob Dylan has often been noted, from the borrowings of lines from favourite films, to his wish to make *Renaldo & Clara* in the mould of one of the French classics, such as *Tirez sur le pianiste* (France 1960) *or Les Enfants du Paradis* (France 1945).[2] What *Masked and Anonymous* reveals, to these eyes, is another part of Dylan's filmic imagination. So many of his songs seem to be attempts to replay films that he has seen, but in the way that he saw them. It is not that life is a film but that films are turning into something else in his mind. It is expressed most obviously in 'Brownsville Girl'—inspired by *The Gunfighter* (USA 1950), or other Gregory Peck films—and 'Tempest,' inspired by *Titanic* (USA 1997)—but the specific is less important than the general. The songs of mysterious narrative or people with strange names who momentarily loom into view, connected, though we do not fully sense how, are part of a creative world where life and story are not separated, the imaginary not yet sorted out from the real. It is a child's view of things.

I have been reading the works of British educational psychologist C. W. Kimmins. His is a forgotten name now, but he once enjoyed a considerable vogue, sufficient at one time to come to the attention of film director and theorist Sergei Eisenstein.[3] In the 1910s and 20s Kimmins interviewed hundreds of children about their imaginative worlds, including the influence of the new medium of film. Some of the testimonies of cinemagoing that he gathered from children for a 1917 Cinema Commission Inquiry, instituted by the National Council of Public Morals, reveal the great power that films were having on children's minds. Children aged between eight and thirteen were asked to write essays describing films that had made a particular impression on them. These essays read uncannily like scenarios for Bob Dylan songs, even phrased in the way Dylan might chose to do. Here are three examples:

Joan was a young and beautiful girl of about seventeen

---

[2] See C. P. Lee, *Like a Bullet of Light: The Films of Bob Dylan* (London: Helter Skelter, 2000).
[3] See the essay 'Charlie the Kid' in Sergei Eisenstein (ed. Jay Leyda), *Film Essays with a Lecture* (London: Dennis Dobson, 1968), pp. 132-133.

years of age, who worked in the mines. Her friend was Lizzie, a pretty girl of about the same age, but fragile and obstinate. Their 'boss' as they called the manager, was a young man, handsome and kind. Many a time had he saved Joan from blows from the foreman, and she had grown to love him. Joan's father was a bully and the terror of the mine.

It was a dull day, and a heavy storm was raging overhead; and a man, evidently a newcomer, entered the inn. He was tall and respectable, with large bright eyes, which seemed to influence everybody. Having had his fill, and the storm having abated, he left the inn and proceeded homewards. On arriving there he sat down and seemed lost in meditation.

A girl had an extremely heroic mother whose husband was locked up in a den of tigers. The woman, who was determined to save her man, boldly went to the circus train where she begged pitifully and melancholily [sic] to give her the keys of the den. After a long argument they answered in the affirmative. When she got to the place they said ' You can have the keys on one condition only,' and that was, when she got to the door and unlocked it they must give back the keys. At first she answered in the negative, afterwards she agreed. The second she got into the gloomy cavern she heard her husband's voice. 'Is that you, John?' 'Who is that?' came a dreamy and fatigued voice. 'It is me your wife, Charlotte.' Then the tears flowed.[4]

It is too fanciful to link Dylan's songwriting to the impressions of short films from the 1910s on London schoolchildren, but nevertheless it is worth thinking about the way film becomes a part of memory, merging story with experience, driven as we are to feature in the films of our mind's devising. Dylan has done so through song; in *Masked and Anonymous* he finally got to do so through film itself.

---

[4] *The Cinema: Its Present Position and Future Possibilities* (London: Williams and Northgate, 1917), pp. 277-278.

Tinashe Kachingwe singing 'The Times They Are A-Changin"
in *Masked and Anonymous.*

What may be most distinctive about *Masked and Anony-mous* is how it recreates, or at least acknowledges, such an imaginative world from a film's point of view. It depicts a world where dream and reportage have intermingled. It may be particularly telling that what could be the film's single most arresting moment is supplied by a child. A young girl (Tinashe Kachingwe) is introduced to Jack Fate and sings an a cappella version of 'The Times They Are A-Changin'.' It is breathtaking, like one clear moment of truth in that world gone wrong. One thinks of the young Dylan, turning up with cap, guitar and harmonica at Gerde's Folk City, sixty years ago now, shaking up his audience: the boy who saw something, in the real world and in his series of dreams.

Originally published as 'Simple Twist of Fate,' 30 May 2021, https://lukemckernan.com/2021/05/30/simple-twist-of-fate, and reproduced here with small emendations. C. W. Kimmins summarises his view of children and cinema in his chapter 'The Child and the Cinema' in *The Child's Attitude to Life: A Study of Children's Stories* (London: Methuen, 1926). His evidence to the Cinema Commission Inquiry is given in *The Cinema: Its Present Position and Future Possibilities* (London: Williams and Northgate, 1917) and is reproduced in Luke McKernan, *Picturegoers: A Critical Anthology of Eyewitness Experiences* (Exeter: University of Exeter Press, 2022), pp. 57-64.

27.

Playing Power

Adam McKay's Vice *and William Shakespeare's* Richard II

> Was this face the face
> That every day under his household roof
> Did keep ten thousand men? Was this the face
> That like the sun did make beholders wink? ...
> A brittle glory shineth in this face.
> As brittle as the glory is the face.[1]

To the cinema, and the next day to the theatre, to see productions which I had not thought would be so closely aligned, yet it seems they are. One was the feature film *Vice* (USA 2018), a biopic exposé of US vice-president Dick Cheney. The other was about another Richard, William Shakespeare's *Richard II*, playing at the Almeida Theatre. Both are studies of the assumption of power, and the faces of power.

I was looking forward to seeing *Vice*, having greatly admired director Adam McKay's earlier film *The Big Short* (USA 2015), on the financial crisis of 2008. *Vice* similarly takes on recent history, in a deconstructed, mocking style that McKay has made his own. Sadly I found the film to be quite poor, even dull. It tried too hard, had a narrator reeling out selective facts from an *Idiot's Guide* to American politics, and gave us a diatribe when what we wanted was understanding. We know what Dick Cheney did (or some of it), we know he was a dark character operating in dark times, but why? From where did that thirst for power come, and why did Cheney pursue it in the way that he did? Consequences are not the same as answers.

---

[1] William Shakespeare, *Richard II*, in Stanley Wells and Gary Taylor (eds.), *The Oxford Shakespeare: The Complete Works* (Oxford: Oxford University Press, 2005), Act 4, Scene 1, ll. 273-278.

Dick Cheney (Christian Bale) in *Vice*.

There is a lot about the film that is fun, with the director breaking down the illusion of reality on repeated occasions, including end credits in the middle of the film when it might have been that Cheney's life would carry on in quiet retirement breeding prize-winning golden retrievers; a Fox News commentator who comments on herself; a focus group that ends up telling us its thoughts about the film we have just seen (and then gets into a fight over it); and Cheney turning to the cinema audience and saying what else was there to do given the threats that the nation faced after 9/11. That is the only point where we see just something of what drove the man, and it is not enough.

One of the gags in *Vice* has Cheney and his wife turning to cod-Shakespearean dialogue at the height of their political machinations. The joke is that you do not get people in dramas telling us their thoughts as events unfold about them as you do in a Shakespeare play, but the film might have been that much better if the Shakespearean conceit had been extended. *Richard II* is a model example of how speech can serve both an exterior and an interior purpose, showing how characters explain themselves to themselves (and us) while becoming ever more trapped by circumstances, as their story progresses. Action is thought; thought is action.

The Almeida's production of *The Tragedy of King Richard the Second* (to give the play its full title) is quite an experience.

Directed by Joe Hill-Gibbins (as much as iconoclast in his field as McKay), and starring Simon Russell Beale as the king, it is a rapid (100 minutes), frenetic roller-coaster interpretation of the play. Much is cut or re-ordered, a cast of just eight stay the entire time on a grey metal box of a set, the only added colour being blood which is thrown about liberally from buckets placed on the stage. It is so choreographed as to be more like a dance piece than conventional theatre, while the single set robs the play of its variety and hence some of its sense.

As ever, Shakespeare comes to the rescue. *Richard II*, one of the most beautifully written plays in the English language, is a profound study of the nature of power. It shows power as a quality of mind. The fall of Richard and the rise of Bolingbroke, who succeeds him as Henry IV, is to a degree a matter of geographical and military manoeuvrings. But (aided by the utter anonymity of the set) what we witness is a battle of minds, as Richard loses power the more he thinks upon it, doubts that Bolingbroke inherits in his turn (the production ends with a bitter, dry laugh from Bolingbroke at his supposed moment of triumph). Power is only power where you believe you are in power. You can no longer be a king once you question your own kingship.

> What must the King do now? Must he submit?
> The King shall do it. Must he be deposed?
> The King shall be contented. Must he lose
> The name of King? A God's name, let it go.[2]

What Richard loses, Cheney seizes. *Vice* makes much of the unitary executive theory of US politics—essentially all power resides ultimately in the one person—suggesting to us that Cheney turned disappointment at coming bottom of a poll of potential presidential candidates into the pursuit of ultimate power by stealth. He converts the meaningless role of vice president into a platform for the exercise of true power, simply by force of will and the unwitting connivance of a weak president (George Bush), whom Cheney keeps in the air during 9/11 while he makes the key decisions. This coup culminates in the decision to invade Iraq, because that is what the focus groups find easiest to understand, and the move will make Cheney's company Halliburton very rich.

This is cartoon history. Simon Jenkins, in an article for *The Guardian*—'Fake-history films like Vice and The Uncivil War

---

[2] Shakespeare, *Richard II*, Act 3, Scene 3, ll. 142-145.

are the new threat to truth'—says that the falsities and misleading simplicities of historical films are a dangerous misrepresentation of history. 'If a newspaper declared on its front page, "These stories are based on real events, and some of them are true," it would be laughed out of court. When films do it, they claim Oscars.'[3] The argument is well made, though the answer is not to demand that history films keep strictly to factual truth but rather to educate audiences to understand better the complexities involved. Film-makers have a duty to story, not history. The problem with *Vice* is that it asserts the latter, and in so doing fails to succeed as the former.

How much better might *Vice* have been if it had focussed more on George Bush than Dick Cheney. The story of the man unsuited to high office but driven there by the demands of his family, only to find power slipping from his hands through the machinations of another who has the greater understanding of (and desire for) power—now there is a subject worthy of a Shake-speare play. *Richard II* may not provide the perfect analogy, but its theme of the transfer of kingship is grounded in the idea of the divine right of kings, the unitary executive theory of its time. Where does the right to power lie? Should they who understand best how power works be those who end up exercising it?

There was something else that I saw in the two productions, and it lay in the faces. Among the pleasures that *Vice* offers is its lookalike performances—Christian Bale as Cheney, Steve Carrell as Donald Rumsfeld, Sam Rockwell as George Bush, with cameos along the way for Henry Kissinger, Condoleeza Rice, Gerald Ford, Colin Powell, Karl Rove and many more. It is not just the snap-shot recognition, but in some way power (for that is what it must be) that is transferred to the audience through the act of viewing. To be impersonated is to be captured, to suffer some loss of power. It is why we value cartoons, but there is something more in seeing how an actor can inhabit greatness and so reveal that which is less than great. They become a key to our understanding, just as many a celebrity or politician has become that which an impersonator uses to portray them. We are only ever what people think we are.

It may have been the same when *Richard II* was first staged. One of the challenges modern audiences have with Shakespeare's history plays is all those dukes named after places. Which is

---

[3] Simon Jenkins, 'Fake-history films like *Vice* and The *Uncivil War* are the new threat to truth,' *The Guardian*, 26 January 2019, https://www.theguardian.com/commentisfree/2019/jan/26/history-vice-uncivil-war-dick-cheney.

Richard II (Simon Russell Beale) in
The Tragedy of King Richard the Second.

Northumberland and why is he arguing with Carlisle? What is
Gloucester to York, or Surrey to Salisbury? Their motives and
allegiances may all be there in Raphael Holinshed's *The Chroni-
cles of England, Scotlande, and Irelande*, faithfully transferred to
the stage by Shakespeare, but they seem almost interchangeable.
It must have been different in 1595. Though the figures were not
contemporaries—it was far too dangerous for the Elizabethan
stage to depict living characters—they would have been far better
understood, as relatively recent history. Moreover, the audience
must have seen parallels with those who did have power over
them. Those named after those same places still ruled the land, yet
here they were on the stage before us, the victim of forces the same
as the rest of us. They became the actors who portrayed them.

Famously, supporters of the Earl of Essex, who planned a
revolt against Queen Elizabeth in 1601, sponsored a performance
of *Richard II,* presumed to be Shakespeare's version, because of
the political resonances. 'I am Richard II, know ye not that?' Elizabeth is supposed to have said. It is not certain, but if it makes for
questionable history it makes for a good story. *Richard II* was a
mirror for its troubled times.

We see our world reflected on our stages and screens. In doing
so we gain some understanding, and through that some satisfaction. Plays and films order that which for us had been disordered.

That is why adherence to factual truth should not be the governing factor behind history films, but understanding must. *Vice* fails because it does not explore its own certainties. *Richard II* is the very antithesis of certainty, a model for any deep study of power and the mind that must wield it.

> But whate'er I be,
> Nor I, nor any man but that man is,
> With nothing shall be pleased till he be eased
> With being nothing.[4]

Originally published as 'Playing Power,' 27 January 2019, https://lukemckernan.com/2019/01/27/playing-power, and reproduced here with small emendations. *The Tragedy of King Richard the Second* ran at the Almeida Theatre in London 10 December 2018 to 2 February 2019. A performance was broadcast live to cinemas in the UK and internationally on 15 January 2019, in partnership with National Theatre Live.

---

[4] Shakespeare, *Richard II*, Act 5, Scene 5, ll. 38-41.

28

Joyce, Film and Allusion

The Joycean connection in Richard Linklater's Before *trilogy*

I recently watched the Richard Linklater trilogy, *Before Sunrise* (Austria/USA 1995), *Before Sunset* (USA 2004) and *Before Midnight* (USA 2013), which traces the romance over nineteen years between Céline (played by Julie Delpy) and Jesse (played by Ethan Hawke). They are much loved films and have been much discussed. All I need to say about what I thought of them in general is that the first was very good, the second looked a bit rushed, and the third was better than the second.

But one aspect of the trilogy intrigued me, and that was the connection to the works of James Joyce. The first film, *Before Sunrise*, takes place on 16 June (the date is specifically referenced in the film), which is the day on which Joyce's novel *Ulysses* is set ('Bloomsday'). *Before Sunrise* takes place on a single day and involves the traversing of a city, substituting Vienna for Dublin. Joyce chose the date 16 June 1904 as the setting for *Ulysses* as it was the first day that he stepped out with his future wife, Nora Barnacle, and the accidental meeting of Céline and Jesse (who tells her that his real name is James), and the romance that then follows, consciously echoes this. And, just to add to the associations, while at university James Joyce translated a play by the German writer Gerhart Hauptmann—its title, *Vor Sonnenaufgang*, or 'Before Sunrise.'

It does look like Linklater read James Joyce's biography around the time that he first conceived of the film: the young man touring Europe on his way to becoming an author, with the guiding point of his imaginative and personal life being that crucial day when he met up with Céline/Nora. The film, as with the novel, is about a life in a day. And this idea continues with its successors.

Before Sunset, the sequel which takes place nine years later, opens with Jesse giving a presentation on a novel he has written (based on his meeting with Céline, who comes to the reading, thus triggering the romance once again). It is at Shakespeare and

Company, a celebrated bookshop on the Left Bank in Paris. The original Shakespeare and Company, which was run by Sylvia Beach in the 1920s, was located at the 6th arrondissement; the present shop is in the 5th arrondissement, and was named in honour of Beach's shop. James Joyce visited the original shop regularly, and it was Shakespeare and Company that published *Ulysses* in 1922.

So the Joycean connection is continued, but it is the third film, *Before Midnight*, that is the most intriguingly if obscurely Joycean in theme. Jesse and Céline are now a couple with two children, and are holidaying in Greece. Greece is the home of the Homeric myths, of course, but the specific Joycean reference occurs when Céline recalls a black-and-white film from her teenage years which had a powerful impact on her, particularly a scene in which a couple visit Pompeii and see the bodies mummified by the volcanic explosion. She does not name the film, but it is *Viaggio in Italia* (*Voyage to Italy*) (France/Italy 1954), Roberto Rossellini's film about a couple's sterile marriage, the couple being played by Ingrid Bergman and George Sanders.

Céline and Jesse are similarly becalmed, and that might be all there is to the subtle referencing of Rossellini's film. But V*iaggio in Italia* is also loosely based on James Joyce's short story, 'The Dead,' the tale of a seemingly happy marriage troubled by lingering thoughts about the past. It is not a scene-for-scene remake; rather it is a loose *homage*, with a specific echo when Bergman's character recalls a boy who may have died for love of her, just as Gretta Conroy does in Joyce's story. It is a reference point for those who want to think more deeply about the film, though just in case you have missed the point there are the names of Sanders and Bergman's characters: Mr and Mrs Joyce.

How much further can we play this game? Jean-Luc Godard's *Le Mépris* (France 1963), known in English as *Contempt*, is partly an *homage* to *Viaggio in Italia*, being as it is the story of an estranged husband and wife (Michel Piccoli and Bridget Bardot) in Italy. Much of the drama concerns the production of a film of Homer's *Odyssey, or Ulysses*.

Literary films are too often produced, and subsequently critiqued, as facsimiles of what appears on the printed page, the plain conversion of a narrative from book to screen, with all of your favourite scenes and characters intact, or so you hope. This is a very narrow way of looking at literary adaptation. What is far more interesting is the oblique reference, the quoting of particular scenes, the echoing of themes, the suggestion of a connection to

Céline (Julie Delpy) and Jesse (Ethan Hawke) in *Before Midnight*,
at the point where Céline recalls seeing *Viaggio in Italia*.

enrich appreciation. I have had a lot to do with Shakespeare on film
in my time, and one thing I have been keen to promote is how a
Shakespeare film can be just as much one with sly references to the
plays as the plain transference of stage text to screen. It is just the
case with other writers.

Back in 1995 I co-programmed a season of James Joyce
films at the National Film Theatre with Phil Crossley. We put
our programme together in Joycean spirit. We included obvious
titles like Joseph Strick's *Ulysses* (Ireland/UK/USA 1967), Mary
Ellen Bute's *Passages from Finnegans Wake* (USA 1966), John
Huston's *The Dead* (UK/USA/West Germany 1987), and television plays based on Joyce's work, including the little-known BBC
play, *Bloomsday* (UK 1964), based on *Ulysses*. We had a special
programme of films known to have been shown at the Volta
cinema in Dublin, which Joyce briefly managed at the end of 1909.
But we also showed *Viaggio in Italia* and *Le Mépris*, and then had
much fun including *Groundhog Day* (USA 1993), whose theme
of a man caught in an eternal daily round might be seen to have
Joycean echoes, but chiefly we chose it because Groundhog Day is
2 February, which was Joyce's birthday.

I wish we had been bolder. I wanted us to include *The
Producers* (USA 1968), simply because Gene Wilder's character

is called Leo Bloom, the same as Joyce's hero. That did not seem to be connection enough, even if the director Mel Brooks was consciously referencing Joyce's hero. But later someone pointed out to me that Wilder's co-star, Zero Mostel had achieved great success in 1958 playing Leopold Bloom in the play *Ulysses in Nighttown*. We really should have included it in the programme.

Others have played at this game. In the collection edited by John McCourt, *Roll Away the Reel World: James Joyce and Cinema*, in which I write about the Volta cinema, American writer Jesse Myers argues for the Joycean-ness of *The Producers*, *American Beauty* (USA 1999) and *The Departed* (Hong Kong/USA 2006), as well as pointing out metaphorical references to Joyce in *The Third Man* (UK 1949), *The Manchurian Candidate* (USA 1962), *Annie Hall* (USA 1977) and several more.[1]

Metaphor and allusion matter more than adaptation. The film that tries to reproduce a novel merely creates a surface impression, and a body of critical work unpicking differences between screen and source text which is, if not futile, then certainly wildly over-done. It is the signposting of references to literary works in films (and *vice versa*) that delights the imagination that much more, and breaks down the barriers between one artistic form and another. It is the knowing transference of ideas, keeping them eternal.

Richard Linklater's *Before* trilogy is more subtly and reward-ingly Joycean than any literal transcription of his work to the screen. Whether Linklater knew of Rossellini's referencing of 'The Dead' in *Viaggio in Italia* I do not know, but I suspect so. There had to be a place for Joyce somewhere, to complete the odyssey.

Originally published as 'Joyce, Film and Allusion,' 19 July 2014, https://lukemckernan.com/2014/07/19/joyce-film-and-allusion, and reproduced here with small emendations. Julie Delpy and Ethan Hawke appear as Céline and Jesse in a scene in Richard Linklater's animated feature film *Waking Life* (USA 2001).

---

[1] Jesse Myers, 'James Joyce, Subliminal Screenwriter?' in John McCourt (ed.), *Roll Away the Reel World: James Joyce and Cinema* (Cork: Cork University Press, 2010), pp. 174-185.

29

A Hero of the Valleys

The lost and found film The Life Story of David Lloyd George

How do we judge a film that no one saw? The audience gives a film meaning, or at least historical specificity. There are many examples of films that have never been seen because they were deemed uncommercial, and other grand projects that were never completed, such as Sergei Eisenstein's *¡Que viva México!* or Orson Welles' *Don Quixote*. But the completed film that stands up as an exceptional work of art, that was a strong commercial possibility in its time, and whose exhibition could have changed film history (in a modest way)—such examples are rare.

One such example has just found its way to a DVD release after a remarkable history of idealism, political intrigue, slander, subterfuge, disappearance, rediscovery and restoration.[1] *The Life Story of David Lloyd George* was made in 1918, vanished before any cinema audience had a chance to see it, and re-emerged to astonished acclaim in 1994. Its place must be in virtual history rather than actual film history, because its story is one of if onlys and maybes. But what a story it is.

The story begins with the Ideal Film Company, formed by the brothers Harry and Simon Rowson in 1911 to distribute films, before moving into production in 1915. Excited by the interest shown by the public in official government films of the war, the Rowsons decided to make an epic drama about the origins and purpose of the war, employing none other than Winston Churchill, then in the political wilderness following the Dardanelles disaster, to furnish ideas which would be turned into a scenario by professional screenwriter Eliot Stannard. When Churchill returned to the cabinet in summer 1916 the original project was dropped, only to transmogrify into a biography of the new Liberal prime minister, David Lloyd Geoerge (the Rowsons were strong supporters of

---

[1] *The Life Story of David Lloyd George*, two-disc DVD, National Library of Wales, 2009.

the Liberal party). Conceived as an epic story of a man who from humble beginnings rises to lead his country through to victory in the greatest war known, it was an undertaking unlike anything attempted in cinema to that date, nor would it have any subsequent parallel until the American and Soviet biopics of the 1930s onwards — *Young Mr Lincoln* (USA 1939), *Wilson* (USA 1944), *Lenin v oktyabre* (*Lenin in October*) (USSR 1937). But those conformed to the classical dramatic conventions of their time, and their subjects were long dead — *Lloyd George* was, and remains, unique in subject and form.

The script was written by a noted historian, though one without film experience, Sidney Low. The director was Maurice Elvey, gradually rising to the top of his profession, at least in British film terms. The cast were a mixture of Ideal stalwarts and lookalikes, most notably in the latter case the stage actor Norman Page, whose uncanny performance as Lloyd George carries the film (Page watched Lloyd George in full flow in the House of Commons and gives us what is probably a highly accurate record of his mannerisms). Alma Reville, later to marry Alfred Hitchcock, plays Lloyd George's daughter Megan, and Ernest Thesiger can be spotted as Joseph Chamberlain. Helen Haye (not credited on the DVD but recently identified) plays Lloyd George's mother.

The film's production was announced to the trade press in February 1918, under the title *The Man Who Saved the Empire*. It was not the only propagandist feature film epic to be made in Britain at this time, with American directors brought in by British official film interests to make *Hearts of the World* (USA 1918, directed by D. W. Griffith) and *Victory and Peace* (UK 1918, directed by Herbert Brenon), but it was the only one made on such a scale with private money only. Filming proper began towards the end of August and astonishingly was completed by the end of September. It took place in several of the historical locations, including the north Wales of Lloyd George's childhood, Birmingham and London. Shaping up to be two-and-a-half hours long, there were suggestions that the film could be released as a serial, but excitement was high at what promised to be the outstanding British film release of the year.

In October the trouble started. Horatio Bottomley, the rabble-rousing, influential owner of the nationalistic journal *John Bull*, began a campaign against the film. Essentially his line was that the film was a disgrace because it was being made by Germans. The Rowsons were Jews, real name Rosenbaum, and in Bottomley's nakedly

Elderly inhabitants of the workhouse materialise outside the
workhouse walls in *The Life Story of David Lloyd George.*

bigoted mind, Jews were equated with Germans. Bottomley's
campaign against the film—Ideal won a libel suit against him—
brought a lot of unwelcome publicity, and may have added to a sense
of awkwardness felt by some in the government at the production
of a film lauding the achievements of the prime minister at the time
of an impending general election (one took place in December 1918,
just after the war ended).

In the end, none of the evidence that we have really explains
what happened next. The Ideal company were paid off, to the sum
of £20,000, around half a million pounds in today's money, which
was the cost of the film's production—though no recompense for
the anticipated returns. Lawyers for the government turned up,
paid Ideal in twenty one-thousand pound notes, took the negative
away with them in a taxi—and that was the last that anyone saw
of it, publicly at least. Someone in power thought it worth a lot of
money to prevent the film from being shown, but to this day no
one can really say why, and the documentary record, including a
memoir written by Harry Rowson, is tantalisingly vague.[2]

---

[2] The section from Harry Rowson's unpublished memoir on *The Life Story
of David Lloyd George* is reproduced in Sarah Street, 'The Memoir of Harry
Rowson: David Lloyd George, MP—The Man Who Saved the Empire (1918),'

The weeping woman in *The Life Story of Lloyd George.*

The only evidence we have for the film after this date is a reference in the diary of Frances Stevenson, Lloyd George's secretary and mistress, over a year later. On 24 February 1920 she wrote:

> Last night went to see a film of D's life which Captain Guest had put on the screen in No 12 [Downing Street] — a perfectly appalling thing. The idea was all right but the man who was supposed to be D. was simply a caricature. I begged D. not to let it be shown. Mrs Ll. G. very angry with D. because she said I had put D. against it because I had objected to the domestic scenes in it![3]

Were there plans to show the film in 1920? Is Stevenson referring to this time, or 1918, when she says 'I begged D. not to let it be shown'? Might she be speaking of a different film entirely? We do not know. *The Life Story of David Lloyd George* was no more,

---

in David Berry and Simon Horrocks (eds.), *David Lloyd George: The Movie Mystery* (Cardiff: University of Wales Press, 1998), pp. 30-51. The full memoir is held as part of the Harry Rowson Collection, British Film Institute, Special Collections.
[3] Frances Stevenson, diary entry for 24 February 1920, Parliamentary Archives, FLS/4.

unseen by anyone, little more than a footnote in a history or two. British film historian Denis Gifford interviewed Maurice Elvey in 1967, shortly before he died, when Elvey said (with remarkable *sang froid* in the circumstances):

> This I suppose must have been one of the best films I ever made or ever shall make ... It is such a shame it has disappeared.[4]

In 1994 the film was discovered. It was in a barn at the home of Viscount Tenby, David Lloyd George's grandson. It was in pristine condition, though in an unassembled form. Considerable effort and ingenuity was required from the only recently-formed Wales Film and Television Archive to piece the film together. As the first sequences were constructed and shown to film historians and Lloyd George experts, the general reaction was astonishment. Instead of the quaint drama that, to be honest, we had been expecting, here was a film of skill and power, possessed of a fervour and a commitment to the issues of the day that was electrifying.

The film had its premiere—literally so—on 5 May 1996 (preceded by a showing on 27 April for an invited audience) at the MGM cinema, Cardiff, accompanied by the Cardiff Olympia Orchestra playing a score by Welsh composer John Hardy. Since that time it has had screenings around the world, usually with Neil Brand accompanying on piano, and it has gained recognition as a unique classic. But there has been a huge struggle on the part of the National Screen and Sound Archive of Wales (as they are now called) to get the film issued on DVD. Now, at last, with pseudo-orchestral score by Brand, it is available for all to see—and it is a film that demands to be seen.

The Life Story of David Lloyd George tells the story of its subject from childhood to wartime victory (the film was completed before the war ended), relayed in key scenes selected to demonstrate a calling to national duty and a desire to overturn injustice. The early scenes, showing Lloyd George's upbringing in Wales, have not been given the praise that should be their due. They capture an atmosphere of modesty, devoutness and dedication towards one's fellow man which is moving in its general effect, and deeply touching in its detail, grounded as it is in an affectionate portrait of late Victorian Welsh society.

---

[4] Denis Gifford, 'The Early Memoirs of Maurice Elvey,' *Griffithiana*, 60-61, October 1997, p. 97.

Lloyd George is shown triumphing in the law and local politics through his oratory and commitment to noble causes. He gains
notoriety through his anti-Boer War (1899-1902) stance, illustrated
by a speech he gave at Birmingham Town Hall which occasioned
a near riot in the streets. This the film recreates with truly extraordinary newsreel-style realism, helped by many hundreds of extras.
If these scenes impress by their documentary quality, the film's
greater power comes in how it illustrates the revolutionary effect
of Lloyd George's time as Chancellor of the Exchequer, introducing old age pensions and the National Insurance Act (1911). Its
effects are memorably illustrated by a scene where we are shown
the wall of a workhouse, through which its elderly inhabitants
materialise and walk away to freedom. The very rightness of the
actions moves us now, and surely must have had—or would have
had—an overpowering effect on a contemporary audience, for
whom these great changes were recent occurrences.

Other vigorous tableaux follow, clearly inspired by the newsreels (Lloyd George himself was a consummate performer for the
news cameras), notably the Queen's Hall suffragette riots. The film
makes much use of an impressive House of Commons interior set,
peopled by lookalikes, shot and performed with an easy realism that
could fool some into thinking they were watching actuality. The film
dips somewhat in its second half when the First World War begins.

Lloyd George served brilliantly as minister of munitions
before becoming prime minister in 1916, but there is paradoxically less drama on show once the film has arrived at the climactic
stage to which its first half has been building. The battle scenes are
convincing, likewise Lloyd George's visit to the Front, and there
is a prolonged sequence inside a munitions factory which may
lack dramatic interest but as a seemingly documentary record is
superbly shot. But our emotions are not re-engaged until the film's
final scenes, when the war comes to an end. Troops line up on the
parade ground in their hundreds, fall out, then run to their waiting
loved ones, at which point they materialise into civilian clothes.
Amid all the happiness, one woman turning her head and weeping
stands for all those whose loved ones were not returning home.
Shown live, it catches the audience's breath every time.

It is not a film for every one. Those hoping for either a more
conventional human interest story, or a political drama, may be
disappointed. Its newsreel-style—a deliberate aesthetic choice to
reflect the way in which many of the audience were most familiar
with Lloyd George as a public figure—lessens the emotion while

it heightens the sense of living history. It is unlike any other silent film in intent and form. But watch *The Life Story of David Lloyd George*, and then try and take seriously one of the conventional dramas of the war made during the war—*Hearts of the World* for example—and they come across as pitiable, not so much in their execution or use of dramatic convention as in their absence of real social and political feeling. *The Life Story of David Lloyd George* is not realistic as such, despite its newsreel inspiration. It is pure hagiography. But more than any other film of the period it manages to articulate what people were fighting for—which is what the Rowsons had wanted for their epic war film, right from the beginning.

At the end of *The Life Story of David Lloyd George Lloyd*, George (Norman Page) speaks to the camera to say 'There must be no "next time"'

The film runs for 152 minutes. Viewers will see from time to time sequences which clearly do not quite fit. Titles referring to Moses are followed by film of Boadicea (the film has several such emblematic sequences); Lloyd George's vision of his prime ministerial predecessors has obvious re-take shots; longueurs in the latter half would undoubtedly have been edited down had the film been completed for release. The film had to be pieced together without a running order, and a place found for every extant shot, somehow. Tinting records came with the film, the colour richly but sensitively reproduced by the Wales archive.

On the DVD you get forty-seven minutes of extras, including an interview with composer Neil Brand which goes beyond the thinking behind his sumptuous score to consider the value of silent film generally. It is a *tour de force* which can be recommended to anyone wanting to understand what the silent film means for us today. Silent film historian Kevin Brownlow is interviewed, stating that the film would have changed film history, particularly in the UK, had it been shown—Britain's *The Birth of a Nation*. Would it have been a huge financial success though? I think Ideal may have ended up with a problem on their hands—a long film, without stars, partisan in politics, perhaps too reliant on the patriotic uplift occasioned by the war. But we will never know.

The Life Story of David Lloyd George will never fit easily into film history, because it was never seen, and because there has never been anything else like it. But it is a major work irrespective of film history, and the National Screen and Sound Archive of Wales have done us a great service in making it available to all.

Originally published as 'A Hero of the Valleys,' 11 March 2009, https://thebioscope.net/2009/03/11/a-hero-of-the-valleys, and reproduced here with small emendations. David Berry and Simon Horrocks' book *David Lloyd George: The Movie Mystery* (University of Wales Press, 1998), includes an extract from Harry Rowson's memoir, and essays by Lloyd George's biographer John Grigg, Nicholas Hiley, Sarah Street, Roberta Pearson, John Reed (who restored the film) and others. The National Screen and Sound Archive of Wales is now called Screen and Sound Archive / Archif Sgrin a Sain.

30.

Worlds and Mirrors

Tarkovsky, Solaris *and Ukraine*

In a time of conflict, sing the songs of the other side.

I watched *Solaris* (USSR 1972) again the other night—the Soviet film, not its pale 2002 American remake. At the time of the crass, blind adventurism of the invasion of Ukraine, I felt the need to experience the finest of Russian culture. The film has long been a favourite. I think I first saw it when a teenager, bewildered but entranced, much as the scientists in Andrei Tarkovsky's film are bewildered but entranced by the planet Solaris.

Solaris tells of a spaceship in close orbit around the mysterious, sentient planet Solaris. The two surviving scientist crew members are joined by a psychologist, Kris Kelvin, who has been sent to investigate tales of strange behaviour on the ship. He succumbs to the same fate as the others, which is to be haunted by human-like figures, in Kelvin's case his wife Hari, who had committed suicide ten years earlier. These 'visitors' are the creations of the planet, whose swirling, living ocean can in some way read their minds and re-animate their memories. Kelvin tries to rid himself of Hari by firing her out of the station on a rocket, but each time she returns, more human-like in her understanding of her situation. Realising the truth of her manufactured existence, Hari attempts suicide by drinking liquid oxygen, only painfully to come back to life again. Finally she and the other visitors are eliminated after the two scientists transmit Kelvin's brainwaves to Solaris. Kelvin returns to Earth, or seems to.

Solaris succeeds so well as a film because it is an exposition of pure myth. It combines the clearest of ideas with the most resonant of results. A man encounters an alien world that can read his mind and bring memories back to life. In doing so the film touches on the most profound feelings about memory, loss, love, identity and place. It does so without the need for words—though there are plenty of them, since this is a Tarkovsky film and there are stretches in which men with gaunt faces exchange philosophical ideas, trying to find their place within the world in which they have found themselves. But the viewer does not much need the words, or they are not what one remembers. What we retain—the memory—are those haunted faces, the bewilderments and agonies of Kelvin and Hari's love, of Hari the suicide brutally coming back to life, of the cuts from the action to the swirling, unknowable ocean of Solaris, playing with our minds. The familiar and the alien have never been brought together so well as they are in *Solaris*.

The film is based on a 1961 novel of the same title by Polish science fiction novelist Stanisław Lem. Although the film faithfully recreates many elements of the book, the two are significantly different in several respects. Lem's novel is a rich, complex work, but at heart it seeks to explain the inexplicable, whereas Tarkovsky focusses on its effects.

Lem, like any science fiction writer who wants to hold their head up high, impresses on us the science behind the fiction. The 'visitors' are explained by their basis in neutrinos rather than atoms. They are human-like but never entirely human. There is a scientific explanation for them. In the novel Rheya (the name is changed to Hari in the film) imitates a dead person. In Tarkovsky's film she is the true Hari. A residue of the scientific explanation has been retained for the film, and we understand that her agony increases the more 'human' she becomes, but the visible truth is that she is the Hari who once was. We see it from the start. The progression lies in Kelvin's understanding of this. It is their shared love that confirms it.

Lem goes to considerable trouble to describe the extraordinary landscape of the Solaris ocean, with its vast limb-like formations, its geysers, membranes, waves, ever-changing formations and its propensity for recreating objects. Tarkovsky simply gives us long shots of swirling seas made out of acetone, aluminium powder, and coloured dyes. It is impossible to visualise what Lem tries to make us see. With Tarkovsky, we see all.

Lem collaborated with Tarkovsky on the film's script and like so many authors before him he became exasperated by the deviations from his original. This was not just a question of tone but of narrative balance. The greatest difference between the two is the scenes on Earth. Lem's novel takes place entirely in space, orbiting Solaris. The first quarter of Tarkovsky's 166-minute film takes place on Earth, with several flashbacks to Earth thereafter, and in the film's unforgettable final image. The film's first shots are of grasses swirling in the waters outside the home of Kelvin's

The space station in orbit over *Solaris*.

father. We do not know it as yet, but we are seeing a presentiment of the restless ocean of Solaris. Earth is as strange a place as Solaris; it is just as much a place of strangeness that plays on our memories, bringing that which was lost back to our consciousness. Knowing Earth is our best way of understanding Solaris.

We see more of Earth with the interviewing of space pilot Burton, whose account of fantastical figures conjured up by Solaris is dismissed by a sceptical committee as hallucinations. To the viewer his recollection of a four-metre tall baby feels like an uncanny presentiment of the Star Child in Stanley Kubrick's *2001: A Space Odyssey* (USA 1968), but the image is there in Lem's 1961 novel), while Burton's prolonged car journey into a faceless city feels like a parody of Kubrick's 'Star Gate.' Kelvin and Hari watch home movies in which Hari herself features, and at the end of the film a wretched Kelvin returns to his father's home, a scene which is then revealed to be taking place on Solaris, their little piece of Russia a floating island in a sea of memories.

Maybe the whole film has been nothing but a creation of the planet Solaris, drawn from the memories of author and director, playing with our minds.

Lem is never so fanciful, but his novel embraces many more ideas than does the film, or at least explicitly so. His ideas on contact—the urge to communicate with the alien—are cited in Tarkovsky's film, but almost as an aside rather than as a central theme. For Lem the compulsion and the failure to connect with the other bind everything together. His most celebrated words are put into the mouth of scientist Snaut:

> We are humanitarian and chivalrous; we don't want to en-
> slave other races, we simply want to bequeath them our

values and take over their heritage in exchange. We think of ourselves as the Knights of the Holy Contact. This is another lie. We are only seeking man. We have no need of other worlds. We need mirrors. We don't know what to do with other worlds.[1]

This is a bitter corrective to the romantic notion of exploration and discovery, but it is also a damning of the imperialist urge. Conquerors seek only to gain more of themselves, because they fear that which contradicts what they are, or appears to do. They would do better to understand themselves first, if ever they are able to do such a thing. Says Kelvin (in the novel):

I am a murderer unawares. Man has gone out to explore other worlds and other civilizations without having explored his own labyrinth of dark passages and secret chambers, and without finding what lies behind doorways that he himself has sealed.[2]

Tarkovsky's film does not have Kelvin's lines, and may have Snaut say 'We have no need of other worlds. We need mirrors' as much because the famous words are expected to be there as because they need to be. It is the point where novelist and film-maker diverge. Tarkovsky was no imperialist, or nationalist, or prey to any other such false dreams, but his political view was shaped by his world. He defied the dictates of the state by extolling the private and the individual, eventually exiling himself from the Soviet Union so that he could continue to make the films he saw he had to make: *Nostalghia* (Italy/USSR 1983) in Italy, *Offret (The Sacrifice)* (France/Sweden/UK 1986) in Sweden.

Lem came from another world. He was Polish, but he was born in Lwów, which at the time of his birth (1921) was in Poland, but is now familiar to all news followers as Lviv, in Ukraine. Lviv has a long history of invasion, absorption into the worlds of others and imposition of alien identities. It has been part of Galicia, Poland, the Soviet Union, Ukraine, and kingdoms and empires long forgotten, its name ever-changing—Lvihorod, Lemberg, Lwów, Lvov, Lviv. For three years it was held by Nazi Germany, when thousands of its Jewish inhabitants were exterminated. It

---

[1] Stanisław Lem, *Solaris* (London: Faber and Faber, 2016), p. 75. In the English translation, by Joanna Kilmartin and Steve Cox, Snaut is renamed Snow.
[2] Lem, *Solaris*, p. 164.

forms the geographical centrepiece of Philippe Sands' modern classic, *East West Street: On the Origins of Genocide and Crimes Against Humanity*. Sands has been in the news himself, reviewing the terms under which the present Russian leader may be tried for war crimes. Lviv, for Sands, is 'a microcosm of Europe's turbulent twentieth century, the focus on bloody conflicts that tore cultures apart.'[3] It is a place of great beauty, yet with dark secrets that our minds must bring to the surface, if we are human. It is a Solaris, of its kind.

Solaris is the mirror of our world, conjured out of our mind's understanding of that world. It is God-like, of course—in the novel Snaut concludes that 'Solaris could be the first phase of the despairing god.'[4] It is a place of conscience and consequences. Lem tries to analyse it; Tarkovsky shows the anguish of the process of discovery on his protagonists' faces. The contact they have made is with themselves.

Solaris, the film, is a beautiful work of Russian art (though one must note that Tarkovsky's poet father Arseny was Ukraine-born). One cannot imagine its like coming out of any other place. It is there in the combination of land and longing, of a particular coming together of romanticism and religion—an icon painted by Andrei Rublev, the artist subject of Tarkovsky's previous film, *Andrei Rublev* (USSR 1966), can be seen in Kelvin's room—of privacy in the face of a state that wants the reflection of everyone to be the same. *Solaris* the novel is the product of a different, perpetually overrun land, again and again made to belong to the worlds of others, a mirror of our follies.

Originally published as 'Worlds and Mirrors,' 26 March 2022, https://lukemckernan.com/2022/03/26/worlds-and-mirrors, and reproduced here with small emendations. Russia launched a military invasion of Ukraine on 24 February 2022. President of Russia Vladimir Putin is reported to have said he joined the KGB after seeing the actor Donatas Banionis in a 1968 spy film, *Myortvyy sezon (Dead Season)* (USSR 1968).[5] Four years later Banionis played Kris Kelvin in *Solaris*.

---

[3] Phillipe Sands, *East West Street: On the Origins of Genocide and Crimes Against Humanity* (London: Weidenfeld & Nicolson, 2016), p. xxvi.
[4] Lem, *Solaris*, p. 208.
[5] Asawin Suebsaeng, 'How the Actor Donatas Banionis Inspired Vladimir Putin to Become a Spy,' *The Daily Beast*, 5 September 2014, http://www.thedailybeast.com/articles/2014/09/05/how-the-actor-donatas-banionis-inspired-vladimir-putin-to-become-a-spy.html.

31.

Spotless

Spotlight and its immaculate shirts

I went to the cinema to see *Spotlight* (USA 2015) and I was very impressed. It is fully deserving of its best picture Academy Award. It is a gripping, sobering account of priestly child abuse in Boston, but also champions the noble practice of investigative journalism, highlighting the best of newspapers at a time when the form, and maybe investigative journalism as we have known it, is under threat. It also shines an understanding and positive light on archives and libraries, not only demonstrating their value, but making the dogged search for information through papers, bookshelves and directories seem as thrilling as any car chase. It is a film with a heart in all the right places.

But what impressed me most about the film was the shirts. This is a film where all of the men dress fabulously. Their shirts are immaculate, fresh off the hangers, scene after scene looking like it could have been posed for a clothing catalogue. Despite the late hours, the grimy spaces in which some lived or worked, and all the running around that they did, the journalists of the *Boston Globe* never failed to look at their very best.

Did they have a huge number of shirts at home? Did they iron assiduously in the little free time they had? Did unseen wives or girlfriends take on the burden? Or were they making constant use of the best laundry service in the whole of America? I focussed on Michael Keaton (playing Walter 'Robby' Robinson) to see just how many shirts he got through. For a while it looked like he was wearing a different shirt for every scene, and I wondered just how large his wardrobe could possibly be, but then I started to see the same shirts come round again. He had to be using the world's greatest laundry service, because those shirts were looking good as new every time.

It has been a much praised feature of *Spotlight* that it does not raise its journalist figures to heroic status, instead concentrating on the plain business of investigation. Nevertheless, they dress like

Rachel McAdams, Brian d'Arcy James, Mark Ruffalo,
Michael Keaton, and John Slattery in *Spotlight*.

angels. Now this could just be the costume designer ensuring that everyone looks their best, but a touch of grime on the shirt collars or a fading crease might have helped the sense of everyday realism that the film otherwise strives hard to achieve. As cleanliness is next to godliness, so signs of wear and tear denote imperfections within. That is the logic of cinema.

A different kind of film would have explored the fallibilities of its heroes, or uncovered a dark past (say, for example, that one of them had been similarly abused as a child). But that would have taken the film away from its scrupulous historical recreation; all of the main characters are based on the actual *Boston Globe* 'Spotlight' investigative team, which went on to win a Pulitzer Prize for its coverage of the scandal. It is story and the method that are in the spotlight, not the investigators. And so their shirts are perfect.

Originally published as 'Spotless,' 13 March 2016, https://lukemckernan.com/2016/03/13/spotless, and reproduced here with small emendations. Spotlight won Academy Awards for Best Picture and Best Original Screenplay. Costume design was by Wendy Chuck, whose work on the film is illustrated at https://www.wendychuck.com/films/spotlight.

32

Playing Dead

Death and holding your breath on screen

Last weekend I sat through six hours and thirty-seven minutes of *Les Misérables* (France 1925), the longest film I have ever experienced at a single sitting. It was shown at the Barbican in London, two comfort breaks and a supper break along the way. Neil Brand provided the live piano score, as he had with this film's acclaimed presentation at the Giornate del Cinema Muto silent film festival in Pordenone, Italy, in 2015, and he was deservedly given a standing ovation at the end of it. It was not just an endurance feat, but a remarkably sustained accompaniment that was sympathetic, inventive, supportive and which never flagged for a single second.

The film itself is a remarkable exercise in sustained invention. Though in 1925 it was soon cut down in size for a more practical release, the film is notable for how it maintains narrative control over nearly seven hours, a model demonstration of pacing, composition and planning by director Henri Frescourt. That said, *Les Misérables* is not a great film. The ecstatic accounts to be found about the film are understandable, given the epic nature of the experience of viewing it, and the film's many virtues: the performances, especially Gabriel Gabrio as Jean Valjean and the precocious Andrée Rolane as the young Cosette; the nightmarish forest with trees coming to life to terrify Cosette; the compelling use of settings seemingly unaltered since the 1830s; the hard-bitten faces true to the bitter times the story reflects. And silent film buffs do love to talk up their subject, which is a forgivable vice.

But there were so many blemishes of a kind to puzzle the sceptic and embarrass the advocate. Mismatched shots (particularly in cuts from mid- to close shots of characters), continuity howlers (the grille to the sewers near the end was a different grille for inside and outside shots), frequent examples of shaky focussing, and even people in 1920s attire seen walking in the background of the scenes set in the Luxembourg Gardens. Why so much effort in some

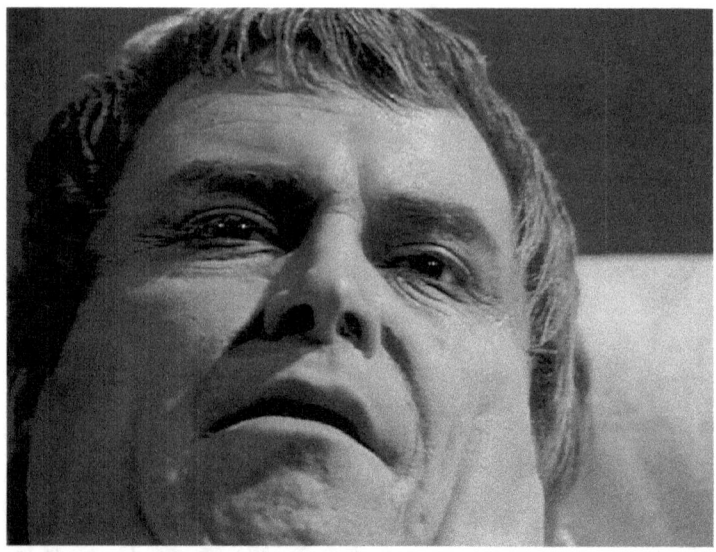

Brian Blessed playing the dying Augustus
in *I, Claudius*, 'Poison is Queen.'

respects, yet such sloppiness elsewhere? Did they not see what we
see?

In particular I was bothered by the dead. I am always interested in scenes of the dead on screen, because I like to see the actor
holding their breath. How long will the director keep that shot
going, I wonder each time. In the BBC's Ancient Rome drama series
I, Claudius (UK 1976) there is an extraordinary scene in which
Brian Blessed, as the dying and then dead Emperor Augustus, is
obliged to lie not breathing at all for over four minutes while Siân
Phillips, playing his wife Livia, confesses to her crimes (she is the
one who has poisoned him). It is a *tour de force*, it is a *memento
mori*, and no corpse could have done it better.

How very differently *Les Misérables* treats the dead. When
Baron Pontmercy (played by Luc Dartagnan) dies in his bed, and
his estranged son Marius arrives just too late to be reconciled with
him, the film shows him in quiet repose, his chest noticeably rising
and falling. The blemish makes things all the more confusing when
Marius himself is severely wounded following the revolt at the
barricades, and Valjean carries him through the sewers. Is he dead
or is he not dead? When we see his bloodied body and notice his
eyes move, is that a sign of hope, or of an actor (François Rozet)

who just could not keep still when he needed too? What were we supposed to believe?

Those of my generation were brought up on unconvincing deaths. The westerns we saw at Saturday morning cinema shows, the war movies and adventure serials on television, were filled with people who clutched at unbloodied chests when apparently shot, lying there at rest until the director called 'cut.' We were convinced that those screen deaths were real, or at least I think that we were. We judged them not by how convincing they were, but accepted what they signified. Perhaps that excuses *Les Misérables*, which puts the idea over the actuality and was presumably content with that.

We have moved on, and now expect our screen deaths to be that much more convincing. Bullets must make a mark, swords cut deep, blood must spurt. But that is the killing rather than the death. For that an essential purity of performance remains. All the actor can do is to lie there, not breathing, playing possum. Like the opossum, which is particularly adept at displaying what is technically known as 'defensive thanatosis' (playing dead to fool a predator), we have the facility to mimic our demise. For all of the realism of the modern-day moving image, which needs to convince a worldly-wise audience for whom the pretences of *Les Misérables* or Saturday morning serials would be laughable, the performance of death is something that must always remain the same, fundamentally false and symbolic. In that *I, Claudius* scene death is not what you see, you do not really even see the Emperor Augustus—you just see poor Brian Blessed motionless, trying not to go red or to betray the minutest evidence of an expelling of air. If we did not see him breathing, we always knew that he might. It is not so different from *Les Misérables* after all.

Perhaps there is a period of time in which we suspend disbelief and experience the sense of the life lost, only for it to be followed by a loss in that belief as the death scene continues. If there is such a moment, it is lost immediately upon its contemplation. The mourners no longer mark a death but are actors in a fiction whose mechanics have been betrayed. It is just a story. Nobody died after all. You can breathe out now.

Originally published as 'Playing Dead,' 27 April 2017, https://lukemcker-nan.com/2017/04/27/playing-dead, and reproduced here with small emen-dations.

33

Looking Up to the Light

The dream of screen rapture

To the cinema to see a film about cinema. Is there any art form, any medium, that has been quite so sentimental about itself as cinema? There is nostalgia in the understanding of every art form or medium which has transformed through time, but cinema's forlornness seems particular to itself. It is summed up by the shot of the viewer, face rapt in light and bright with love, seated in the centre of a row, framed by the cinema seats around them, staring up to follow the light of the projector and the invisible screen. Invisible, because what they are actually looking at is us in the audience (or a little above us), the film besotted with its audience, telling us that what we are looking at is actually a mirror. We must go to the cinema to be like this—the image is what defines it.

That clichéd moment is there, of course, in *Empire of Light* (US/USA 2022), the film that was on show. It is a curious work that tries to blend the stories of two people afflicted the one by schizophrenia, the other by racism, with a love of the traditional experience of cinema. Olivia Colman plays an unhappy duty manager at a Margate cinema who never has the time to see a film, until finally she has the cinema to herself and asks to see one. The title picked, *Being There* (USA 1979), a satirical comedy in which Peter Sellers plays a simple-minded gardener whose words are taken for wisdom by the political establishment, is a peculiar choice, but it is there for exigences of plot. Colman, bathed in that light, tearfully stares up at that point above us and is transported.

When did this image of cinema begin? Pictures of the cinema audience are as old as cinema—starting with a celebrated image of the Cinématographe Lumière on an 1896 poster, with the audience laughing at *Arroseur et arrosé* (France 1895), in which a boy takes his foot off a hose just as a gardener is peering at it. The cinema audience, whether as a mass or with focus on an individual, has remained common in advertisements, posters, postcards, photographs, and in stock image libraries. But these are the views of outsiders. It is in the

Hilary Small (Olivia Colman) weeps at the screen
in *Empire of Light.*

films themselves that we can see how the industry wants us to see
it, and from where the image of centralised figure staring up at the
screen derives.

The image of the individual in the audience wholly engrossed
by what thy see on the screen probably starts in the 1920s. Two
1928 films about film itself, *Show People* (USA 1928) and *Shooting
Stars* (UK 1928), have film actors uplifted by the sight of themselves on the screen, respectively Marion Davies and Brian Aherne.
The latter, playing a screen actor, a failure in life, who is lifted by
the sight of his heroic other self on the screen, is an early indicator
of the viewer who in seeing the film sees inside themselves. But the
film's purpose is satire, not nostalgia. Film needed to have outlived
a generation or two before that could happen.

So one has to pass over films with notable audience or viewer
scenes—*Sabotage* (UK 1936), *Sullivan's Travels* (USA 1941), *Brief
Encounter* (UK 1945), *Bonnie and Clyde* (USA 1967), *Taxi Driver*
(USA 1976), even *The Smallest Show on Earth* (UK 1957) with its
rather forced sentiment about old cinemas and remote silent films—
to films that look back on a cinema that is being lost, by concentrating usually on the one viewer. Maybe it begins with Victor
Erice's *El espíritu de la colmena* (*The Spirit of the Beehive*) (Spain
1973), with its 1930s Spanish child open-mouthed at the sight of
Frankenstein's monster, or Woody Allen's *The Purple Rose of Cairo*
(USA 1985), with Mia Farrow as the 1930s downtrodden cinema
fan, who literally escapes into the films she so loves. However, the
shots of them in their respective audiences are at an angle rather

Bud (Leigh McCormack) at the cinema in *The Long Day Closes*.

than face-on, hence are realistic rather than symbolic. The individual cinema member viewed face-on as they are fixated on the screen is absolutely there in *Nuovo Cinema Paradiso* (France/Italy 1988), where the child Salvatore Cascio becomes enraptured by what he is able to see in his small-town cinema, but the image is pure nostalgia. More needs to be added before the theme is fully in place.

The film that may have established the image of transportation, in its framing and symbolism, is Terence Davies' *The Long Day Closes* (UK 1992). The partly-autobiographical work, set in 1950s Liverpool, focusses on how a child from a working-class background, Bud (played by Leigh McCormack), escapes from the narrow confines of his life through a powerful imagination. This is exemplified in an iconic image of Bud seated at the front and centre of the circle seats in a cinema. He is surrounded by the audience but separate from it, bathed in projector light as though he were the projected image (which for we the audience is the case) while he is fixated on the unseen screen, his face awash with light and love.

The image is both nostalgic and free from time. It looks back to the particularities of the experience of cinema in 1950s Britain, but it is a reflection rather than a recreation. It is understood from our remote perspective. It says this is what we have lost but is yet not lost while we can still remember it. Specifically, by showing what the filmmaker remembers of cinema as place and experience, it enshrines what is being lost of cinema—which is why it is so often used to portray classical cinemagoing. Nostalgia kills the thing it loves.

The Long Day Closes followed on from Davies' similarly autobiographical *Distant Voices, Still Lives* (UK 1988), which also celebrates what was memorable about cinema, in an image of two women family members smiling at the screen, but the image from the latter film is the more acute for concentrating on the individual. It is an image that has been emulated—whether deliberately or inevitably—in films such as *Amélie* (France/Germany 2001), *Hugo* (USA 2011) and *La La Land* (USA 2016). The latter two feature couples caught up by the screen, which may dissipate the power of the image, but in *Hugo*'s case it adds an almost didactic tone, showing children enjoying films of the past the way that they tend not to, but (the film implies) should.[1]

However, the rapturous quality of the image, which is so powerfully there in *Empire of Light*, is not necessarily to be traced through scenes from other films that show cinema audiences. Films where protagonists look up to some object above us (i.e. in film observer terms) that seems to pierce their very soul, are films where they are supposed to be having a sight, or sense, of God. Falconetti in *La Passion de Jeanne d'Arc* (France 1928), a scene from which is memorably intercut with shots of Anna Karina empathetically watching the film in a cinema in *Vivre sa vie* (France 1962), or Jennifer Jones in *The Song of Bernadette* (USA 1943), are two examples where the characters are similarly transported, taken out of this world in their eyes and in how they are framed. They look beyond the screen to something the viewer can only sense but not see for themselves, an iconography of course taken from centuries of Christian art.

There is a difference, in that the protagonists in religious films are often looking at what cannot be seen. The vision is frequently in their minds only, whereas the cinema-goer sees what they see. Hence Falconetti sees beyond us, but Anna Karina sees Falconetti. There are close parallels nonetheless. Both cinema experience and religious experience invite absolute love.

It is all sentimental nonsense. When I saw Olivia Colman weeping over *Being There*, alone in a huge cinema, I could not help but think that there was no real difference between the physical experience as shown and watching the film at home on television.

---

[1] My views on *Hugo*'s didactic tone are given in 'The Age of Innocence,' *The Bioscope*, 1 January 2012. https://thebioscope.net/2012/01/01/the-age-of-innocence.

Nana (Anna Karina) looking up at Falconetti, in *Vivre sa vie.*

Of course, large flat-screen television sets were not around in 1981, but the film is preaching a lesson to the people of 2023, not those of four decades ago. This what you are losing it instructs us—rapture, absolute love.

Of course there can be rapture, and cinema in its traditional form has meant so much to so many. But it has also been quite ordinary. It was the routine aspect of cinema, the habit of going twice a week because that is how often the films were changed in cinema's heyday, that gave cinema meaning. It was convenient and belonged to the daily round. That is no longer the case. Cinema has become a staging post for some visual entertainments before they reach their mass audience further down the line—on phones, tablets, television screens or whatever. Those viewers may be enraptured, or mildly entertained, depending on their point of view. The cinema has only ever been a means to an end.

What films such as *Empire of Light* may actually be about is a loss of power. Those raised eyes, that look of supplication, that blind faith, are past. The films, in an age of the domestic big screen experience and hand-held devices, are at our level, and in our hands. Those who would have us look up to the light no longer wield such power. A film like *Empire of Light* pleads for us to believe, but we do not need to. Cinema makes for beautiful memories, but film has moved on, and the audience with it.

Originally published as 'Looking Up to the Light,' 23 January 2023, https://lukemckernan.com/2023/01/23/looking-up-to-the-light, and reproduced here with small emendations. *Empire of Light* was written and directed by Sam Mendes. Though not autobiographical, the Olivia Colman role is inspired by Mendes' mother, who had a bipolar disorder.

34.

Open All Night

A tragedy in miniature

It was on again the other night. In these days of DVD and streaming services it can seem hard to think of the film that is difficult
to find—as films once were, aside from current releases, when
you had to search long and far before tracking down that rarity
of which you had read but had seen perhaps no more than a tanta-
lising still. The film was *Open All Night*, a British title from 1934,
which turned up on the schedules of vintage film and television
channel Talking Pictures TV at the challenging hour of 2:50am. But
once a film has become a part of your blood, then you must see it
each time it recurs—to recover that sense you had when first you
saw it and understood, to reaffirm some special sense of yourself.
You have to make time for it.

I think I first saw the film in the late 1980s, when Alexander
Walker, then film critic of the *Evening Standard*, noted its appearance in the television schedules (again at some unsociable hour,
as I recall), saying that here was something little-known that was
worth waiting up for. As a budding aficionado of British 1930s
films, and a shameless seeker out of the obscure, I needed no
further prompting.

The film did not disappoint. A tragedy in miniature, everything about it denoted quality in straitened circumstances, a humble
production from the 'quota quickie' era of British production that
reached out to offer something more. It touched the heart.

I have seen the film a couple of times more since, though not
yet on a cinema screen, and then again on that Tuesday morning
amid the advertisements for back pain relief, lottery tickets and
bed mattresses—ironic in view of a scheduling time known only
to insomniacs—that give Talking Pictures TV its special flavour.
Presumably I was not the only viewer, even at ten to three in the
morning, but it felt that way. The film had to be seen, and I was
fulfilling my duty in seeing it.

Double-page advertisement for *Open All Night*,
from *Kinematograph Weekly*, 18 October 1934.

Open All Night tells of a Russian grand duke, fallen in the
world, who proudly serves as night manager at a London hotel,
the Paragon. Anton, played by character actor Frank Vosper
(surely his only leading role), is an expert manager of people,
who puts his skills to solving the problems of two young couples
over a night at the hotel, while dealing with the disappointment
of having been given his notice when he had expected a promotion. One of the film's distinguishing features is that it takes place
entirely at night, practically in real time, weaving a number of
narratives together that can only be resolved through the film's
tragic dénouement.

The film was made at Twickenham Studios, run by enter-
prising producer Julius Hagen, who specialised in films made on
the cheap, the notorious 'quota quickies' that were the product
of the Cinematograph Films Act of 1927, which ruled that a
certain proportion of films shown in British cinemas had to be
British-made. Hagen exploited the situation through distribution
deals with American distributors and ruthless financial manage-
ment. Economies were made by hiring old hands whom no one
else would now employ as directors, such as the veteran George

Pearson, director of *Open All Night*. Pearson writes in his autobiography of the strictures under which such films were made:

> The usual budget for a 'quickie' was determined solely on length, based on a fixed charge of £1 per foot on screened film—hence the 'quickies' were sarcastically termed 'Pound-a-Footers.' Their average length was between five and six thousand feet, enough for an hour of screen time sufficient for the Quota. To make a talking film with £6,000 only to meet the costs of studio space, subject, script, director, technicians, film stock, lights, artistes, overheads, and end up with a profit, needed a spartan economy and a slave-driving effort, for the time allotted on the floor was strictly limited to twelve days, less if possible![1]

Hagen economised further by making the studio available day and night—Pearson records that three of the eight 'quickies' he made there were shot at night. I have not been able to determine it for certain, but it would have been more than appropriate for *Open All Night* to have been made that way.

Despite the economies, there were talents on hand able to achieve the remarkable on next to nothing. *Open All Night* never looks anything other than humble, but the hotel sets are ingenious, including the foyer over which the many extras constantly mill, picked up by Pearson's prowling mobile camera, and eye-catching staircases (movement up and down floors as a reflection of whether one is going up or down in society is one of the film's motifs). The art director was James A. Carter, revered in the industry for his ability to conjure up small miracles. Pearson's fellow 'quickie' director Bernard Vorhaus many years later recalled:

> the quite amazing art director Jimmy Carter, who managed to get an amazing quantity of sets over night ... He had an amazing effective plaster department with a tremendous number of moulds. He would whip up scenes with elaborate plaster Tudor beams, trees, God knows what, which were quite out of proportion to the meagre resources in general.[2]

---

[1] George Pearson, *Flashback: The Autobiography of a British Film-maker* (London: George Allen & Unwin, 1957), pp. 192-193.
[2] Quoted in Linda Wood, 'Julius Hagen and Twickenham Studios' in Jeffrey

Also working on the film were reliably efficient cinematographer Ernest Palmer, occasionally conjuring up striking compositions and with some interesting low-angle shots of the protagonists; editor Lister Laurance, who shows great aplomb in building up the tempo between the interlocking stories as the tension mounts; and music director W. L. Tyrtel, notorious for routine scores that churned away in the background unaffected by change of scene or mood, but who does well in weaving his score alongside the unobtrusive band playing in the hotel.

Stills for *Open All Night*, clockwise from top left: Frank Vosper, Gillian Lind, Michael Shepley, Geraldine Fitzgerald, Margaret Vines, Vines with Lewis Shaw. From *Kinematograph Weekly*, 18 October 1934.

So much for efficiency. What makes *Open All Night* something special? It starts with the story, which is credited to John Chancellor, a hack writer of crime and science fiction stories under numerous aliases, none quite as exotic as his real name, Ernest Charles de Balzac Willett. Some sources state the film came from a play, but it is more likely to have been an outline or magazine story; George Pearson's only mention of the film in his autobiography is as a type of film that 'were typical magazine stories [...] hackneyed situations of conflict and comedy.'[3] What-

Richards (ed.), *The Unknown 1930s: An Alternative History of the British Cinema, 1929-1939* (London/New York: I. B. Tauris, 1998), p. 43.
[3] Pearson, *Flashback*, p. 195.

ever the source, it is practised screenwriter Gerard Fairlie who created an efficient scenario, if not one graced with too many memorable lines. The plot is intricate and meticulously worked out, with not a word wasted in taking things to their climax. One of the particular qualities of the film is how the figures involved are neatly imprisoned by narrative, lost people propelled by circumstances they cannot control.

The story revolves around Anton, whose fate recalls Emil Jannings in *Der letzte Mann* (*The Last Laugh*) (Germany 1924) as much as the setting suggests an economical *Grand Hotel* (USA 1932) (*Open All Night* cheekily starts with a line about nothing ever happening at the Paragon, echoing the famous opening—and closing—line of *Grand Hotel*). Frank Vosper is superb. Whiskered-up to look thirty years older than his actual age of thirty-five, he excludes authority and vulnerability, enterprise and disillusionment all in one, effortlessly managing the human crises that come before him while being helpless in the face of those that beset him. It is only towards the end of the film, when someone has been found dead in the hotel and Anton is implicated that he tells a detective that he is a 'grand duke of the Holy Russian Empire,' his bearing rising as he speaks the words that take him far above the petty world in which he finds himself. We are told nothing of his back story—he simply represents fallen greatness, and acceptance. In the film's memorable final scene Anton returns to his Soho flat and toasts a portrait of Tsar Nicholas II on his wall, before taking the only course of action that will solve the problems of the young people he is trying to save, and spare him shame, by shooting himself. So another of *Open All Night*'s distinctive qualities is that it ends with the suicide of a character all in the film and all watching can only admire. Such is fate.

It is hard not to see in Anton a reflection of George Pearson himself. Pearson was a film veteran of twenty-two years, who had entered the film industry in 1912, aged thirty-seven, only after a substantial career as a schoolteacher and headmaster. Something in the medium's power to transmit a message spoke deeply to him when he gave up security to join the British branch of Pathé as a director. He did not want to make educational films but rather story films that investigated the heart. His ambitions—eloquently expressed in his autobiography—were not always realised by his abilities, but he enjoyed a fair amount of success (especially with the 1920s *Squibs* series of films starring Betty Balfour) before finding himself left behind by the changing film world of the

Anton (Frank Vosper) toasts the Czar in *Open All Night.*

1930s. Anton too, for all his goodness, is an abandoned figure, because time is no respecter of virtue. All he can do is help out the young, knowing that they must leave him behind, because that is the way the story must go. Anton is Pearson the director, whether consciously or no, seeing how life must carry on, guiding as best he can, even as he guides himself out of the picture.

Then there are those young people. All have made a mistake in life: Maysie (a sprightly touching performance from Gillian Lind), the out-of-work chorus girl who befriends Anton; sick wife Elsie (Margaret Vines) and her young husband, Bill (Lewis Shaw), whose desperation causes the accidental death that could have him accused of murder, until Anton writes a suicide note declaring that it was he who killed the man; and Jill (Geraldine Fitzgerald), guilty of petty theft, trapped between a 'well-known weekend husband,' the lecherous Hilary (Michael Shepley) and her distraught waiter fiancé, Henry (Colin Keith-Johnson).

None were well-known names; only Fitzgerald would have a notable career thereafter, though Shepley became a familiar film character actor (Frank Vosper would die in mysterious circumstances in 1937). As with many performers in the 'quickies,' they came fresh off the stage (sometimes literally so—they could be in the theatre in the evening and join the studio that night), hired by Twickenham because they were cheap. There is a lost air about them—going through the motions efficiently enough, not quite sure what story they were telling, victims of fate quite as much as their characters. The three young women, in particular, each have a look of forlorn hope, not seeking escape because what would be so different about what they were escaping to? (the grievously ill Elsie would rather listen to the hotel band playing than fall for her husband's hopes).

There is splendid summary of fiction films attributed, from around this time, to Carl Koch, German film director and husband of the animator Lotte Reiniger: 'Entertainment films are merely monstrous documentaries of actors at work.'[4] One can apply this mischievous insight to any fiction film, of course, and probably all of us do so to some degree when watching any film, as we step back momentarily from the spectacle that would engulf us. But it is particularly relevant to *Open All Night*. It is profoundly a film about itself. Its hapless young protagonists, inexpert in life, still finding their way in their profession, cannot find their way out of the hotel. They sit alone at tables, drinking champagne they cannot afford, as the indifferent crowd passes by. They need Anton, they need George, to steer them to the freedom their youth merits, even though it is he who must pay the price for this.

All films are about time. They cut up its flow and explore the effects of this distortion on humans. *Open All Night* establishes its particular dictate by taking place in near real-time, with no flash-backs and arguably no parallel action. The clock is ticking, just as it does for Pearson and his crew to make the film in twelve days at so many thousand feet and no more (*Open All Night* was filmed in July 1934, cut in August, released in October, its running time sixty-two minutes). The film will be shown in a cinema, cheap fodder to fill out an hour in the programme, an entertainment constrained by time, whose special appeal to the audience is that it may eliminate time entirely, or at least conquer it for a while. *Open All Night* is a tragedy to pass the time. Its ending therefore becomes entirely logical—its lead calling time on himself, before the dawn breaks and yet another day can begin.

Open All Night's protagonists are caught in story, because what else is there to make sense of chaos? They follow the lines, they keep to time, they make their exits only to start up all over again in the next play, the next film on the schedule. They under-

---

[4] 'Sayings of the Month,' *World Film News and Television Progress*, April 1936, p. 5.

stand that it is all a monstrous documentary, but how may they escape? Only Anton finds a way to end the story.

Originally published as 'Open All Night,' 29 April 2021, https://lukemckernan.com/2021/04/29/open-all-night, and reproduced here with small emendations. *Open All Night* gained some good notices at the time—the *Kinematograph Weekly* praised it as being an 'ingenious, colourful drama of London's night life... refreshingly comprehensive and its appeal is addressed to all classes. Good popular booking.' *Variety* called it 'good, average entertainment anywhere and not long enough to provoke much criticism.' After its initial American release it was re-issued there under the extraordinary, and quite misleading, title *Murder by Appointment*. The film has not had a release on any domestic format to date (2025). George Pearson moved on to the Colonial Film Unit, where he ended up its Director-in-Chief. He died in 1973, aged ninety-seven. His memoir *Flashback: An Autobiography of a British Film Maker* (George Allen & Unwin, 1957) is a little fusty, but informative and inspiring, much like its author.

35.

The Big Parade

The fading hopes of a silent film masterpiece

When did I last see *The Big Parade* (USA 1925)? I cannot remember where, or when. On a big screen, probably, and at least twenty years ago. My memory of it, apart from its huge emotional impact, chiefly centred on the soldiers marching slowly through woods in the face of gunfire. I saw the film again recently, the new Blu-ray release of Kevin Brownlow and David Gill's Thames Television restoration, and I was surprised at how much I had forgotten.[1] The march through the woods is as much of a cinematic coup as ever it was, but so much of the film was as if new to me—which, though it makes me worry about my memory, made it in all other respects a great pleasure because it was as though watching a film classic for the first time.

The film tells a story now so familiar that you have to make a special effort to remind yourself that nothing like it had ever been seen on the screen before, and that it was shown to an audience for whom the First World War was but a few years ago, with its impact and consequences still being digested. Directed by King Vidor in 1925, it tells of Jim, a young American playboy (John Gilbert) who enlists when America joins the war and becomes close friends with two men from humbler working backgrounds, Bull and Slim, played by Tom O'Brien and Karl Dane. They train for war, travel over to France, and while stationed at a French village waiting for the fighting to begin, Gilbert falls in love with a French girl, Melisande, played by Renée Adorée, despite neither being able to speak a word of the other's language. Gilbert has left a fiancée back in America, so the romance is touched with doubts if not guilt.

The soldiers go to the front. Having been strafed by a German airplane as they march down a road, they meet proper action at Belleau Woods. This sequence has been much praised for its realism, as the soldiers proceed slowly through the trees in the bright

---

[1] *The Big Parade*, Blu-ray, Turner Home Entertainment, 2013.

Melisande (Renée Adorée) and Jim (John Gilbert) in *The Big Parade*.

light of day, one by one falling as they are picked off by sniper fire and machine guns. It comes as a huge shock after the Arcadian interlude in the French village, but what struck me was how stylised the whole sequence it, so that realism is a quite misleading concept. In its gentle rhythm, in its play of light and shadow, in its intercutting between propulsive and repulsive elements, it seems a very formalised, almost balletic sequence—a dream of war with the reality of death.

The fighting continues at night on open ground, where the trio find themselves in a fox hole. Slim goes out on a doomed solo mission and is killed. Jim goes out to try and rescue him, and in another of the film's heart-stopping sequences, he shoots a German soldier and then pursues him, both dragging themselves through the mud. Coming together, Jim is unable to bayonet the man but instead gives him a cigarette, before his young enemy dies. It is the kind of sequence advocates of the silent film hold up as being the quintessence of the medium. Nothing is said, everything is only felt and read through the eyes until it becomes a scene that could only have been told silently. Its power is the very model of what was lost when cinema found sound.

Jim returns home after the war, where we and his family learn for the first time that he has lost a leg. Again, one has to think back to how it must have come across in 1925 to see a star of Gilbert's romantic appeal so disfigured. His family—and conveniently his fiancée—seem repulsed by him, even as his mother has a sweet vision of the different stages of her child growing up, but this is a part of Jim's new maturity. He has to reject his inherited comforts and discover his true self back in France, where Melisane toils in the fields dreaming that he might return one day. But who is that figure she sees hobbling on the brow of a hill, coming toward her? It is no less powerful for being the only ending that the audience would ever have allowed the filmmakers to make.

The Big Parade has its occasional lapses and absurdities—Karl Dane's eye-rolling comedy; Melisande clinging onto the truck which is taking Jim away from her raises more of a smile than a tear—but no more than must inevitably occur with the passing of time. It rings true in both narrative and performance. It was arguably the most successful film commercially of the silent era with a worldwide box office of $22,000,000, against a production budget of $245,000.[2] Watching, however, I kept thinking of how what was once hugely popular becomes the reserve of the specialist. The cinephiles laud *The Big Parade* as the peak of silent film craft, with performances, technique and theme that could hardly be bettered. I myself have just said how it rings true. Yet for the general audience these things are not true. It is quaint. It is false. It has been rendered implausible and unpersuasive by the passing of time and by the many films that have adapted its template for the tastes of their own times. Some in that general audience would fall for it, or at least appreciate its lasting values with a bit of context, but ultimately *The Big Parade* is much like any other film, in that its relevance is fundamentally tied to its popularity, and that is measured in a small number of years before tastes move on.

---

[2] *The Big Parade* (1925), *The Numbers*, n. d., https://www.the-numbers.com/movie/Big-Parade-The-(1925). *The Birth of a Nation* (USA 1915) is sometimes credited as being the highest-grossing silent film of all time, but its box office figures are uncertain.

When is dramatic art ever eternal? Art on a wall achieves this, perhaps because it is static and not so dependent for its meaning upon an audience—it is constructed to stand out of time. Of course dramatic plays have lasted down the centuries, but their performances do not, as any vintage filmed or televised Shakespeare play will demonstrate. It all changes, from what was generally understood to what is selectively understood and requires apologetics. What is past is lost, or is in an ever-increasing process of being lost. As John Gilbert's embittered face towards the end of *The Big Parade* suggests, film's great hopes never last.

Originally published as *The Big Parade*, 25 October 2013, https://lukemckernan.com/2013/10/25/the-big-parade, and reproduced here with small emendations.

36.

Film and the Historian

Mike Leigh's Peterloo *and the role of the historical consultant*

Few arguments can be more engrossing to take up, yet with so little hope of resolution, than the relationship between history and film. It is almost as if one of the chief functions of film is to bring history into confusion. Actuality film — newsreels, newsfilms, documentaries, home movies — appears to capture moments of historical time, and gets re-used as the building blocks of historical documentaries. But the image of the event is not the event itself, while the presence of the camera brings its own influence to bear on what it is ostensibly recording. The more you look, the more uncertain you must become about what it is that you are looking at.

And as for the fiction film... So much has been written on the distortions of historical fact perpetrated by feature films and television fiction where the imperative has been to tell a story and to entertain. Critics and historians have winced, wailed and wept at the heresies made by filmmakers. Many indulge, with a mixture of sadness and smugness, in the game of pointing out the most egregious examples. There are numerous books devoted to the subject and writers who have become specialists in this particular field, notably Robert Rosenstone, who became intrigued by the historical film's paradoxes after working as a consultant on Warren Beatty's Russian Revolution drams *Reds* (USA 1981).[1]

Historians get employed by filmmakers, undoubtedly welcoming the pay cheques, but ultimately must cut sorry figures, as advice is overturned by expediency. The American Historical Association has these optimistic words in the careers section of its website, where it considers opportunities for consultants:

---

[1] See, for example, Ted Mico, John Miller-Monzon, David Rubel (eds.), *Past Imperfect: History According to the Movies* (London: Cassell, 1996), Robert A. Rosenstone, *Visions of the Past: The Challenge of Film to Our Idea of History* (Cambridge, Mass./London: Harvard University Press, 1995), K. R. M. Short (ed.), *Feature Films as History* (London: Croom Helm, 1982).

> An increasingly sophisticated audience is demanding greater historical integrity in media productions. Producers of documentaries, dramatic films, and educational programming often hire historical consultants to advise on costumes, scenery, props, dialect, and content accuracy. Most television networks and large production companies will require the services of a historian...[2]

Well, indeed they may, but the historian is there to advise and suggest, not to construct. History, to be told, must be subservient to the medium that expresses it. Film operates to the (perceived) logic of its audience. Historical truth must always bow to narrative necessity. If there is no story, there is no history.

I thought on these things while watching Mike Leigh's new film, *Peterloo* (UK 2018), because it is a historical film unlike almost any other that I can recall. The film tells of the Peterloo Massacre, the famous—though not famous enough—incident on 16 August 1819 in which a cavalry regiment charged a peaceful demonstration of some 60-70,000 people who had met at St Peter's Field, Manchester, to protest over parliamentary representation. Eighteen people were killed, and hundreds wounded. It is a story that demands telling, though it is not one that has been filmed before now.[3]

I enjoyed the film very much, both for what it tried to do and how it went about doing so. Firstly, though I have said that Peterloo is a story that demands telling, *Peterloo* the film does not tell a story. It appears to do so, given that it follows a course of action with its roots and their consequences, and it has characters whose fates intertwine. It shows a lesson learned through time, which is probably all that a story is. But what story exists is incidental to its purpose. That purpose is to produce an historical document.

Peterloo aims to be actuality, early nineteenth-century newsreel if you will, the stuff that captures moments of historical time, from which one must then derive information from which to derive a history—which is the telling of a story. This is done most obviously through the scrupulous recreation of meetings and the speeches given at meetings, which we witness verbatim,

---

[2] American Historical Association, Professional & Career Resources, https://www.historians.org/community-careers/professional-career-resources.
[3] The main character in *Fame is the Spur* (UK 1947) is a British left-wing politician inspired by his grandfather's role at Peterloo.

albeit shortened from reality. The words people use, their means of expression, the clothes they wear, the way that they wear them, their habits and incidental manners (for example, people sitting up in bed to go to sleep), all aspects which offer nothing in themselves that will propel a story, all are foregrounded. We are so used to historical films and television programmes where the past is populated by twenty-first century people. They have the costumes of the past, but they think like us, talk like us, and share our preoccupations. In *Peterloo* we are not invited to recognise ourselves, even while it hopes that we must sympathize with the predicament of our ancestors. Of course *Peterloo*'s recreation of the sounds, sights and manners of the past is not *authentic* (it is 200 years too late for that), but its efforts towards authenticity exist of themselves. They do not simply serve a story, to be distorted when the demands of story say that they must.

The massacre, in *Peterloo*.

Peterloo is being called here a film by Mike Leigh (its writer and director), but it is really a Leigh and Riding film. Jacqueline Riding, who worked previously with Leigh on *Mr Turner* (France/Germany/UK 2014) is named high up the credits as 'Historian' (not the more usual 'historical consultant' that is found buried among the lesser credits of other films). If you read Riding's complementary book, *Peterloo: The Story of the Manchester Massacre*, the parallels in technique between the two are remarkable.[4] Riding collects evidence and presents it in good order. She pays particular

---

[4] Jacqueline Riding, *Peterloo: The Story of the Manchester Massacre* (London: Head of Zeus, 2018).

attention to the look of things (we are told about the appearance of even the most minor of characters if she has the details to hand). It is scrupulous, a little pedantic, and it works well on film. She and Leigh have made an evidentiary historical film.

It is interesting to look at the history of historians and fiction films. It does not seem to be a history that has been written, and except for recent years the evidence is not easy to find (as opposed to historians and actuality film, which is better documented). Historians were probably first involved, unwittingly, by D. W. Griffith, whose *The Birth of Nation* (USA 1915) lays claim to historical veracity by citing various written histories or classic images in its intertitles. Perhaps the first historian to be involved in the production of a film was the British journalist and constitutional historian Sidney Low, who wrote the scenario for *The Life Story of David Lloyd George* (UK 1918), converting very recent history into a feature film entertainment that likewise asserted veracity through the recreation of specific incidents. A notable early contribution was that of French historian Pierre Champion, who was hired as historical consultant for Carl Th. Dreyer's *La Passion de Jeanne d'Arc* (France 1928), following Champion's editing, in 1921, of the transcript of the trial of Joan of Arc.

For the classical years of Hollywood studio production, there must have been instances where historians were called in to help verify (or justify) artistic decisions, but they seem little documented. There are some references to historical consultants, but invariably associated with documentaries, or drama-documentaries. The earliest of these I have traced is James T. Shotwell, historical consultant for *Land of Liberty* (USA 1939), a documentary on the history of the USA, edited by Cecil B. De Mille. Historical films were almost invariably adapted from novels, and if anyone was going to be consulted it was the novelist. There was little urge towards authenticity. It was the dream that mattered.

Things appear to have changed in the 1960s, as cinema itself changed with a new breed of filmmaker looking beyond the artifice of the studio era. One of the first historical consultants as we now understand them was Andrew Mollo. He was an authority of British military uniforms, who co-directed Kevin Brownlow's alternative history about a Britain occupied by the Nazis, *It Happened Here* (UK 1964), after which he served as consultant on a number of popular war-themed films, such as *The Eagle Has Landed* (UK 1976) before joining Brownlow again for *Winstanley* (UK 1974), whose meticulous and sympathetic account of the

proto-communist Diggers of the Civil War era, bears close affil-
iation with *Peterloo*. Brownlow and Mollo's film also uses texts
of the time, in the form of Gerrard Winstanley's pamphlets, as
foregrounding texts to which the images serve as verification, or
commentary. Both pare away cinema's decorative tendencies to
present something like an unvarnished truth.

Probably the most celebrated example of a historian's collaboration with a filmmaker is Natalie Zemon Davis and *Le Retour
de Martin Guerre* (*The Return of Martin Guerre*) (France 1982).
Of this famous tale of imposture set in sixteenth-century France,
Davis wrote, 'Rarely does a historian find so perfect a narrative
structure in the events of the past with such dramatic popular
appeal.'[5] The story of Martin Guerre, the man who left his wife
and child, was then replaced by someone claiming to be him, only
for the real Martin Guerre to return, is classically dramatic—even
if it hinges on the unlikely hope that the audience will be in doubt,
at least for a time, as to whether 'Martin Guerre' is telling the truth.
It made for an entertaining film, directed by Daniel Vigne and
featuring Gérard Depardieu and Nathalie Baye, weakened (ironically) by too heavy a reliance on that classical narrative structure.
Perhaps for the medieval historian it is filled with small absurdities that would never be a part of French medieval life, but aside
from some excusable lapses (everyone has perfect teeth and skin),
it looks like the past come to life. It looks like the past inviting me
to understand it.

The connection with Davis stands out because of her great
reputation as a historian, and for her thoughtful writings on the
experience of working closely on the film's production, for which
she was co-writer as well as historical consultant. As with Jacqueline Riding, she wrote a history book, *The Return of Martin
Guerre*, that was published in 1983, a year after the film was
released. In the preface she writes:

> Watching Gérard Depardieu feel his way into the role
> of the false Martin Guerre gave me new ways to think
> about the accomplishment of the real impostor, Arnaud
> du Tilh. I felt I had my own historical laboratory, gener-
> ating not proofs, but historical possibilities. At the same
> time, the film was departing from the historical record,
> and I found this troubling. The Basque background of

---

[5] Natalie Zemon Davis, *The Return of Martin Guerre* (Cambridge, Mass./Lon-
don: Harvard University Press, 1983), p. vi.

the Guerres was sacrificed; rural Protestantism was ignored; and especially the double game of the wife and the judge's inner contradictions were softened. These changes may have helped to give the film the powerful simplicity that allowed the Martin Guerre story to become a legend in the first place, but they also made it hard to explain what actually happened. Where was there room in this beautiful and compelling cinematographic recreation of a village for the uncertainties, the 'perhapses,' the 'may-have-beens,' to which the historian has recourse when the evidence is inadequate or perplexing?[6]

This anguish, partly a worry over cinema's (apparent) simplifications, and partly a worry over the power of cinema to take stories beyond the control of the historian, particularly if you can call on actors of the calibre of Baye and Depardieu to enrich the telling, gets voiced again and again by the historical consultants of the modern era. Why have there been so many of them? It may have something to do with the emergence of videotape at around the time of *Le Retour de Martin Guerre*. Films which previously were seen only the cinema, or some years later on television, could now be rented. The details could be pored over, and failings—such as historical errors—more easily verified and shared. This went hand-in-hand with increased audience appetite for credible history, and was only accentuated by the arrival of the Web, which increased opportunities for anyone to analyse, discuss and share.

Now every film and television programme that looks to the past has a historical consultant. Not all are major names—the humblest professor for a university's historical department is likely to have received the call asking to verify some turn of phrase, choice of costume or architectural construction. Some notable names have got involved, however. They include Robin Lane Fox (*Alexander*), Robert Lacey (*The Queen*, *The Crown*), Orlando Figes (*Anna Karenina*), and Kathleen Coleman (*Gladiator*), who was so disgusted with the results that she had her name taken off the credits, a despairing act undertaken by numerous other historical consultants. All report mixed experiences, arguing for a middle ground between authenticity of detail and truth to the spirit of the past. Robert Lacey's comments on the ambiguities of historical authenticity making the Netflix series *The Crown* (UK/USA 2016-2023) may sum it up best:

---

[6] Davis, *The Return of Martin Guerre*, p. viii.

'Martin Guerre' (Gérard Depardieu) and Bertrande de Rols
(Nathalie Baye) in *Le Retour de Martin Guerre*.

People say 'is it true or is it false?' ... I say, 'I don't like
the word false.' I'd rather say is it true or is it invented? Is
it true or is it imagined? Because, you see there is a difference between history and the past. The past is one thing.
The past is what people lived through: lived and loved
and betrayed each other and were true to each other. Most
of the past vanishes. We don't know the details.[7]

Robert Rosenstone, the doyen of those who have studied the fiction film's engagement with history, explains the difference between written history and filmed history, in a way that seems to
complement Lacey's thoughts on history (something recreated)
versus the past (something lost):

The world on the screen brings together things that, for
analysis, or structural purposes, written history often has
to split apart. Economics, politics, race, class and gender
all come together in the lives and the moments of individuals, groups and nations. This characteristic of films
throws into relief a certain convention—one might call it

[7] Quoted in Catherine Hallemann, 'What It's Really Like to Be a Historical Consultant on *The Crown*,' *Town and Country*, 18 December 2017,
https://www.townandcountrymag.com/leisure/arts-and-culture/a14107357/
the-crown-history-consultant.

a fiction—of written history: the strategy that fractures the past into distinct topics, categories and chapters; that treats gender in one chapter, race in another, economy in a third.[8]

Films must show what the written word alone cannot reveal. Films imagine. They do so by a process of synthesis, showing people caught in time, subject to process. They recreate events, they treasure any moments of authenticity that may be achieved, but they do not analyse as a historian must want to analyse. Instead they encourage identification with times past. They provide experience.

Peterloo has its limitations. It fails to show much in the way of suffering (the workers of Manchester do not seem to be leading a bad life, except for those unfortunate enough to get transported). The fear of a version of the French revolution occurring in Britain, that so animated those in power, is insufficiently explained. Thus the drivers behind the Peterloo Massacre are taken too much for granted. It has also been sold as the great entertainment film that it is not. The couple next to me in the cinema pronounced it to be the worst film they had ever seen—though they sat through all 154 minutes of it just to make sure.

Its greatest limitation is its great virtue. It boldly and beautifully tries to do what few historical films attempt, which is to be the evidence, forming its own kind of historical document. It can claim, with some confidence, to show us how things were, because of its integrity and because it allows nothing else to distract it from this purpose. It is the historian's dream. But we, the audience, must dream of other things.

Originally published as 'Film and the Historian,' 19 November 2018, https://lukemckernan.com/2018/11/19/film-and-the-historian, and reproduced here with small emendations.

---

[8] Rosenstone, *Visions of the Past*, p. 60.

37.

On the Deaths of Famous People

Fame and mourning

The first person of whose death I became aware was Pete Duel. He was an American actor, star of the popular television series *Alias Smith and Jones* (USA 1971-1973), which followed the adventures of two outlaws in imitation of the film *Butch Cassidy and the Sundance Kid* (USA 1969). Duel committed suicide on the last day of 1971, and I remember the shock and the puzzlement that I felt. It was not so much that his life was lost but the realisation that he had had a separate life to the happy character of Hannibal Heyes that he played on the screen. His real life had been somewhere else, but equally a part of his life had been mine.

Thereafter I was greatly moved by the death of rock singer Marc Bolan, who was such a figurehead to those of my generation; was indifferent to the death of Elvis Presley, who I really only knew as a bad actor; and shocked as the whole world was at the murder of John Lennon. I did not know these people, but those whose passing I felt, mattered to me. It was not as though I knew them, or even felt that I knew them, but even so in some way I had lost their company.

Years have gone by, and I have experienced deaths of friends and family, inevitably, and of many people I knew only through their fame. This week David Bowie died, and the worldwide outpouring of grief has been genuine, well merited, but also curious. So many people mourning a person they never met, or saw only in concert, indeed many mourning he whose golden years had taken place years before they were born. What was it that they were mourning?

Glen David Gold's novel *Sunnyside* opens with a case of mass delusion in which Charlie Chaplin appears in eight hundred different places simultaneously.[1] Supposedly based on a true case from November 1916, the conceit shows how an idea of the motion picture

---

[1] Glen David Gold, *Sunnyside* (London: Sceptre, 2009).

Pete Duel.

actor could be shared by many different people in a collective understanding that was nevertheless different for each individual. There
was only one Charlie Chaplin, yet everyone felt they knew him—that
they experienced him—in their own particular way.

There had been no one else like this previously in human
history. Gerben Bakker, in his book *Entertainment Industrialised*,
goes into the economics behind it:

> When Charlie Chaplin was nineteen years old he ap-
> peared in three music halls a night. On one fine day he
> started in the late afternoon at the half-empty Streatham
> Empire in London. Directly after the show he and his
> company were rushed by private bus to the Canterbury
> Music Hall and then on to the Tivoli. This constituted the
> maximum number of venues an entertainer could visit on
> an evening, and thus the inherent limit to a performer's
> productivity.
>
> Yet, barely five years had passed before Chaplin
> would appear in thousands of venues across the world
> at the same time. His productivity had increased almost
> unimaginably.[2]

---

[2] Gerben Bakker, *Entertainment Industrialised: The Emergence of the International Film Industry, 1890-1940* (Cambridge: Cambridge University Press,
2008), p. xix.

Charlie Chaplin, c.1916.

Bakker is interested in the economics of Chaplin, how cinema prices were lower than those of music hall, so that he could only capture a small percentage of revenues, yet nevertheless ended up as the world's highest-paid performer. But the cinematic distribution of Chaplin enabled him also to be shared in an emotional sense. People felt they knew Chaplin, Mary Pickford, John Bunny, Florence Lawrence, and the other first film stars of the 1910s. They increased people's social circle. Previously most people knew very few people. They knew their own family, their neighbours and their work colleagues. They were constrained by a narrow social set. People had lived like this for centuries, knowing few others, who on the whole were only of interest because they were family, neighbours or work colleagues.

Cinema extended who you knew. You shared an intimacy with people who were glamorous, capable, versatile, popular and who seemed familiar even as they were utterly remote. The deaths of John Bunny (in 1915), Wallace Reid (1923) and Rudolph Valentino (1926) consequently became occasions for widespread grief, of a kind that had never existed before. Each was a universal loss, felt on an individual level.

Of course there had been famous people before films stars, be they theatrical performers, sports figures, military leaders or royalty, whose lives were followed by those who never saw them, or only occasional images of them, and whose passing was the cause of extensive grief. And newspapers, magazines, posters and other media from the mid-nineteenth century onwards distributed images of the glamorous and famous that could be widely shared. But cinema not only greatly widened the potential for appeal (across national boundaries as well) but created something on top of this: a feeling of closeness. Cinema's performers openly appealed to you, that individual member of the audience. There might be eight hundred other people with you in the cinema who shared the experience, but you along with them also felt it individually.

The memoirist C. H. Rolph identifies something of this in his book *London Particulars*, where he writes about seeing a Chaplin film in a London cinema in the 1910s:

> The universal Chaplin impact was something I shall never really understand. For years it seemed to me that there are so many totally humourless people in the world that success on the Chaplin scale simply shouldn't be possible, that it is a phenomenon calling for some transcendental explanation. Then I saw that this point of view merely rationalizes the feeling, in the breast of each Chaplinite, that Chaplin really belongs to him alone, that there is no one else who quite understands just how funny life can be.[3]

The reach that David Bowie enjoyed was greater than even Chaplin enjoyed. Multi-channel television, the internet, social

---

[3] C. H. Rolph, *London Particulars* (Oxford: Oxford University Press, 1980), p. 106.

media, a proliferation of forms in which the sound and vision of the man can be produced, shared, consumed and reused creates a saturation effect *en masse*, but each individual experiences this differently. There are, or were, eight hundred, or 800 million, David Bowies out there.

The quality of the experience seems different to that of Chaplin's time, however. Chaplin became a friend to millions, but he was remote for all that, an impossible figure whose real life was only really understood there on the big screen. David Bowie you could imagine meeting, and having a chat about anything ('So, David, that line you wrote about Mickey Mouse having grown up a cow—what were you thinking?'). This is what television and social media have done, of course, making familiar that which the predecessor medium made distant.

But if the quality of our knowledge of these people has changed with the media over the years, the fact remains that cinema ushered in a key aspect of modern life, which is that we know more people than we know. We know more of people, we invest more emotionally, because of the world that has opened up for us through what is beamed onto screens. We are, logically speaking, more sociable than our ancestors.

And so we mourn the passing of those we have never met, because we knew them anyway, and they were a part of ourselves.

And I still feel sad about Pete Duel.

Originally published as 'On the Deaths of Famous People,' 13 January 2016, https://lukemckernan.com/2016/01/13/on-the-deaths-of-famous-people, and reproduced here with small emendations. David Bowie died on 10 January 2016.

38

Every Picture Tells A Story

William Scott, James Scott and what is seen and felt

Just under thirty years ago I went to a tiny cinema, the Minema, off Hyde Park Corner, London, to see a dramatised documentary about the Irish painter William Scott. It was directed by the painter's son, James Scott, who had recently won an Academy Award for the short film *A Shocking Accident* (UK 1982), adapted from a Graham Greene short story. It was called *Every Picture Tells a Story* (UK 1984). Humble a production as it was, it nevertheless made a great impression on me. It told the story of the painter's childhood up to the time when he left Northern Ireland for the Royal Academy of Arts in London.

It was a costume drama intercut with commentary from William Scott himself, and three elements have remained stuck in my memory, along with the general sense of a fine film. One was when the teenage Scott is asked by an art teacher (played by Natasha Richardson) to draw an apple, to show what he can do. The very simplicity of this made a great impression on me. Another, oddly, was the abrupt ending, when Scott says that everything in art was changed by Cézanne, and the film ends there (I now know it was intended as part one of a trilogy, but the remaining parts were never made).

The third element was the film's most distinctive feature. One would witness a scene from Scott's childhood, played out by actors, when abruptly the film would cut to one of his abstract or semi-abstract works, as a kind of flash-forward showing how what impressed the child's mind was later recapitulated as art. It was a startling, exhilarating innovation, which impressed me as a film enthusiast and turned me into a lifelong admirer of Scott's art. The visual coup stayed with me, and though I never had the chance to see the film again I filed it away as a hidden gem, forever confirmed as one of my favourite films of that period.

2013 was the centenary of Scott's birth and was marked by a major exhibition at the Ulster Museum in Belfast. I managed to get there on the very last day of the exhibition, 2 February 2014, when it so happened that there was a screening of *Every Picture Tells a Story*. Would it still stand up? I spent the morning touring the exhibition. It was a thrilling experience being in the huge white space of the Museum's main gallery, with Scott's immaculate works all about me, and not a soul there, bar the occasional guard. What a rare joy to have an art gallery all to yourself. Scott's paintings are best known for their use of domestic images such as tables, saucepans, jugs and cutlery, and for the skilful arrangement of line and plain blocks of colour. The works are abstract to a degree, but figurative also—they relate to something, yet need not relate to anything. To be in a room filled with them is heavenly.

And so to the film, shown in the Museum's lecture room. It did not disappoint. I had forgotten much of it, so mostly it was like seeing the film for the first time, but its special economy of style, at one with its subject, was what arrested me back in 1984 and which remained true. The film shows the Scott family living in Scotland when the father (a loving portrait played by Alex Norton) returns from the First World War. He moves the family to his home town of Enniskillen in Northern Ireland and makes his living as a sign painter. Among his large brood of children, his son William is drawn to art, sketching objects on the kitchen table and helping out with his father's work. The father takes him to a local art teacher, and after the father dies in an accident the local Presbyterian community see to it that the talented son is able to go to the Royal Academy in London.

The narrative is irrelevant, however. What matters is what is seen, and felt. There are the saucepans, plates, pots and tables that most obviously recur in Scott's later art, which is revealed—as I remembered—by the startling cuts from figurative memory to abstract expression as the film cuts from story to paintings. There is the collapsing of time, between the unfolding story and the figure of William Scott himself, heard speaking but filmed sitting wordlessly, and between past and present most ingeniously (and economically) where Scott's father prepares to go on an Orange parade in the 1920s before we see a 1980s parade taking place outside. Nothing, incidentally, is made of politics or religion, in the film. It is simply a part of the picture, of what is seen and felt.

Which leads us to the film's title. This was the part of it that had always bothered me. 'Every Picture Tells a Story' is a tired cliché, and an odd thing to say about art works which tend towards abstraction. The beauty of abstract art is that it does not tell a story.

William Scott (John Docherty) draws an apple.

It is not dependent on narrative, be that figures arranged in a recognisable setting (e.g. historical) or a portrait, where we are encouraged to think who that person was, what thoughts lie behind their eyes. It is art that requires a key. In the film someone asks the young Scott why a book of paintings has no descriptions to say what the pictures signify, to which he replies that 'pictures are for looking at — the picture tells the story.' The real-life Scott then tells us that 'every picture tells a story.'

This is not 'story' as in narrative, but the abstraction of things seen and felt. They signify something of the story of William Scott, and that was obviously part of the filmmaker's intentions, and his reason for the choice of title. But what 'every picture tells a story' really means is that the picture renders the story unnecessary. The pictures do not need a narrative explanation. The paradox could have made *Every Picture Tells a Story* a weak film, but instead it is a film that is able to have it both ways. The pictures spring out of the story of William Scott, and they have no story at all. All that is there is all that you can see.

I returned to the gallery after the film screening, and passed through the rooms once more, which were now filled with people. The spell cast in the morning had been broken. Too many other eyes were looking, interpreting, confusing the narrative, breaking up the abstraction.

But do we ever have pure abstract art? Every picture plays upon something in our memories, even the simplest shape or a single colour must connect with something in the way that we see the world, or we would not see the picture at all. Art, in that respect, is the distillation of experience. Perhaps purely abstract art only exists in an empty gallery, where no one can see it, where there are no stories to be told. So I like to feel that, being in that gallery in the morning, when there was only me, I might have come close to seeing it.

Originally published as 'Every Picture Tells a Story,' 7 February 2014, https://lukemckernan.com/2014/02/07/every-picture-tells-a-story, and reproduced here with small emendations. The website https://william-scott.org has examples of his work, a biography, details of collections, news and events. James Scott's website https://www.james-scott.com has information on his art works and films, including *Every Picture Tells a Story*. The film is available, together with other art films made by James Scott, on the BFI DVD *Every Picture Tells a Story: The Art Films of James Scott*.

39

Jiří Menzel's Closing Shot

How cinema says goodbye

One of the cinema's great gifts to us all is the closing shot. Each art form becomes distinctive through its ability to tell stories through devices unique to itself, and so there is nothing in the novel, theatre, opera or any other dramatic method that has anything to compare with the closing shot of cinema. Where something similar does occur, it is invariably a failed attempt to capture that which belongs only on a screen, at the end of a story of around two hours' duration, whose meaning for its audience must always lie beyond words.

Not every film has a memorable closing shot—indeed most do not—but those that we cherish help define the medium. Charlie Chaplin and Paulette Goddard silhouetted as they walk away from us down a road in *Modern Times* (USA 1936); Alida Valli walking past and ignoring Joseph Cotten at the end of *The Third Man* (UK 1949); the solitary John Wayne, grasping his right arm, as he leaves the door of the homestead in *The Searchers* (USA 1956); the young Jean-Pierre Léaud running into the sea with the freeze-frame on his bewildered face in *Les Quatre Cents Coups* (*The 400 Blows*) (France 1959); the shoot-out in *Butch Cassidy and the Sundance Kid* (USA 1969); Klaus Kinski alone on a swirling raft, his mad dreams all dead, in *Aguirre, der Zorn Gottes* (*Aguirre, the Wrath of God*) (Mexico/Peru/West Germany 1972)—are iconic in themselves, but show how cinema can resolve itself, at the end of those two hours of storytelling, into a single, lingering image. All that we have seen, or all that we have to learn from what we have seen, is contained in the shot that will most powerfully imprint itself on the mind. It is time contracted into a memory.

I thought about closing shots when hearing yesterday of the death of the Czech film director Jiří Menzel. The films he was allowed to make were too few, but three of them enjoyed the highest acclaim: *Ostře Sledované Vlaky* (*Closely Observed Trains*) (Czechoslovakia 1966), *Rozmarné léto* (*Capricious Summer*)

Pavel (Václav Neckář) and Jitka (Jitka Zelenohorská) in *Skřivánci na niti.*

(Czechoslovakia 1968) and *Skřivánci na niti* (*Larks on a String*) (Czechoslovakia 1969). The first two, products of the marvellous Czechoslovak new wave of filmmakers during the political thaw of the Prague Spring, are bittersweet comedies that were widely seen at the time. The third, *Skřivánci na niti*, was made as the Soviet tanks rolled back in, forcing it to be banned before any screening. It was not seen officially until 1990, the year after the Velvet Revolution, when it shared the Golden Bear at the Berlin Film Festival. It has one of the greatest of closing shots, and is therefore by definition one of the greatest of films, since the one cannot be without the other.

The film is set in a scrap metal yard in the Communist Czechoslovakia of the 1950s, a time of leaden Stalinist ideology, political purges, labour camps and show trials. A group of political dissidents work, in desultory fashion, at the yard: a librarian, a philosopher, a saxophonist, a barber, a dairyman, each condemned for having thought the 'wrong' way. The objects they recycle are reminders of a ruined past, much as they are themselves. All must be smelted into something new. Every now and again one of them asks someone in authority why things are the way they are. In the following scene we learn that he who asked the question has disappeared. So the next in line has to ask the question.

But though set against the bleakest of circumstances in the most unpromising of settings, this is a lyrical and uplifting film,

The closing shot.

filled with humour both sad and mischievous. It is beautifully shot—cinematographer Jaromír Šofr conjured up shots of exquisite colour amid the piles of rusting metal in the scrapyard, of which the grimy dissidents seemed almost to be an organic part. Amid the absurdities of ideology (a group of children is taken to see the dissidents, their earnest teacher pointing out the sad and kindly women as having 'repugnant, imperialism-soaked faces'), the men ponder philosophical questions, keeping understanding alive.

Fleeting romance occurs between the separated male and female detainees; the light touch of hands as they tenderly pass pieces of metal between them as part of a chain has a blissful edge to it. The women's guard, a sad young man married to a disaffected Roma, becomes entranced by a sentimental painting of an angel he finds on a scrap heap. Becoming a guardian angel himself, he furtively allows the women the little happiness he cannot find. In every scene, the prison in which they find themselves is undermined by minds that question and hearts that beat true.

A young man among the dissident group, Pavel (played by Václav Neckář, the hero of *Ostře Sledované Vlaky*), falls in love with one of the women. He marries her by proxy, but before the marriage can be consummated, again at the guard's connivance, Pavel is hauled away in a car for having asked the question about why some of his number have disappeared. Our last sight of him is in a mining party. Before they go underground, he sees his bride Jitka (played by Jitka Zelenohorská) bidding him farewell. The mineshaft lift hurtles downwards. One of those who had disappeared, the philosopher, is in the cage. He ends a disquisition with the words 'I am happy, I have found myself.'

Elated by love and truth, when he should be suffering punishment for questioning the state, Pavel looks up. He sees the bright light above shrinking as his party descends into the depths, a receding sign of hope that only seems to increase as the light grows smaller. It encapsulates all that has taken us to this point. It is defeat, hope and irony all in one. It is symbolic of the film itself, which was consigned to darkness before it could be seen, yet had such light and life within it. The day would have to come when it would be seen again.

Like film, like country. I saw Jiří Menzel once. It was at the National Film Theatre, for a screening of his film *Vesničko má středisková (My Sweet Little Village)* (Czechoslovakia 1985) at the 1986 London Film Festival. It was when the protests in Poland were making us sense that the Soviet grip on Eastern Europe was failing, but before the Velvet Revolution overturned the one-party system in Czechoslovakia. Menzel was asked if change might come to Czechoslovakia. Unable to commit himself, yet equally unable not to look up and see hope, Menzel said that his country was like a sleeping beauty, only waiting to be wakened, at who knew what time. It was but three years away.

That bleak era has gone, to be replaced by the troubles of our own times. *Skřivánci na niti* can be seen on DVD, and included on the 2011 Second Run release is a short, self-filmed interview with Menzel.[1] He has a comfortable home. I admire his bookshelves. Things ended well enough for him. He looks back on the film's history, comments wryly on its recovery, then ends with a mild tirade at modern cinema, which he finds too fond of violence and digital trickery. It is an old man's complaint, but his recollection of cinema as being at its best when it showed compassion is something to make us think.

Compassion is what *Skřivánci na niti* is all about, and compassion lies at the heart of that extraordinary closing shot. It says everything about the nonsensical prisons that we continually build for ourselves, and how we must always see beyond them. It is the perfect end to the finest of films.

Originally published as 'Jiří Menzel's Closing Shot,' 8 September 2020, https://lukemckernan.com/2020/09/08/jiri-menzels-closing-shot, and reproduced here with small emendations. Jiří Menzel died on 5 September 2020, aged eighty-two.

[1] *Larks on a String (Skřivánci na niti)*, Second Run DVD 057 (2011).

REALITIES

40.

The Running Man

The sequence photography of Eadweard Muybridge

It is perhaps the most iconic of all photographic images. Eadweard Muybridge's running man—he made several photographic sequences of a man running, but I am thinking of the one illustrated here—conjures up the very idea of photography. It has captured the instant, has brought a moment out of its specific time into all time. We can hear the click of the shutter. It is one of a sequence of twelve, any one of which can seen as representative, as all document the same action, but the point where both legs leave the air is the most quintessentially photographic. It is the image for which photography was made.

It is the point where the nineteenth century turns into the modern age. It does not just offer a view of the past—it makes the past coterminous with us. He started running in 1885 and he is running still in 2010. The plain background accentuates the timelessness, leaving us nothing to contemplate save bare, unaccommodated man. It sums up who we are: hurtling forward from who knows where to who knows where, yet never really going anywhere. It simultaneously celebrates and laughs at progress.

The image has classical resonances. There is an echo of Ancient Greek statuary and the Olympic ideal, but the stronger echo is with Leonardo da Vinci's 'Vitruvian Man' or the 'Proportions of Man,' the idealised, perfectly proportioned figure inscribed within a circle and a square. Muybridge's man, similarly ideally proportioned, is inscribed within a square. And da Vinci's image has an intimation of motion about it—the figure's body is static but there are two sets of arms and two sets of legs, indicating that idealised man can only be revealed in movement. I run therefore I am.

The image is about time itself. Just as in times past a skull might be used as a *memento mori*, a means for the observer to contemplate the death that must come to us all, the running man obliges us to contemplate the ceaseless flow of time. The image seeks to defeat time by capturing the moment—the science of sequence photography that Muybridge inspired was called chronophotography, which means 'picturing time.' A photograph does not capture time in any actual sense; it is a chemical (or now digital) illusion. But it does capture the idea of time, a thing for contemplation.

The image also represents the historical moment between the still image and the motion picture. Muybridge was interested in dissecting motion by capturing that which could not be detected by the naked eye, namely the individual elements of motion. He was not trying to create motion pictures, though he did experiment with these as a sideline. Motion pictures do not reveal the invisible as such; they replicate visible reality. But Muybridge's vision and technical accomplishment led the way to motion pictures as others built on the logic of what he had established. It is right that he is the usual starting point for histories of film.

The running man is also telling us a story. One of the most engrossing elements of the Muybridge exhibition currently at Tate Britain is how it leads us to imagine Muybridge playing out the psychodrama in his head following his acquittal for the murder of his wife's lover (and she died soon after). Much has been made of the women in his sequence photographs, shown as they are in submissive, playful, dancing, teasing, eroticised or domestic roles. The men, however, are all going somewhere, doing physical, masculine things—lifting, wrestling, throwing, marching, chopping, running. Muybridge himself appears (naked) in some sequences, and just as we can see all of the women in the photographs as Flora Muybridge, so all the men are Eadweard Muybridge, emblematised as the man running for the sake of running, wanting to be doing something that it is good for man to be seen doing, without really knowing why.

Then there is athletics itself. This is not just an image of a man out of time. It is a photograph, or a set of photographs, of an athlete. Competitive sports became hugely important in the late nineteenth century, and in 1878 Muybridge photographed members of the San Francisco Olympic Club. In 1884 he started work at the University of Pennsylvania, producing hundreds of photographic sequences, many of them showing athletes from the university. American universities were hotbeds of the new enthusiasm for sport, and sport was becoming an important expression of what it meant to be a (male) American. The running man is someone who ran with a purpose, who knew what it meant to run.

The sequence photographs of the running man did not come out of nowhere. Produced as part of Muybridge's *Animal Locomotion* series published in 1887, they came as the culmination of an exceptional career in photography.[1] As the exhibition makes clear, Muybridge was a photographer of considerable accomplishments long before he started photographing galloping horses and running men. His work ranged from stereoscopes (3D images) to extraordinary panoramas. He was a photographer of landscapes and cityscapes, always able to capture something beyond the mere replication of a reality. Even before he began his motion studies in the late 1870s he was revealing something of the mystery of time and motion in his work. The necessarily long exposures that came with wet plate photography meant that the apparent instant is really a record of the passage of seconds. The passing of time is reflected in the stillness.

The running man as an instantly recognisable symbol of what it is to be human is a part of modern culture. The man running ever forwards yet getting nowhere has been used in pop videos such as Talking Heads' 'Road to Nowhere' and U2's 'Lemon.' Videos inspired by Muybridge's work, often inspired by the figure running endlessly against a black background with white lines, can be found all over such sites at *YouTube* and *Vimeo*, as modern artists demonstrate a compulsion to revisit his vision. Muybridge sequences have been used on posters, book covers, murals, television trailers and T-shirts. The running man even runs endlessly across twelve frames on the lenticular ruler I bought at the exhibition.

---

[1] Eadweard Muybridge, *Animal Locomotion: An Electro-Photographic Investigation of Consecutive Phases of Animal Movements* (Philadelphia: University of Pennsylvania, 1887).

And then there is the science. For all that we can philosophise about time, or see the images as depicting a crisis in the idea of masculinity, or see them for the inspiration they gave to artists such as Duchamp, Bacon and Twombly (and Muybridge wanted to inspire artists), the running man and all the other *Animal Locomotion* sequences were commissioned by a body of scientists. The University of Pennsylvania paid him $40,000 to undertake work of a scientific character, and the committee that oversaw his work included an anatomist, a neurologist and a physiologist. The running man was there to be studied. He was demonstrating the processes of human motion, revealing action and musculature as it had not been possible to show them before. The white grid on the black background is there for scientific reasons: to gain the measure of a man.

The running man is not a complete work in itself. It/he is part of Plate 62 of *Animal Locomotion*, one of twelve images taken in succession, plus another twelve images giving a side-on view of the same action. It is one twelfth of a work that one cannot ever pin down. Looking at the twelve images in sequence does not really tell us what the work signifies; looking at one of the images does not give us the full work; looking at the sequence animated falsifies what Muybridge tried to achieve. And the man did not run forever, as the animations suggest. He ran from one end of the track to another. Then he stopped. Muybridge's work is endlessly mysterious to contemplate.

The Muybridge exhibition at the Tate is a marvellous experience. It covers every aspect of his remarkable career, clearly explained and illuminatingly displayed. There are his haunting images of Yosemite, the breathtaking panoramas of San Francisco, hypnotically beautiful cyanotypes (the blue-toned contact proofs from which published collotypes were made), and a Zoopraxiscope projector with which he exhibited proto-animation 'films' on disc, based on his photographic sequences. A little more context, in the form of the works of his peers and those he has influenced, would have been welcome, but about his work there can be no complaint. OK, perhaps just one. In the exhibition there is no Plate 62. There is Plate 63, in which the same athlete runs a little faster, and not quite as iconically—he leans forward too much. The quintessential Muybridgean image is not there.

Originally published as 'The Running Man,' 22 September 2010, https://thebioscope.net/2010/09/22/the-running-man, and reproduced here with small emendations. The 'Eadweard Muybridge' exhibition ran at Tate Britain in London 8 September 2010-16 January 2011. The book of the exhibition, Philip Brookman (ed.), *Eadweard Muybridge* (London: Tate Publishing, 2010) is a good guide to the different aspects of Muybridge's work, with contributions from Marta Braun, Andy Grundberg, Corey Keller and Rebecca Solnit. According to Muybridge's notebooks, the name of the running man was Percy C. Madeira (1862-1942).

41.

The Colours of War

Turning monochrome into colour in They Shall Not Grow Old

The image shows two opposing forces. On the left-hand side, British officers standing in a French village in 1916 during the Battle of the Somme are seen in monochrome: monochrome skin, monochrome clothing, monochrome buildings behind them. On the right, facing them, are British troops in colour: pink faces, khaki-green uniforms, blue and red buildings behind them. They seem lined up for a battle over archives and historical truth.

The still—derived from the 1916 documentary *The Battle of the Somme* (UK 1916)—has been published by the UK First World War centenary art organisation 14-18 NOW. It is promoting an as yet unnamed documentary film on the war, directed by Peter Jackson and made by his company WingNut Films, in association with the Imperial War Museums. The film is scheduled to be premiered at the London Film Festival in November 2018, with a BBC One broadcast, school and cinema screenings to follow. It is clearly being planned as a major contribution to the events marking the centenary of the end of the war. What is distinctive about Jackson's film is that, in words of the press release, it is to use 'modern-day techniques such as colourisation to portray the Great War as never before,' promising 'to provide a 21st-century public with a unique new perspective on the 20th century's most shocking conflict.'[1]

Colourisation has long been anathema to anyone with a respect for film history. Introduced commercially in the 1980s, it was intended to breath new commercial life into monochrome film libraries. A generation had grown up without black-and-white film or television, and which rejected monochrome as an annoyance. Hence the video shelves started fill with colourised Laurel

---

[1] 'A New Film by Peter Jackson,' *14-18 NOW*, January 2018, https://web.archive.org/web/20180122201825/https://www.1418now.org.uk/commissions/new-film-peter-jackson.

and Hardy. The colour itself was garish, unnatural, upsetting even. The film community reacted with alarm, demanding that films designed, dressed and lit to be shown in monochrome should only be seen that way. Cinephiles shivered in horror at the thought of a *Citizen Kane* or *Casablanca* in colour.[2]

They Shall Not Grow Old (via *The Battle of the Somme*).

Colourisation proved not to be a major commercial opportunity for the studios. Colour might put red on the cheeks of Oliver Hardy, but it could not make the manner or dialogue of old feature films anything other than pertaining to the times in which they were made. Colourised videos ended up in bargain bins, and the film heritage community breathed a little more easily.

But colourisation did not go away. Techniques improved, and were applied some time ago to First World War footage. In 2003 a six-part British television series, *World War One in Colour*, narrated by Kenneth Branagh and shown on Channel 5, rode on the bandwagon created by such series as *The Second World War in Colour* (UK 1999) and *The British Empire in Colour* (UK 2002). Those series had both used genuine colour footage; now, all the archive footage had been colourised. A monochrome war had been translated by a computerised paintbox.

---

[2] There is a good account of the original debate around colourisation in Anthony Slide, *Nitrate Won't Wait: A History of Film Preservation in the United States* (Jefferson, N. C./London: McFarland, 1992), pp. 122-133.

The problem with colourising monochrome from the First World War, aside from any ethical or aesthetic consideration, is that films are not a true colour record. Films of that period were made on orthochromatic stock, sensitive to green and blue, but lacking red sensitivity. Only with panchromatic stock, introduced in the 1920s, was sensitivity to all colours established. So the idea that by colourising a First World War film you were using the black-and-white record as a key to a hidden colour record was false. The authentic colour could not be digitally deduced from the monochrome. There were falsities of uniform colours, insignia, skin tones, skies and landscapes. It was a fantasy, the equivalent of a period colour postcard, or the artificially coloured films of the pre-war era, where colours were painted onto the film stock.

How, then, to cater for those who want to see the war in colour? There has been an interesting split in the reactions to the news of Jackson's film. Some, particularly among the film archiving community, have been horrified. For them it is a clear vulgarisation, misrepresenting the past for the cheapest of reasons. For others, the need for a stronger connection with the past outweighs this purist position, if indeed they are aware of it all. We can connect with colour. The alien past is made more meaningful. The people look just like us, and so the magic trick works.

One can argue that film is not reality, but a reflection of reality. Overlaying it with colour is only a further treatment of that reflection of reality, a way of looking at the past rather than the pretence of being the past itself. We will have to see Jackson's film to judge properly. But there is a fundamental issue here about how we treat our actuality film archives. The First World War was filmed in monochrome (a tiny amount of colour film was shot during the war in the Kinemacolor process, of which only a few minutes survive, showing the British fleet off Scapa Flow in 1915). To understand that inheritance we must look at it for what it is. Colourising archive actuality film does not bring us closer to our ancestors; it increases the distance between us. It threatens to make the First World War film archive we have inherited meaningless, because we can no longer look at it sympathetically. It is the effort that creates the understanding.

Yes, on some occasions archive film can and should be manipulated for particular ends. It need not always be treated reverently in its original form alone—that way elitism lies. But, to my mind, using it to show what it is not does more damage than good. If we want people to understand the past, we should not be colouring it.

Originally published as 'Colouring the Past,' 25 January 2018, https://lukemckernan.com/2018/01/25/colouring-the-past. A revised version was published as 'The Colours of War,' *Sight and Sound*, April 2018, p. 15 and is reproduced here with small emendations. When I wrote these pieces, the public had not seen the film that was released later that year as *They Shall Not Grow Old* (New Zealand/UK 2018). My reaction on eventually seeing it was still greater disappointment, as I felt the colourisation itself was unnaturalistic, while the monochrome that starts and ends the film, though run at too fast a speed, had much more to show. Others disagree about the film's qualities and its imposition of colour. See, for example, Ian Christie, 'Strange Meeting: *They Shall Not Grow Old*,' in *What Made Cinema? Visual Culture and Early Film—Selected Essays: Volume 1* (New York: Sticking Place Books, 2025), pp. 383-385.

42.

Pandaemonium and the Isles of Wonder

The influence of Humphrey Jennings on the opening ceremony of the 2012 Olympic Games

> Pandaemonium is the Palace of All the Devils. Its building began c.1660. It will never be finished—it has to be transformed into Jerusalem. The building of Pandaemonium is the real history of Britain for the last three hundred years.[1]

Frank Cottrell-Boyce, the writer behind *Isles of Wonder*, the extraordinary and widely acclaimed opening ceremony for the 2012 Olympic Games, had revealed in a *Guardian* article that a major inspiration for the work was Humphrey Jennings' *Pandaemonium*. Of the creative process with director Danny Boyle he writes:

> We shared the things we loved about Britain—the Industrial Revolution, the digital revolution, the NHS, pop music, children's literature, genius engineers. I bought Danny a copy of Humphrey Jennings' astonishing book *Pandemonium* for Christmas and soon everyone seemed to have it. The show's opening section ended up named *Pandaemonium*.[2]

Pandaemonium, as the BBC commentary noted on the night, was the name that John Milton gave to the capital of Hell in his epic poem *Paradise Lost*. It is also the title of Humphrey Jennings'

---

[1] Humphrey Jennings (ed. Mary-Lou Jennings and Charles Madge), *Pandaemonium, 1660-1886: The Coming of the Machine As Seen by Contemporary Observers* (London: André Deutsch, 1985), p. 5.

[2] Frank Cottrell-Boyce, 'London 2012: opening ceremony saw all our mad dreams come true,' *The Guardian*, 30 July 2012, https://www.theguardian.com/commentisfree/2012/jul/29/frank-cottrell-boyce-olympics-opening-ceremony.

The opening ceremony of London 2012.

posthumously published book which is a collection of nearly 400 contemporary texts dating 1660-1886 that, as the book's subtitle puts it, illustrate 'the coming of the machine as seen by contemporary observers.'

Humphrey Jennings (1907-1950) is generally recognised to be among the greatest of all British documentary filmmakers. In films such as *London Can Take It!* (UK 1940, co-directed with Harry Watt), *Listen to Britain* (UK 1942, co-directed with Stewart McAllister), *Fires Were Started* (UK 1943) and *A Diary for Timothy* (UK 1946), Jennings documented the relevance of the British experience of war to history, art, society and culture. Often described as a poet among filmmakers, he applied a poet's synthetic vision to the British condition at a time of national crisis. If you have not knowingly seen one of his films, you are very likely to have come across sequences from them, because they have been ceaselessly plundered by television for footage illustrating the impact of the war on Britain. For example, Andrew Marr's piece on the history of London that featured as part of the BBC's build-up programme ahead of the opening ceremony used several shots from *London Can Take It!*

That poet's synthetic vision was also applied to *Pandaemonium*, a collection of texts (or Images, as Jennings described them) which he worked on between 1937 and his accidental death in 1950, without ever shaping the material into a finished manuscript or finding a publisher. It was not until 1985 that his daughter Mary-Lou Jennings and Charles Madge (like Jennings, a co-founder of the social investigation organisation Mass-Observa-

tion) edited a version of the work that was close as could be hoped
to Jennings' conception.

Pandaemonium comprises texts from poets, diarists, scientists,
industrialists, politicians, novelists and social commentators who
wittingly or unwittingly document the great changes wrought in
British society by the industrial revolution. It begins with Milton's
description (written c.1660) of the building of Pandaemonium, and
anyone who saw Boyle and Cottrell-Boyce's vision of Glaston-
bury Tor, from which burst forth fire as the tree at its top was
uprooted, ushering in the industrial revolution will recognise its
inspiration in Milton's opening words:

> There stood a Hill not far whose grisly top
> Belch'd fire and rowling smoak; the rest entire
> Shon with a glossie scurff, undoubted sign
> That in his womb was hid metallic Ore,
> The work of Sulphur. Thither wing'd with speed
> A numerous Brigad hastens. As when bands
> Of Pioners with Spade and Pickaxe arm'd
> Forerun the Royal Camp, to trench a Field,
> Or cast a Rampart. Mammon led them on,
> Mammon, the least erectd Spirit that fell
> From heav'n, for eve'n his looks and thoughts
> Were always downwards bent, admiring ore
> The riches of Heav'ns pavements, trod'n Gold...[3]

The quotation at the head of this essay comes from notes
Jennings wrote for an introduction to the work. It confirms the
influence *Pandaemonium* had on Danny Boyle and his creative
team, not least in their sly critique of the corporately-sponsored
Olympics themselves, with the Olympic rings being forged in the
furnaces of the dark Satanic mills. Pandaemonium has been built,
and continues to be built—the task is to transform it into Jerusalem.
So Boyle and Cottrell-Boyce do not look for a return to that green
and pleasant land portrayed at the start of *Isles of Wonder*. Instead
they look with hopes toward what has and can still be built out
of it, to fulfil the vision expressed in William Blake's 'Jerusalem.'[4]

---

[3] John Milton, *Paradise Lost: A Poem Written in Ten Books* (1667), Book I,
ll.670-682.
[4] The last verse of 'Jerusalem' reads, 'I will not cease from Mental Fight / Nor
shall my Sword sleep in my hand / Till we have built Jerusalem, In Englands
green & pleasant Land.'

Vision is the operative word. In his introduction (as reconstructed by Charles Madge), Jennings says that his Images, whose construction he likens to 'an unrolling film,' illustrate 'the Means of Vision and the Means of Production.' The Industrial Revolution he sees as the victory of Production over Vision, of materialism over poetry, which has failed to keep up with, or to master, the changes brought about by industrialisation:

> It would take a large work on its own to show, in the great period of English poets 1570-1750, the desperate struggle that poets had to keep poetry's head into the wind: to keep it facing life. But by 1750 the struggle—like that of the peasants—was over. *In other words poetry has been expropriated.*[5]

Boyle and Cottrell-Boyce were inspired by Jennings, but they also sought to show how the argument has moved on since Jennings' time, to show that there could be a greater balance between production and vision. *Isles of Wonder* was divided into three main sections (with comic interludes featuring the Queen and Mr Bean). The first, 'Pandaemonium,' showed the march of industrial society over the green and pleasant land, but also the changes in society that the process unwittingly led to—women's suffrage, Jarrow marchers, the *Empire Windrush*, the Beatles. The second, 'Second Star on the Right and Straight on Till Morning,' took children's literature as its theme, pitting its villains (Cruella De Vil, Lord Voldemort) against the forces of collective good, represented by the National Health Service and a host of Mary Poppinses. It can also be seen as representing the revival of poetic sensibility and responsibility, the human urge towards the greater good, defeating the forces of Mammon. From thesis to antithesis to synthesis, and the third part, 'Frankie & June say... Thanks Tim' finds great hope in another revolution, the digital revolution (Tim being Sir Tim Berners-Lee, inventor of the World Wide Web). Here an interconnected society, themes from which we had seen prefigured in the earlier parts, overrides the forces that have divided it in the past, moving forward to—perhaps—Jerusalem.

Humphrey Jennings could never have conceived of such a spectacle as *Isles of Wonder*, but he might have understood the technique, not least with reference to his own documentary films. *Listen to Britain*—which could almost have been a subtitle for *Isles of*

---

[5] Jennings, *Pandaemonium*, p. xxxvii.

Wonder—is a portrait of national unity illustrated through the songs and sounds of a country at war. There is no narration, only images of the different corners of the land and different strata of society, bound together by effort and by sound (factories, Myra Hess playing piano at the National Gallery, variety entertainers Flanagan and Allen). *Spare Time* (UK 1939), a film closest in conception to Jennings' brief involvement with Mass-Observation, shows how Britain's working class enjoys its leisure time, from pubs to wrestling matches, from allotments to marching kazoo bands. Such films succeed through a subtle association of ideas, one image illuminating the next by association. As with his films, so it was with the unrolling film of Images in *Pandaemonium*, and now with *Isles of Wonder*.

> If you're trying to celebrate a nation's identity, you have to take things that are familiar parts of the landscape and make them wonderful.[6]

So writes Cotterell-Boyce, and they are words to explain the art of Humphrey Jennings as well. It is what a great documentary filmmaker can do: capture images of common stuff, and transmute them into something wonderful. To do so, it is necessary not just to photograph your subject well, or to edit with a satisfying rhythm. You must have a governing idea to give those images meaning. Humphrey Jennings wanted to see Jerusalem built once more; Danny Boyle and Frank Cottrell-Boyce have encouraged us all to dream of the same.

(And would you believe it, the name of the eleven-year-old boy who sang 'Jerusalem' at the start of ceremony was ... Humphrey. 'While I think his voice is brilliant, I admit I wasn't sure why they picked him at first' says Humphrey Keeper's schoolteacher in a *Times* interview.)[7]

Originally published as 'Pandaemonium and the Isles of Wonder,' 29 July 2012, http://britishlibrary.typepad.co.uk/movingimage/2012/07/pandaemonium-and-the-isles-of-wonder.html, the day after the opening ceremony of the London 2012 Olympic Games, and reproduced here with small emendations. The complete opening ceremony can be viewed on the Olympics *YouTube* channel at https://www.youtube.com/watch?v=4AsOe4de-rI.

---

[6] Cottrell-Boyce, 'London 2012.'
[7] Fay Schlesinger, 'Soloist an "Inspiration" to Disabled Children,' *The Times* [London], 30 July 2012, p. 11. Humphrey Keeper was born without a lower left arm.

43.

Filming Windrush

How and why newsreels of the Black British arrivals of 1948 were made

Newsreel films of the *Empire Windrush* and the arrival of West Indians at Tilbury Docks have been shown extensively in news programmes and documentaries, and widely shared on social media. The danger is that such films may be viewed with assumptions based on current media practice. To understand more fully what we are being shown, it is important to have a knowledge of news archives and contemporary news production. There are technical, as well as ideological, processes that have shaped the news of the past and the news archives that survive today. This essay considers how, and why, the Windrush story was reported in Britain at the time, across the different news media, with particular emphasis on newsreel films.

The passenger liner HMT *Empire Windrush* brought one of the first substantial groups of West Indian immigrants to the UK on 21 June 1948. Of the 1,027 passengers (and two stowaways), 802 had come from the Caribbean, most hoping to find employment following news of labour shortages in the UK, with an intention to settle.[1]

The arrival of these new Black Britons has gained great symbolic significance, with its seventieth anniversary in 2018 being the subject of considerable interest and some political fall-out, after some of the so-called 'Windrush generation' were threatened with deportation, an unintended consequence of a change in the UK's immigration laws. It was a news story back in 1948 as well, but how much of a news story?

---

[1] Lucy Rodgers and Maryam Ahmed, 'Windrush: Who exactly was on board?,' *BBC News*, 27 April 2018, https://www.bbc.co.uk/news/uk-43808007.

Windrush arrivals, from 'Pathé Reporter Meets,' Pathé News 48/51.

Newspapers

In 1948 there were four primary ways in which news was pub-
lished in the UK. The first was newspapers. At this time there
were nine daily national titles—in descending order of popularity,
*The Daily Express, Daily Mirror, Daily Mail, Daily Herald, News
Chronicle, Daily Telegraph, Daily Graphic, The Times* and *The
Daily Worker;* and nine Sunday titles—again in descending order
of readership, *The News of the World, The People, The Sunday
Pictorial, The Sunday Express, The Sunday Dispatch, The Sunday
Graphic, Reynolds News, The Sunday Times* and *The Observer.*
The 1948 Hulton Readership survey found that 87% of the adult
population read a daily newspaper, and 92% read a Sunday news-
paper.[2] Newspapers made the news.

The story was widely covered, but not as prominently as
might be expected. The top two titles put it on their front page on
22 June 1948, but for the *Daily Express,* the story '450 Arrive—
Get Pep Talk' had to compete with over twenty other stories on

---

[2] Mass-Observation, *The Press and Its Readers* (London: Art & Technics,
1949), pp. 12, 110-117.

the broadsheet page.[3] Its focus was on the unpreparedness of the Colonial Office, and the lecture the arrivals were given by an official on how things would not be as easy for those seeking work as they might have imagined.

The *Daily Mirror*, with eight stories on page one, had a brighter headline, '492 Men on Ship of Good Hope Hail England,' but likewise focussed on the difference between hopes and reality. It quoted discouraging words given to the arrivals by an RAF Welfare Officer, including the admonition 'No slackers will be tolerated.'[4] However, the story appears to have been dropped for the later edition that day, though it was the subject of a leader in the 23 June edition.[5]

The most widely-read newspapers reflected official disquiet over the very idea of letting people from the West Indies into the UK, despite the recent British Nationality Act which had defined British citizenship in global i.e. Commonwealth terms. That said, the *Daily Mail* had a welcoming tone to its 22 June story, 'Cheers for Men from Jamaica,' describing the operation as being 'emigration-in-reverse' (but it was on page three, not the front page).[6]

Radio
Then there was radio, which meant the BBC, whose Home Service broadcast six news bulletins a day, reaching a huge audience—there were over eleven million radio licences held in the UK in 1948.[7] The BBC radio bulletin on the Windrush arrivals, entitled 'Here to Work,' the various versions of which throughout the day survive as scripts, is mostly matter of fact about the numbers and arrangements. But it notes, as do the newspapers, the concerns that were being raised by some in government. 'Questions have been asked in the Commons about the wisdom of allowing them to travel,' it reports.[8] The BBC bulletin aspired towards the neutral, but in following the party line could not avoid the tone of official suspicion.

---

[3] '450 Arrive—Get Pep Talk,' *Daily Express*, 22 June 1948, p. 1.
[4] '492 Men on Ship of Good Hope Hail England,' *Daily Mirror*, 22 June 1948, p. 1.
[5] B. B. B. [Bernard Buckham], 'Do We Mean It?,' *Daily Mirror*, 23 June 1948, p. 2.
[6] 'Cheers for Men from Jamaica,' *Daily Mail*, 22 June 1948, p. 3.
[7] David Fisher, 'Media Statistics,' *Terra Media*, http://terramedia.co.uk/reference/statistics/index.htm.
[8] 'Here to Work,' *BBC Home Service*, 22 June 1948, script available at https://tinyurl.com/2p9s9umw. Print originals of BBC radio news scripts for 1930s-1970s are held by the British Library.

John Parsons (right) interviewing, from 'Pathé Reporter Meets.'

Newsreels

Thirdly, there were the newsreels. It might seem extraordinary to some now that people ever saw the news in cinemas, but the immediate post-war period, when cinemagoing was at its peak in the UK (there were 1,635,000,000 cinema admissions in 1946), practically every one of the UK's 4,700 cinemas showed a newsreel as part of its programme.[9] There were also some dedicated newsreel cinemas, which showed just newsreels, cartoons and travel films, mostly found in cities. Newspapers and radio were dominant, but newsreels nevertheless played a major part in building up people's picture of the news.

That idea of 'building up' is an important one. Much as we pick up our idea of the news today from different media—mostly online or on television, with newspapers of diminishing importance—so it was with a different balance of media in 1948. The newsreels were not able to be issued as frequently as newspapers or radio because they were made on film, which took time to develop, edit and distribute. The newsreels were issued twice a week—that is, they produced a new issue on Mondays and Thursdays; so, if

[9] Fisher, 'Media Statistics.'

you happened to go the cinema daily for some reason, you would have seen the same news for three or four days. This matched the traditional public habit of going to the cinema twice a week. It meant that the newsreels often showed stories that people already knew about from the papers or the radio. What the newsreels could do was provide moving pictures. They did not tell the whole story; they filled out the story.

There were five newsreels in the UK in 1948 — *British Movietone News*, *British Paramount News*, *Gaumont-British News*, *Pathé News* and *Universal News*. So, as with newspapers, but not radio, not everyone saw the same newsreel. Often the five newsreels covered the same story, but that was not the case with the Windrush arrivals. Two of the newsreels, *British Movietone* and *British Paramount*, did not bother.

Why was this? It is hard to say for sure, but the likeliest answer is that it was not seen as that big a story. It had had some coverage in the newspapers, but it was hardly a huge event, and the newsreels were as much in the entertainment business as they were in the news business. They selected stories for their visual interest and novelty as much as their currency.

It is interesting to see what stories each of the five British newsreels covered for Thursday 24 June 1948, the first release date after the Windrush story took place (21 June). We can see this from their issue records on the News on Screen database:[10]

> *British Movietone News*, issue no. 994A
> 'Wimbledon Opens'
> 'Beauty on Water Skis'
> 'Upsets Mar Soap-Box Derby'
> 'The Queen Starts the Marathon'
> 'And Sees Model Planes Fly'
> 'Sweden's King is 90 Years Old'
> 'Palestine — The Truce'
>
> *British Paramount News*, issue no. 1807
> 'Jews and Arabs Observe Truce in Palestine'
> 'Wimbledon Tennis Stars Get Going'
> 'News from the Junior Front: Children's Dog Show in
>   Hyde Park'
> 'News from the Junior Front: World's Smallest Dog'

---

[10] *News on Screen*, http://learningonscreen.ac.uk/newsonscreen.

'News from the Junior Front: Soap Box Derby in Germany'
'Western Germans Get New Currency'
'Veteran of Forty Wins Twenty-Six-Mile Marathon'

Gaumont-British News, issue no. 1510
'Opening of the Wimbledon Championships'
'Thrills and Spills on Land and Water'
'Roving Camera Reports: King Gustav's 90th Birthday'
'Roving Camera Reports: Palestine Truce'
'Roving Camera Reports: Jamaicans Arrive'
'Marathon Race Started by the Queen'

Pathé News, issue no. 48/51
'Queen Starts Marathon'
'Druids Hail the Dawn'
'Mayor Gives Chopstick Lunch'
'Abdullah Worships in Jerusalem'
'Pathé Reporter Meets' [Ingrid Bergman interviewed by
    film director Alfred Hitchcock on her arrival at
    Heathrow]
'Pathé Reporter Meets' [Jamaicans come to Britain to
    look for work. Interviewed by Pathé Reporter]

Universal News, issue no. 1872
'Open Air Art Exhibition'
'News in Brief' [safety devices]
'News in Brief'[Belgium—canoes 'shoot the rapids']
'News in Brief' [Monsieur Spaak's daughter weds]
'News in Brief' [Mr and Mrs Attlee visit 'Surrey Hills
    Clinic']
'News in Brief' [Germany—Boy's soap box race]
'News in Brief' [Children's dog show in London]
'News in Brief' [Polytechnic marathon at Windsor]
'News in Brief' [Jamaicans arrive for work in England]
'Lawn Tennis Championships at Wimbledon'

So there were three newsreel reports on Windrush. One of them,
produced by *Universal News*, does not survive in the archives, but it
was quite probably the same footage as featured in *Gaumont-British News* because the two newsreels were both part of the Rank
film company and co-operated closely. Therefore we have two
newsreel films available to us. Happily both can be seen online.

Newsreel operator filming the Windrush arrivals at Tilbury,
from 'Pathe Reporter Meets.'

The most significant, and the most widely-seen today, is that
produced by *Pathé News*, entitled 'Pathé Reporter Meets.'[11] It is a
fabulous film. The West Indian young men come across as engaging
and earnest, radiating an optimism that makes you want to cross
somehow into the screen and shake their hands. It culminates
in calypso singer Lord Kitchener (real name Aldwyn Roberts)
singing an acapella ode to his new home, 'London is the Place for
Me.' The commentary (by Pathé stalwart Bob Danvers-Walker) is
notable for its positivity, which would be a characteristic of British
newsreel coverage of West Indian immigration over the next few
years. There is reference to the less than kind reception that was in
the minds of some in government, which Danvers-Walker pointedly counters by stressing public favour, reminding the audience
of their best intentions: 'Prodded by public opinion, the Colonial
Office gives them a more cordial welcome than was at first envis-

---

[11] 'Pathé Reporter Meets,' *Pathé News*, 48/51, 24 June 1948, video file at https://
youtu.be/QDH4IBeZF-M and https://www.britishpathe.com/asset/84440,
shotlist at http://learningonscreen.ac.uk/newsonscreen/search/index.php/sto-
ry/102428.

aged.' The difference in tone to that adopted by newspapers and radio is notable.

The bright spirit of the film is aided greatly by the interviewer, John Parsons. His presence makes the newsreel story come across as more recognisable to us, as we are used to reporters asking questions before the camera. In 1948, however, this was a radical approach. Parsons was a former army officer who in 1947 had been recruited by Pathé's forward-thinking boss Howard Thomas to bring a new personal touch to the newsreel. On-screen reporters were seldom seen in the newsreels, which generally relied on an unseen commentator speaking over a musical background. Pathé's experiment was admired, but not adopted widely until television news as we understand it, with a presenter and reporter inserts, took off in 1955. The *Pathé News* report on the Windrush arrivals is therefore atypical of the average newsreel, but does show a medium that saw the need to develop.

That need to develop was recognised by the Pathé editor of the time, G. Clement Cave. He was keen to see the newsreel address social and political issues, setting aside some of the trivial filler material which had diminished the newsreel as a source of news in the eyes of critics. The Windrush story could be seen as one manifestation of this policy, though when it was released Clement Cave had been relegated to news editor after more overtly political coverage that analysed the background to topical stories had caused adverse comment from audiences and exhibitors.[12] Newsreels were obliged to be politically cautious. They were a part of the cinema programme, but occupied only a small part of that programme — ten minutes out of a show of three hours or more meant that they lacked sufficient muscle to be more challenging. Where they were shown determined their whole approach to the news.

We know more about how the Windrush newsreel was produced from the surviving paperwork.[13] The shotlist report submitted by the camera operators gives their names: Cedric Baynes and John Rudkin. The fact that there were two camera operators, alongside the reporter Parsons, indicates that this was a story that Pathé saw as being important. The average newsreel story usually had one camera operator and often no live sound. Money was spent on 'Pathé Reporter Meets' to give the story what they felt it merited. It was constructed to make an impact.

---

[12] Luke McKernan (ed.), *Yesterday's News: The British Cinema Newsreel Reader* (London: BUFVC, 2002), pp. 227-230.
[13] 'Pathé Reporter Meets,' shotlist.

The other newsreel film that survives is more perfunctory. *Gaumont-British News* could usually be relied upon for interesting coverage with smart commentary, but 'Roving Camera Reports Jamaicans Arrive,' from issue no. 1510, gives us a mere snapshot. There is just enough space for commentator Ted Emmett to tell us that these '400 happy Jamaicans' are here to help the Motherland—'so let's make them very welcome'—and it is all over in twenty seconds.[14] It would be an error, however, to judge a newsreel story only by its length. The Pathé coverage is noteworthy for the extra effort put into its production, but newsreels often functioned as visual reminders of a story that already had news currency. It was presence, not duration, that was significant.

The newsreels, despite their positive tone, were no less selective in what they chose to tell than the other news media. They all refer to Jamaicans, though there were passengers from other parts of the Caribbean, plus Polish refugees who had come via Mexico. The pictures suggest that young men predominated, but there were over 250 adult women on board, and eighty-six children.[15] Some had served in the Royal Air Force, but from the tone of the Pathé report you might think this applied to most of them (you sense Parsons' approval in the tone of his questions). Any news story is selective: a story, in effect.

Television

There is one other film of the Windrush migrants. Fourth among the news media types that reported on the story was television. It was the minor medium, as there were only 46,000 British households with television receivers at this time.[16] The BBC, which was the only television broadcaster in the country, had started broadcasting a bi-weekly news programme in January 1948, but it was unlike the news programmes we have today. Instead, *BBC Television Newsreel* was exactly like a cinema newsreel, with an unseen commentator and music playing over the stories.[17] It was, in effect, a cinema product shown on the small screen.

It covered the story for its broadcast of 25 June 1948. Sandwiched between stories on druids celebrating the Summer Solstice

[14] 'Roving Camera Reports: Jamaicans Arrive,' *Gaumont-British News*, 1510, 24 June 1948, video file at https://tinyurl.com/2983ntd2, see also http://learningonscreen.ac.uk/newsonscreen/search/index.php/story/66887.
[15] Rodgers and Ahmed, 'Windrush: Who exactly was on board?'
[16] Fisher, 'Media Statistics.'
[17] McKernan, *Yesterday's News*, pp. 239-245.

and the ninetieth birthday celebrations of King Gustav of Sweden, 'Jamaican Emigrants Arrive' nevertheless follows Pathé in letting one of the emigrants speak, though sadly the soundtrack is lost.[18] The surviving mute two-minute film, held in the BBC archives, shows the *Empire Windrush* at Tilbury, with the emigrants on deck. One is interviewed by an unseen reporter, speaking into a large microphone. They gather up their luggage and proceed down a gangway. It is a witness, but little more.

Television news had started humbly, and with few viewers. But it would soon evolve, coming up with presenter-led, live programmes by 1955, with the commercial ITV channel offering the BBC keen competition through Independent Television News (ITN). The millions moved from the cinema to the living room, and with that the newsreel, irredeemably out-dated, faded from British screens. The last *Pathé News* was released in February 1970.

What was different about the newsreel coverage of the Windrush migrants was not only its cordiality but how it was experienced. Newspapers, radio and television news were all consumed privately, or in a grouping no larger than a family. Newsreels, however, were seen in a cinema, where the viewer was joined by hundreds if not thousands of others. The newsreels understood that they were speaking to a crowd rather than an individual, which affected their whole tone of address. They spoke to a visible us.

This collective experience of news has been lost since the newsreels disappeared from British cinemas in the 1970s, but maybe there is some sort of inheritance in the way we read news on social media today. We each view our phone and computer screens as individuals, but we can follow the debate that a news story generates with an audience (mostly of our own choosing). We understand the news as something shared.

Despite this possible affinity with social media, there is much about the newsreels that will now seem strange. Some understanding of the conditions under which newsreels operated will, however, make them function once again for us as vital news forces. We are fortunate that so much of the British newsreel heritage is available on *YouTube*, including all of the Movietone and Pathé newsreels, covering much of the twentieth century. The newsreels added something important to the news, and in Pathé's report on Windrush we see the medium at its best. We feel ourselves to be

---

[18] 'Jamaican Emigrants Arrive,' *BBC Television Newsreel*, 25 June 1948. Held by BBC Archive.

part of that crowd, sharing in a news that was everyone's news, a news that spoke to all.

Originally published as 'Filming Windrush,' 26 September 2019, https://lukemckernan.com/2019/06/26/filming-windrush. An amended version was published online on the Sir Lenny Henry Centre for Media Diversity site, 22 June 2023, https://tinyurl.com/2s398nf6, and in print in *Representology: The Journal of Media and Diversity*, issue 5, Summer 2023. The above version is taken from the *Representology* version, with small emendations.

44

Another Time

Reliving the past through episodes of television football show
The Big Match

My favourite television programme of the moment is *The Big Match Revisited* (UK 2008-) on ITV4. This is a series of repeats of the revered ITV football highlights show, *The Big Match* (UK 1968-1992), which at the time that I remember it best—the 1970s—was shown on Sunday afternoons. It was never quite as good as the BBC's *Match of the Day* (UK 1964-), which stole its thunder by being shown, as it still is, on Saturday evenings, but was nonetheless essential viewing. It was presented by the avuncular Brian Moore, whose delivery, a combination of wry authority and moderate enthusiasm, was ideally suited to its times. It earned the trust of viewers, players and managers equally.

The Big Match Revised, after a brief modern voiceover, presents the original programme as broadcast, with only the advertisements changed. Currently it is showing games from the 1979-80 season. By that date I had lost most of the fervent interest I once had in the game, but the series nevertheless feels satisfyingly nostalgic—and something more than that.

There is plenty there for the nostalgist—the names of the past (whose destiny, for good or ill, you know but they cannot), the dreadful haircuts, the quagmires that passed for pitches, the huge shirt collars with complementary ties worn by the players in post-match interviews, the rules now lost (look, they can back-pass to the keeper), the standing fans, the perimeter advertisements that do not move, the shirts with numbers only, not sponsors' logos. In that simpler age there were no wingbacks, no one was credited for making an assist, no Video Assistant Referee...

All of this has great appeal, as do the games themselves, which do not show much of the skills and tactical thinking that we expect of Premiership matches today, but are fine contests for all that, particularly praiseworthy given all that mud. But the particular

The Big Match Revisited.

appeal to me, which the nostalgia naturally complements, is the sense of the playing out of lost time.

It is so rare to see extended actuality footage from the recognisable past. When television shows us historical programmes they are usually fictional or light entertainment. If we are shown actuality, it is shown in the form of archive clips used to illustrate a topic, or documentaries which have themselves turned the visual materials to hand into a particular didactic or narrative shape. On the rare occasions when we are permitted to see extended actuality, so lightly edited that it can pass for actual time, then it is of a notable historical event—the 1953 coronation, for example, or a high-profile sporting contest, such as the 1966 World Cup Final.

There is nothing historic about the matches on offer on *The Big Match Revisited*. They are, almost without exception, quite average. They are everything that anyone bar the most dedicated of fans of one or other side would forget. They are all style and little substance.

Their ordinariness, their forgettability, however, is what makes watching the repeats so compelling. Here is the extended here and now, only in the past, for an hour's broadcast (the programme generally shows highlights from two or three games). This ordinariness, alongside the tolerable colour video, and unobtrusive camera technique and editing, makes the programmes feel like now, or some other time that could be now. In another world, recognisably the one we share, these games are going on in the present. They are not so much repeats as an alternate time that might be the time in which we find ourselves, were it not for a few historical twists that are not in themselves of any great significance (VAR, logos, mud-free pitches, shorter hair). Fundamentally they share the pattern of the present.

I said 'recognisable past,' because there will be a limit to that sense of past time being time now. The colour over monochrome, the affordability of the extended record of mundane matches because of the cheapness of video as opposed to film, the change in the commentators' voices from the public school tones of the past to Moore's demotic, all help eliminate the sense of alienation that archive film can bring. The recognisability aids the affinity.

But you also need the extended time. You need to let the past unfold for a while, in its own form, making its time become your time. It needs time to persuade you of its normality, to persuade you that this other time is where you belong quite as much as the current time to which you believe that you belong. It is a liberating feeling—if anything, the complete opposite of the nostalgic. It is not time lost, or regained, because it was never lost in the first place. Instead it is happening now.

It can be argued—it has been argued—that film made a wrong turning when someone invented editing. It stopped letting things simply unfold before the camera, which is maybe all that film needs to do. Editing broke up time to make a point, to tell a story, to jolt us out of our reveries while equally propelling us into dreamworlds. Meanwhile, an ordinary reality kept rolling on, mostly eluding the camera, emerging fitfully in those overlong shots in home movies, in CCTV, and in weekly football highlights shows.

They are highlights, not the full game, but they extend things for long enough to give the sense of uninterrupted time. They are edited, naturally, and highly selective. We see the game but little of the crowds, and we always see the same kinds of shots because the shape of the pitches remain standard and the camera positions pre-determined to what depicts the game best. Just to point the camera anywhere is to be selective, and maybe what is real is only everything that the camera does not see. But in *The Big Match Revisited* I see that dilemma resolved. I see that which I need to see, which is the satisfactory passing of time. It does not matter whether I remember that time or not, because it is not about the past as a memory but rather the past as coterminous with the present.

The repeat that is new. This feels to be the special quality that belongs to programmes like *The Big Match Revisited*—not that there many other programmes like *The Big Match Revisited*, more's the pity. They are literally time-shifting. They make you think that perhaps nothing is lost after all.

Originally published as 'Another Time,' 6 October 2021, https://lukem-ckernan.com/2021/10/06/another-time, and reproduced here with small emendations. *The Big Match Revisited* was first broadcast on ITV4 on 7 February 2008. By 2025 it had reached its ninth series.

45.

The Dead

The impact of The Battle of the Somme

> Is it right to let us see men dying? Yes. Is it a sacrilege?
> No. If our spirit be purged of curiosity and purified with
> awe the sight is hallowed. There is no sacrilege if we are
> fit for the seeing [...] I say it is regenerative and resurrec-
> tive for us to see war stripped bare. Heaven knows that
> we need the supreme katharsis, the ultimate cleansing.
> We grow indifferent too quickly [...] These are dreadful
> sights but their dreadfulness is as wholesome as Tolstoy's
> 'War and Peace.' It shakes the kaleidoscope of war into
> human reality [...] I say that these pictures are good for
> us.[1]

Those words were written by journalist James Douglas on 25
September 1916. He was reacting to a screening of the film *The
Battle of the Somme* (UK 1916), a film whose impact upon audiences was unprecedented and—it could be argued—has never
been repeated. Douglas, like many commentators, was trying to
rationalise what he saw, to express the meaning and to find justifi-
cation for a film whose stark images of the war that was still raging
shocked audiences into a realisation of sacrifice and death. It was
the images of death in the film that so disturbed many. If soldiers
were not shown being killed (and some apparently were), then
every face that stared at the camera was likewise facing death. The
audience had been made witness to this, complicit in the soldiers'
fate.

While some called for the film not to be shown, for most it
was justified, to the point of becoming almost a moral obligation.
Through watching *The Battle of the Somme*, they gained a sense
of the enormity of what troops in their name were undergoing,

[1] James Douglas, *The Star,* 25 September 1916, p. 2. James Douglas was a British
journalist, editor of *The Star* newspaper from 1908 to 1920.

what the sacrifice (the optimum word) was that army and nation were making. Douglas' evocation of religious feeling put the film in terms that many would understand. It is not a pure reaction to the film itself—that is not possible. Instead he saw the film through his own thoughts on the meaning of war. Any image, any film, is identified by us through expectations and understandings that are informed by time, place and culture. *The Battle of the Somme* in 1916 was a different film to *The Battle of the Somme* in 2008.

This we can now judge through the release of the film for the first time on DVD, produced by the Imperial War Museum, whose archive preserves the film.[2] Alert to the complexities of authenticity, the IWM presents the film in a form that encourages us to question how we see what we see. Firstly, the film, for which no original negative survives, has undergone a digital restoration which has brought out details which were hitherto obscured. Even for those familiar with the film (and most in Britain must be familiar with it to some extent, given the widespread use of sequences from the film in television documentaries), it is like seeing the film anew. But the major coup is the music. We are given two music tracks. One is a modern score by Laura Rossi, a symphonic work for full orchestra. The other is a recreation by Stephen Horne of a likely original score, taken from a contemporary cue sheet which suggested the sort of musical passages musicians might want to adopt in accompanying the film in 1916.

The latter will amaze many. Jaunty marches and popular airs accompany scenes of troops marching to the killing fields of the Somme, the scenes of battle and their aftermath. What were they thinking of in 1916? It is a complicated question to answer. Partly the musicians of the time were responding to what might have seemed just another war actuality film, which required patriotic accompaniment. But also the audience of the time saw heroism and uplift where we, after almost a century of awful contemplation of the futility of that war, bolstered by poems, novels and films, see something profoundly pitiable. It is with consciousness of such modern expectations, but equally with a sense of being true to the film's original vision, that Rossi supplies a rich, subtle and binding score that connects 2008 to 1916. Which of these two very different scores will you prefer to listen to, and why? Or might your preferred option be to witness the film in silence?

---

[2] *The Battle of the Somme.* SN6540. Strike Force Entertainment/Network/Imperial War Museum (2008).

Recreated 'over the top' shot from *The Battle of the Somme.*

The digital restoration, which allows us to see so much, is perhaps most striking when it comes to the famous 'over the top' sequence. This is the part of the film that will be most familiar. It is shown on television (at least in the UK) every time a shot is needed to evoke the First World War. Troops clamber over the top of a slope, then march slowly over barbed wire away from the camera, a couple of men falling down as they do so.

Oh God, they're dead!

Such are the words a woman is reported to have exclaimed in a cinema showing the film, and it was this sequence that aroused the greatest comment at the time, the greatest need to explain the film's significance.[3] But they were not dead. As is now known, the sequence is a fake, set up in a trench mortar battery school some time afterwards, simply because the actual scenes taken of troops going over the top were deemed disappointing. At the time, no one knew of this subterfuge, and as far as reception is concerned, it did not matter. People believed they were witnessing death on screen; and producers and exhibitors felt this to be an acceptable thing to show. Which you may think is extraordinary.

---

[3] 'Rambler,' 'Round and About,' *The Bioscope*, 24 August 1016, p. 671.

What seldom gets shown on television is the shot that immediately follows the 'over the top' sequence in the film. This shows genuine footage of troops going over the top. But we see them only in the far distance. The cameramen—there were just two, J. B. McDowell and Geoffrey Malins, the latter of whom shot both 'over the top' sequences—were greatly restricted in what they could shoot. Their hand-cranked cameras had single 50mm lenses with poor depth of field, they had no telephoto lenses, the orthochromatic film stock was slow, making filming action in the distance or in poor light difficult. But there was also military control and official censorship, each preventing them from filming anything other than officially-sanctioned images. And there was the danger. The most obvious indication of the 'fake' nature of the first sequence is that the cameraman would have been in absolute peril of his life had it been genuine. But for the shot that follows, Malins is a long way off, and far in the distance we can just pick out tiny figures on the horizon—British troops, coming over the top and marching into no-man's land. Looking closer into the middle ground, the digital restoration now reveals to us a sight not previously detected in the film: a number of troops proceeding leftwards, one or two of whom fall down. Oh God, they're dead.

Do we want to look that closely? Can they really seem dead when viewed at such a distance? Is the death we seek not in the falling bodies, or even in the corpses seen later in the film, but rather in the eyes of the still living, whose fate awaits them, and who are all dead now of course? That was a line the film historian Denis Gifford would sometimes come out with when we were in the basement theatre at the British Film Institute, watching some collection of British silent short films. The figures would parade to and fro, some of whom he knew, having interviewed them in the 1960s, but then that sad moment of realisation:

They're all dead now, of course.

This is a poignancy that seems particularly linked to the non-fiction film. Dramatic films, of whatever age, are attempting to entertain. Either they do or they do not. But the film of actuality trades on the depiction of life, and then the distance created by time. This was recognised even in 1916. Sir Henry Newbolt wrote a poem inspired by the experience of watching the film, entitled 'The War Films,' made memorable by its opening line:

O living pictures of the dead,
O songs without a sound,
O fellowship whose phantom tread
Hallows a phantom ground —
How in a gleam have these revealed
The faith we had not found.[4]

The Battle of the Somme captures the point of loss, the ghosts on the screen, the living pictures of the dead. Of course it is a deeply partial record. It shows no real fighting beyond shellfire, no serious injuries, no pain, little hatred (look for the shove that one British soldier gives to a captured German who stumbles past him). And of course it shows only the Allied point of view; the Germans would respond with their own film, *Bei unseren Helden an der Somme* (*With Our Heroes on the Somme*) in 1917. But we recognise it for what it is able to show, not for what it leaves out. It is a profoundly memorable expression of the hopes and fears of its age.

The Battle of the Somme was filmed by Malins and McDowell, two experienced newsreel cameramen, who knew well how to capture plain packages of actuality. McDowell was the senior of the two, who ran his own film company, British & Colonial. Malins had been filming on the war front for longer, and is the better known, not least for his somewhat vainglorious memoir, *How I Filmed the War*.[5] The film was edited by producer Charles Urban, with some assistance from Malins. Urban saw that the footage Malins and McDowell had shot would work best at feature length, rather than as a series of ten-minute shorts which had been the practice up until then. His vision gave the film the presence it needed to capture the audience that it found. The producer was William Jury, and the film was made for the British Topical Committee for War Films, a trade body working under War Office sanction, which would be replaced by the War Office Cinematograph Committee once the film started to enjoy huge success. It has been estimated that it was seen by 20,000,000 people in the UK in six weeks—almost half the population.[6]

---

[4] Sir Henry Newbolt, 'The War Films,' *The Times* [London], 14 October 1916, p. 7.
[5] Lieut. Geoffrey H. Malins, *How I Filmed the War: A Record of the Extraordinary Experiences of the Man Who Filmed the Great Somme Battles etc.*, (London/Nashville, Tennessee: The Imperial War Museum/The Battery Press, 1993) [facsimile edition, book originally published 1920].
[6] A figure calculated by Nicholas Hiley in *Making War: The British News Media and Government Control, 1914–1916*, vol. II. PhD thesis, Open University, 1985, p. 735.

Genuine 'over the top' long shot from *The Battle of the Somme.*

The DVD comes with the alternative music scores, commentaries, interviews with archivists and musicians, and five 'missing' scenes and fragments. We do not know what the original *The Battle of the Somme* was like exactly; the version that survives was re-edited, and the footage used in other films, during and after the war. Rather than insert these extra scenes where it is not quite certain they should go, the IWM has chosen to present them (without music) separately. There is a booklet as well, with information on the film's production, reception, restoration and particularly its music. It is a magnificent achievement, one whose influence on research, teaching and the appreciation of First World War history is likely to be considerable. The only possible disappointment is the menu, which simply divides the film into its five parts, where a more detailed use of chapters could have helpfully guided researchers to particular points of action, regiments, location etc.

More will follow. The booklet notes the future publication of Alastair H. Fraser, Andrew Robertshaw, and Steve Roberts' *Ghosts on the Somme*, a book which analyses the film in great detail, overturning some of the traditional understanding of who filmed what, which regiments are shown, and which locations are featured, while confirming that the vast majority of the film is genuine actuality.[7] There is still more to be discovered about *The Battle of the Somme*. It is a film we will have to return to, again and again.

Originally published as 'The Dead,' 1 November 2008, https://thebioscope.net/2008/11/01/the-dead, and reproduced here with small emendations. The DVD was reissued in 2014 by Strike Force Entertainment and Imperial War Museums (as the IWM is now called). *The Battle of the Somme* was recognised by UNESCO in 2005 by being accepted for inscription on its Memory of the World register.

---

[7] Alastair H. Fraser, Andrew Robertshaw and Steve Roberts, *Ghosts on the Somme: Filming the Battle, June-July 1916* (Barnsley: Pen & Sword Military, 2009).

46.

The Siege of Sidney Street

Anarchists before the news cameras in 1911

On the night of 16 December 1910 a group of Latvian revolution-aries attempted to rob a jeweller's shop at 119 Houndsditch in the City of London. Their aim was to obtain funds to support revo-lutionary activity in Russia, and to support themselves, but their efforts to break in were overheard and nine policemen were called to the scene. The Latvians were armed; the policemen were not, and in the ensuing confrontation three of the police were shot dead and two injured.

The public was horrified by what swiftly became known as the Houndsditch Murders, which followed on from the 'Tottenham Outrage' of the previous year when two Latvians had shot dead a constable and a child following an interrupted robbery. One of the Houndsditch gang, George Gardstein, had died of his inju-ries, having been shot accidentally by a confederate, but a huge manhunt built up to track down all of the gang, a number of whom were arrested before two (neither of whom it is now thought were present at the Houndsditch burglary) were tracked down to 100 Sidney Street, Stepney in London's East End.

The Siege of Sidney Street (or the Battle of Stepney) that was to follow took place 100 years ago on 3 January 1911. It has gained lasting fame for unprecedented scenes that brought armed police and troops onto the streets of London to conduct a siege with desperate revolutionaries, all of which took place before the star-tled, and undoubtedly thrilled, eyes of the public and the press. Among those recording the events as they happened were five film companies, and it is their story that justifies centenary account.

The besieged Latvians were Fritz Svaars and William Sokoloff, known as Joseph. They had taken refuge at 100 Sidney Street only for their position to be given away by an informant late in the evening of New Year's Day. Detectives were sent under cover of darkness to watch over the building while they tried to determine the two men's movements by contact with a lodger and the informant. Keen not to have the men slip out their grasp, but knowing they would be armed, the police felt they had to act. In the early hours of Tuesday 3 January, armed police were positioned in houses and shops surrounding the block which contained 100 Sidney Street. By 3.00am there were 200 policemen in place. It was realised that storming the building by its staircase would be too hazardous, as the two men would have the advantage by firing down on the police officers, so the adjacent buildings were cleared of other people and the police waited for daylight.

As dawn broke, people started to gather around the police cordon, trying to find out what was happening. The police threw stones at the second-floor window where they believed the two men were hiding. Nothing happened. Then someone threw a brick and smashed a window pane. From the floor below shots fired out and a policeman was hit. A hail of bullets followed as they tried to move the wounded man. The two men were well-armed, certainly better munitioned than the police, and well-positioned. An order was sent to bring in troops from the Tower of London. Scots Guards were sent, on the authority of the Home Secretary, Winston Churchill, who thought upon hearing the news that it would be interesting if he were to go along and see things for himself.

By this time the press had got wind of the story, and reporters, photographers and newsreel cameramen were arriving on the scene. Five film companies were present: Pathé, Gaumont, Andrews Pictures, Co-operative and the Warwick Trading Company. Pathé (*Pathé's Animated Gazette*), Gaumont (*Gaumont Graphic*) and Warwick (*Warwick Bioscope Chronicle*) had each recently established newsreels and were companies with well-established news-film credentials. Co-operative specialised in Shakespeare productions, so it is something of a surprise to see them involved, while Andrews Pictures was a small-scale film renter and exhibitor. Presumably any firm who learned what was happening and had a camera operator at the ready made the most of the opportunity.[1] Three of the five films taken that day survive: those of Pathé, Gaumont and Andrews.

The troops assumed positions around the building and around 11.00am began firing. The barrage of fire from both sides was relentless and was to continue for around two hours. The crowds around the perimeter were now considerable, and policemen had

---

[1] Frame stills from each of the films made of the siege, including those made by Co-operative and Warwick which are now lost, are reproduced in 'The Battle of London,' *The Bioscope*, 5 January 1911, p. 9.

Newseel images of the Siege of Sidney Street
from *The Bioscope*, 5 January 1911.

a difficult time holding them back, as the newsreel record make clear. The films show the heaving crowds, the troops getting into position, policemen armed with rifles, and gunfire coming from the buildings either side of Sidney Street.

The Home Secretary had not been able to get the better of his curiosity. He arrived by car at midday and positioned himself at the corner of Sidney Street and Lindley Street, peering round to see what was happening. It was an extraordinarily foolhardy action, one which would soon lead to much criticism, and regret on Churchill's part, but at the time the idea went round that he was directing operations. Pathé's cameraman gained a huge scoop by obtaining close shots of Churchill, though a story which circulated that film was taken of a bullet going through his top hat is quite false. It seems that no other newsreel filmed him — Gaumont certainly did not, as they were positioned on the other side of the street, while Andrews resorted to deceit, declaring that its footage of men looking down at the siege included a rear view shot of Churchill (Churchill did not take up any rooftop position).

Home Secretary Winston Churchill (in top hat) watching the Siege of Sidney Street, part of the *Pathé's Animated Gazette* coverage.

Then 100 Sidney Street caught fire. The gunfire ceased momentarily as wisps and plumes of smoke started to pour out of the building, which is vividly shown in the film record. Flames could be seen from the windows, then the shooting started up again — not just from the soldiers, because, extraordinarily, the men inside were still returning fire. Joseph may have been shot dead at this time (the fire started around 1.00pm), while Fritz Svaars died in the flames when the roof caved in and part of the first floor collapsed. Soldiers fired further volleys, then ceased. No one had escaped from the building and it was clear no one could have survived such an inferno. Fire engines arrived and poured water on the charred remains. As firemen entered the building, part of a wall collapsed and one of them, Charles Pearson, later died of his injuries—the third and final death caused by the siege of Sidney Street.

The bodies of Fritz Svaars and Joseph were discovered inside, the second only as late as 8.00pm, by which time the newsreel films had been processed, printed and were on show in some London cinemas, scooping much of the press. In the manner of newsreels at this time, the films let the pictures do the talking. Intertitles on the extant films are matter-of-fact and offer little in the way of explanation, though they do employ loaded terms such as 'assassins,' 'murderers,' 'aliens' and 'outrage.' The sensational nature of the films was all that was needed. Detailed description and background speculation was for the newspapers; the newsreels had simply to show audiences what the event looked like, to present the moving pictures of what everyone was talking about. The audience themselves would supply the rest.

These were the Houndsditch Murderers, or at least their associates, and most of the public would not have been greatly interested in their affiliations and what drove them to such desperate actions. Their war was not with the British authorities *per se*, but rather with Tsarist Russia. They—and there were a dozen or so associated with Houndsditch and Sidney Street—were refugees in Britain, which they used as a base for fund-raising and plotting revolution back in Russia. They had strong ideological motivation, and would have been contemptuous of the British police and army as tools of the oppressors. For the popular press they were all anarchists, but most had Social Revolutionary or Marxist affiliations, and had fought in terrible encounters with Tsarist forces, some of them undergoing savage beatings and torture. They believed they would receive similar brutality from the British police should they be caught, which helps explain some of their actions (Fritz Svaars in particular feared that he would break under torture after beatings he had received in Riga a year before). They used robbery to raise funds to support themselves and associates at home, and in some cases for gun-running or the production of propagandist literature.

Most were Jewish, and were part of the wave of refugees driven out of Russia by the pogroms of the late 1800s and the savage reprisals that followed the failed 1905 revolution. Britain had a reputation as a haven for such refugees, though most ended up in the sweatshops of the East End, desperately poor and roundly despised by the rest of society as 'aliens.' British film contributed to this climate of hostility. Hepworth produced *The Aliens' Invasion* (UK 1905), in which English workmen were shown being thrown out of work because of Jewish immigrants accepting low wages; the Precision Film Company produced *Anarchy in England* (UK 1909), which recreated the Tottenham Outrage; while Clarendon made *The Invaders* (UK 1909), in which armed foreign spies occupy a British house disguised as Jewish tailors. However, most often films portrayed anarchists as figures of fun, as in Walturdaw's *The Anarchist and the Dog* (UK 1907), in which he throws his bomb, but the dog retrieves it. The siege of Sidney Street itself was not dramatised at the time, but the basic details contribute to the climactic scenes of Alfred Hitchcock's *The Man Who Knew Too Much* (UK 1934) and a close recreation was attempted in Hammer's *The Siege of Sidney Street* (UK 1960).

The causes that drove the revolutionaries of 1911 have faded into history, even if terrorism on British shores inspired by overseas conflict and a different set of beliefs has not. But the films remain, and the press reports, and the photographs, and the many picture postcards that were produced, as tragedy was turned into commerce. The films not only show extraordinarily exciting things happening on the streets of London, but they show us an area of London never before visited by the motion picture camera. The wretched, run-down area of Stepney of 1911 would not have attracted cameras in the normal course of events, but humble Sidney Street, its environs and inhabitants gain some sort of fleeting immortality each time we run the films again, before disappearing back into history as the cameras once more turn to focus elsewhere.

Originally published as 'The Siege of Sidney Street,' 2 January 2011, https://thebioscope.net/2011/01/02/the-siege-of-sidney-street, and reproduced here with small emendations. For further information on the Sidney Street siege, Donald Rumbelow's *The Houndsditch Murders and the Siege of Sidney Street* (London: Macmillan, 1973, revised W. H. Allen, 1988) is the classic account, outstanding in the dramatic detail and in its understanding of both police procedure and the revolutionaries' motivations. Andrew Whitehead, *A Devilish Kind of Courage: Anarchists, Aliens and the Siege of Sidney Street* (London: Reaktion Books, 2024) has a useful focus on the role of the media, including the newsreels. Three of the five newsreels made of the Sidney Street siege exist, though some surviving copies are incomplete and/or confused with other films of the events. These are *The Battle of London* (Pathé), copies held by the BFI National Archive and British Pathé; *The Great East End Anarchist Battle* (Gaumont), copies held by the BFI National Archive and Reuters; *Houndsditch Murderers* (Andrews Pictures), copies held by the BFI National Archive, British Pathé and Reuters. The BFI also has a *Pathé's Animated Gazette* newsreel item on the December 1910 funeral of the policemen whose deaths led to the Sidney Street siege, *Funeral in London of the Policemen Murdered by Burglars in Houndsditch* (UK 1910).

.

47

Lumière Forever

Cinema's outstanding start

Most honest histories are untidy; early film history especially so. The first years of cinema were a complex field in which the different elements that would make up the medium were "invented" at different stages, in which the many participants engaged in its creation held widely different understandings of just what the medium meant, and in which the medium was profoundly interlinked with many other cultural, social and economic phenomena. All we should know of early film history is that we do not know it well enough.

Such uncertainty is not reflected in many a written history of the medium. In these, the story is expressed in easy stages: from experimentation, to invention, to illumination, to commercialisation. In this simple history, the work of the Lumière brothers, Louis (1864-1948) and Auguste (1862-1954), is paramount. The one thing someone is likely to know about the birth of cinema is that the two French brothers were pre-eminent, and something about people supposedly running away from film of a train approaching at the first film show. And with that lesson in the medium's roots we can moved on quickly to lesson two, D. W. Griffith, and engage with a cinema that we can recognise.

Why has the legend of the Lumières come to loom so large? It has something to do with the pride of a nation traumatised by defeat in the Franco-Prussian War (1870), which seized on certainties that would confirm its cultural strength in the competitive world of the twentieth century. It has something to do with the cult of invention, the belief in a perfect coming together of conception and realisation (such as is seldom experienced in reality). But it also has much to do with the very excellence of the films that the Lumières made. What other medium could boast such a creative, mature body of work with which to launch itself on the world? For some, cinema has yet to improve on the outstanding start that it made.

Cinématographe Lumière at the Institut Lumière, France.

This is demonstrated in the marvellous two-disc DVD/ Blu-ray set *Lumière!*, recently published by France Télévisions Distribution and the Institut Lumière.[1] It presents 114 of the 1,422 films made for and by the Lumières over the period 1895-1905. The films have undergone a 4K digital transfer, with startling results. We cannot say if the films ever looked quite so good at the time, given the vagaries of the contemporary technology and its operators, but they certainly look better than most of us will have experienced up until now. For those accustomed to grey-ish Lumière short films shown on 16mm in film study classes, or the much-copied titles that have ended up on *YouTube*, the films on *Lumière!* will come as a revelation.

Equally revelatory will be the range of films on offer. The Lumières, having shot their initial films over 1895 and early 1896 themselves—often domestic scenes featuring family members— sent out operators around the world, to exhibit their Cinématographe camera/projector, and to take new films to add to the Lumière catalogue. The Lumières managed a photographic material business, and had extensive contacts upon which they could build this new business. They had a clear vision of what to film: for the most part, postcard-like views of celebrated places, a gazetteer of the renowned. The films on *Lumière!* show scenes from France, Britain, Egypt, Indo-China (Vietnam), Russia, Ireland, Spain, Switzerland, the USA and Japan. There are views from a balloon in flight, ascending the Eiffel Tower, upon an Alpine glacier, in an opium den, and on a Belfast football field.[2] It is the world of 1900 from every conceivable angle, sparkling before us as though filmed yesterday.

But it is not *what* was filmed, but *how* it was filmed, that is so magical. Practically speaking, all Lumière films were exactly the same. There was fifty feet (seventeen metres) of film available for a Cinématographe operator, and consequently all the films are of equal duration. The camera stayed in a fixed position—there were some travelling shots, from trains and boats, to give a panoramic effect, but there is none of the arsenal of cinematographic techniques that would follow in the Lumières' wake. There are some fictionalised films and records of performers, including dancers

---

[1] *Lumière!*, two-disc set, France Télévisions Distribution/Institut Lumière (2015).
[2] The *Lumière!* DVD gives London as the location for *Football* (France 1897), no. 699 in the Lumière catalogue, but recent research has identified the location as Belfast for a match between Glentoran and Gliftonville.

Repas de bébé with Auguste Lumière,
his daughter Andrée and wife Marguerite.

and a puppet skeleton, but for the most part the films are studied actualities.

It is these constraints that formed the great art of the Lumière Cinématographe—that, and a talented team of photographers trusted to do their masters' bidding (Alexandre Promio, Gabriel Veyre, Charles Moisson, Marius Sestier *et al*). They captured *le moment juste*. They composed their images with the greatest care, filming in bright sunshine for the sharpest image, and determining the ideal combination of lateral interest and action in depth. They are compositions in the finest photographic sense.

But there is more to Lumière films than that. In a celebrated essay, 'Let there be Lumière,' the late Dai Vaughan wrote of the films' special quality being that they were created at a time before audience assumptions about cinema existed. With later films,

> [a]s audiences settle for appearances, according film's images the status of dream or fantasy whose links with a prior world are assumed to have been severed if they ever existed, film falls into place as a signifying system whose articulations may grow ever more complex. True, the movement of leaves remains unpredictable; but we know that, with the endless possibility of retakes open to

the filmmaker, what was unplanned is nevertheless what has been chosen: and the spontaneous is subsumed into the enunciated.[3]

Writing of the Lumière film *Barque sortant du port* (France 1895) (sadly not included on *Lumière!*), which shows a boat heading out from a harbour from which a small group watches its departure, Vaughan says that it

> begins without purpose and ends without conclusion, its actors drawn into the contingency of events. Successive viewings serve only to stress its pathetic brevity as a fragment of human experience. It survives as a reminder of that moment when the question of spontaneity was posed and not yet found to be insoluble: when cinema seemed free, not only of its proper connotations, but of the threat of its absorption into meanings beyond it. Here is the secret of its beauty. The promise of this film remains untarnished because it is a promise which can never be kept: a promise whose every fulfilment is also its betrayal.[4]

It is a beautiful conceit, maybe a little too beautiful. Lumière films were not the first films; the brothers had been inspired by the Edison Kinetoscope peepshow with its earthy records of variety acts, and the chronophotographic brevities of the German inventor Ottomar Anschütz. There had been many optical toys depicting motion which had played their part in building up an expectation of the reproduction of movement. The Lumières were already working within a tradition, which 'many of their audience would have understood as well as the Lumières themselves. Vaughan's view is that of someone who is trying to divest himself of a subsequent cinema history; it is acute, but nostalgic.

I would say that what distinguishes Lumière films is their sense of endless time. In some way akin to the repeated significations of movement displayed by optical devices such as the Zoetrope, or the one-second-long image sequences on a rotating disc that Anschütz's 'Electrical Wonder' machine showed, the films of the Cinématographe offer the promise of unceasing repetition. Lumières were not shown on a loop, and their actions

---

[3] Dai Vaughan, *For Documentary: Twelve Essays* (Berkeley/Los Angeles/London: University of California Press, 1999), pp. 7-8.
[4] Vaughan, *For Documentary*, p. 8.

generally show a beginning and an end. But there is something of the eternal about them. That train will always be approaching the station, that boat will always be leaving the harbour, those leaves will always be fluttering in the background as the proud Auguste and Marguerite Lumière feed their daughter Andrée, in *Le repas de bébé* (France 1895), the movement of which so transfixed audiences at the time. They are films that we seem compelled to watch over and over again, trying to unpick their mystery. Reports from the time indicate that the original audiences were driven by much the same compulsion.[5]

Early commentators wrote of how Lumière films offered the illusion of immortality, a simulacrum of life itself. This, I think, derived not simply from the illusion of life replayed that motion pictures offered, but the formulaic, repeatable actions that the films preserved—walking, marching, feeding, dancing, playing. Here was the unending round of life, such as had been mimicked by earlier optical toys, but now made startlingly real through moving photographs. It was what must have so entranced those first audiences, to see the familiar made eternal. They were animated pictures—pictures with the soul of life (*anima*) breathed into them.

There is much more to see in *Lumière!* It is a tour around the world, collecting what were in most cases the first moving images produced in the countries featured. It is a telling document of the comfortable world and fixed outlook of the French bourgeoisie. It is a collection of many examples of great cinematographic art, such as the dazzling backward tracking shot filmed by Gabriel Veyre in what is now Vietnam, *Le village de Namo* (France 1900). It is a collection of many iconic films that are essential for anyone professing themselves to have a knowledge of cinema.

Lumière! is a handsomely-produced set, with much care having gone into its presentation. It is very much a French production, with ne'er so much as a word of English on the box, booklet, titles or commentary. The films are divided into chapters, from first films, to scenes of France, to scenes overseas, to comedies, and so on. You can watch the films without any sound, or with

---

[5] Sample eyewitness reports of Lumière shows can be found on the Picturegoing site e.g. in Paris, *The Referee*, 12 January 1896, p. 1, https://picturegoing.com/?p=5385; in New York, 'Keith's Union Square," *The New York Dramatic Mirror*, 11 July 1896, p. 17, https://picturegoing.com/?p=5176; and in Nizhny-Novgorod, 'I.M. Pacatus' (Maxim Gorky), *Nizhegorodski listok*, 4 July 1896, https://picturegoing.com/?p=230.

commentary, or with music (Camille Saint-Saëns obliges), or with titles giving production information—and choose whichever permutation of these suits you. A second disc comes with an assortment of films with background information and expressions of enthusiasm from the great and good of film. Aside from the absence of multi-lingual options, my only criticism would be the limitation of dividing the films up into chapters, when one would like to have the option of going direct to individual films.

One can feel some resistance to the cult of the Lumière brothers, who have been subject to a little too much uncritical hagiography. The legend has been protected to a point where it becomes unhelpful. There is no good critical history of the Lumières. There have been no proper studies, that I know of, that explain in full how their business worked. It has been made too difficult for a general audience to see these films—it is very late for an official DVD/Blu-ray issue like this to have been produced. A braver, more imaginative gesture would have been to release every film onto *YouTube* (or *Daily Motion*, its French equivalent) for free and let a new audience discover the films and make of them what they will. But the legend has to be protected, or else it ceases to be a legend. More's the pity.

Nevertheless, *vive Lumière*. And, especially now, *vive la France*.

Originally published as '*Lumière Forever*,' 15 November 2015, https://lukemckernan.com/2015/11/15/lumiere-forever, and reproduced here with small emendations. It was written two days after the Islamist terrorist attacks at the Bataclan theatre and the Stade de France in Paris.

48.

A World is Turning

An unfinished film celebrating Black British achievement

Back in my time working as a cataloguer at what was then called the National Film Archive, then the National Film and Television Archive, and is now the BFI National Archive, we used to produce shotlists for some of the films in the collection. They were not, strictly speaking, shotlists, since we cataloguers seldom described the film down to the level of individual shots, but they were detailed descriptions, broken up by footage lengths. The reason for doing so was the provide a clear account of a film without there being the need for someone to view the film (thus saving the print from unnecessary wear-and-tear), particularly for films that did not have descriptions in secondary sources. The focus tended to be on early films, and non-fiction.

When the Archive began in the 1930s, it seems that such descriptions were produced for every film held. As time went on, and the collection grew considerably, this was no longer possible, hence the move to selectivity. Occasionally it was useful, occasionally sheer indulgence. The BFI seldom produces such descriptions these days (it has curators now, rather than cataloguers, and they have to do many things). But the shotlists we produced were useful, sometimes reflected careful research, and were on occasion a thing of beauty.

They certainly looked beautiful. They were printed out on large yellow cards and filed in a wooden cabinet from another age. The look of them alone conferred importance. It was singularly satisfying to leaf through them, with great discoveries to be made each time the enquirer browsed through cards and a word or phrase caught the eye. Ah, so the camera saw that. We must find out more.

There was beauty in the words too. Your task was to sum up the essence of a film, dispassionately yet usefully, so that you were relaying the essence of that over which you had pored at the Steenbeck table viewer, stopping and starting the film to pinpoint that face, that place, those tell-tale words on the side of a passing bus (there is nothing like adverts on buses for helping you work out when and where a film has been made).

Where are those shotlists now? Reverently stored in some British Film Institute vault, I expect. But in the 1990s we moved to producing the shotlists electronically and then printing these out and attaching them to the yellow cards. Those electronic versions are now on the BFI's archive database.[1] Many of the shotlists I produced can be found there, though none has my name attached to it. In each case the effort paid off, because much was done with the films, either at the time or subsequently. Proof, if proof is needed, that cataloguers have to be good thing.

All of which is preamble to one film on which I spent quite some time — it would have been in the mid-1990s — trying not only to describe it but to solve its mysteries, since it was unreleased, had never been finished, and had seemingly left no trace at all. It was called *A World is Turning*, or to give its full, putative title, *A World is Turning (Towards the Coloured People)*.[2]

A World is Turning was to have been a documentary-variety film showcasing talented members of the Black community of Britain. It went into production in January 1948, but was never completed. It was planned to feature Black musicians, dancers, sportsmen, a preacher, a surgeon and an artist, maybe more, all active in Britain, with a slender linking narrative. Its purpose was to overcome prejudice by focussing on talent and contribution to society. It believed that by portraying excellence it could influence opinion. In its small way, it looked to a better world. Or so it would have done, had the film ever seen the light of day.

At the end of the shotlist I summarised what I had been able to find out about the film. These are my notes from the time:

> No details of release for this production have been traced, which was intended to document contributions to British public life made by members of the black community. The camera slates give the director as G. L. Norman and the cameraman as Bernard Hayward. From the slates, filming took place January to March 1948, but further filming in June is mentioned in a *Melody Maker* article. In *The British Film Yearbook 1949-50* p. 429 Robert Ad-

---

[1] *Collections Search*, https://collections-search.bfi.org.uk/web.
[2] The shotlist can be found at https://collections-search.bfi.org.uk/web/Details/ChoiceFilmWorks/150467874.

ams is credited as having appeared in and being associate director of THE WORLD IS TURNING (sic), produced by Norman's, 1948-49. Robert Adams, however, does not appear in these rushes. G. L. Norman ran the Norman's Film Service [incorrect—see below], which provided a stock shot service and produced short interest films (see extract from letter below).

In Sam Edwards, *New Zealand Film 1912-1996* (1997), p. 11, it is mentioned that New Zealand director and cameraman Rudall Hayward worked on a documentary, THE WORLD IS TURNING (TOWARDS THE COLOURED PEOPLE) for 20th Century-Fox. Presumably he is the same person as Bernard Hayward.

Melody Maker reference: 'Felix King and his orchestra, from the Nightingale niterie in Berkeley Square, recently took part in a short propaganda film, the object of the production being the cementing of better relations between coloured peoples and white. Star of the film is Adelaide Hall and the Felix King boys are heard in a vocal accompaniment to her song "Gospel Train", the special vocal arrangement being by George Mitchell. The film was actually made at the Nightingale' (26 June 1948, p. 5).

Letter in NFTVA Norman's file from Mrs I. J. Norman, 9 October 1975: '... We were going to make a film on the negro population, filming such persons as MacDonald Bailey, Turpin Bros, Adelaide Hall, Winifred Atwell, etc. My husband's long illness put a stop to all this developing, but all this material is incorporated in the library.'

I am not unimpressed by the research efforts of my young self in pulling all this information together in those pre-Internet days. How on earth did I know to look in a New Zealand film reference work for information? That is research for you—once you start looking for stuff, the stuff finds you.

But what I did not discover is why the film was made. On the *BFI Player*, someone has speculated that the film may have been made to coincide with the arrival in Britain of West Indian immigrants on the *Empire Windrush* in June 1948, but there is nothing to support such a suggestion.[3]

---

[3] https://player.bfi.org.uk/free/film/watch-a-world-is-turning-1948-online.

Instead the roots of the film lie deeper. An article in *The People* newspaper for 9 May 1948 provides some background.[4] Its genesis came about through the meeting of Gerald Norman (G. L. Norman, the film's director) and one Paul Maingot, shortly after the Second World War. Gerald Leslie Norman (1907-1993) was the younger brother of Emile Louis Norman (1897-1960), founder of Norman Film Productions in the 1930s and in the 1940s of Norman's Film Services, a stock footage business whose surviving collection would eventually make its way to the BFI National Film and Television Archive (so I was wrong to say in the shotlist that G. L. Norman ran the company, at least at that time).

Norman served in the Royal Air Force during the war. Shortly afterwards, he met up in London with Paul Maingot, described by *The People* as 'a former 8th Army colonel.' I have not been able to identify any Colonel Paul Maingot, but one clue might be that the surname is common in Trinidad, being of French origin. The two men had a shared interest: as the newspaper puts it, they were 'determined to help right the injustices they had seen done to coloured people.'

Norman used his film industry links (meaning brother Emile, whose company produced the film) to organise the production; Maingot raised the finance. News of the intended production soon percolated through the leading lights of the Black British community, all keen to take part, it was said. Among the names mentioned in various sources as taking part were singer Adelaide Hall, pianist Winifred Atwell, athletes Jack London and McDonald Bailey, boxing brothers Dick and Randolph Turpin, and actor Uriel Porter (misnamed Parker in *The People* article). Of these, only Adelaide Hall appears in the surviving footage, and it is not certain that the other names were filmed at all.

As noted in the shotlist, the Black actor Robert Adams— a celebrated figure at the time for his leading role in the film *Men of Two Worlds* (UK 1946)—seems to have been involved in helping set up the film, though he did not appear in it, possibly through professional commitments, as he was starring in a touring stage version of Richard Wright's novel *Native Son* at the time. Filming began in January 1948 and continued, probably fitfully, through to June of that year. A brief mention in *The Hollywood Reporter*, 27 August 1948, implies that the film was still in production to that date.[5]

---

[4] 'Challenge Colour Bar for a Film,' *The People*, 9 May 1948, p. 5.
[5] *The Hollywood Reporter*, 27 August 1948, p. 3.

Adelaide Hall in *A World is Turning.*

Contributing to the production's radical edge was camera operator Rudall C. Hayward (1900-1974), who was definitely involved—there is an album of his with photographs from the production held by New Zealand's Ngā Taonga Sound & Vision archive[6]—though it is hard to say why he changed his name to Bernard on the camera slates. Hayward had worked in the New Zealand and Australian film industries since the silent era, producing comedies and dramas on the slimmest of budgets. With his second wife, Ramai Te Miha Hayward (1916-2014), an actor and pioneering cinematographer of Maori heritage, he moved to England for a while, working on small news and documentary subjects; he as camera operator, she as sound recordist.

The couple were committed to left-wing causes—in the 1950s they made films in China, including *Inside Red China* (New Zealand 1958) and *Children in China* (New Zealand 1961), later filming in Albania. They undoubtedly shared Norman and Maingot's sympathies, Ramai in particular having long been the victim of racist attitudes herself. In a 1990s interview cited in a thesis by New Zealand scholar Sian Smith, Ramai Hayward stated that she wrote the script for the film, as well as working behind the camera

---

[6] Ngā Taonga Sound & Vision, https://www.ngataonga.org.nz/search-use-collection/search.

Hospital scene from *A World is Turning*, with unnamed Black doctor.

(as sound recordist, presumably).[7] It is possible, if not confirmed elsewhere. Intriguingly, a woman's voice can be heard calling the takes in the hospital scenes, for which the names of director and camera operator have been wiped from the clapperboard.

Whatever the roles, there were four people involved in the film (plus Adams) who were committed to their cause. Alas, commitment was not matched by ability, or finance. What survives of *A World is Turning* is rushes, with repeated shots, test sequences and so forth, which would not have made it into the finished production, but even so the evidence suggests limited competence. Filmed for the most part in a small Wardour Street studio, the lighting is poor, the interviewees painfully stilted (in particular a scene requiring multiple takes between Indian artist N. R. Rao and an utterly wooden white interviewer, Miss Mitchell), the direction non-existent.

Reflecting the filmmakers' wish to show different aspects of Black and Asian British society, there is a scene in a London church with a Black preacher; a scene in a club with two dancers performing to Roy Fraser and his Calypsonians, watched by a Black man who protests at racial prejudice in British society before

---

[7] Sian Smith, '*It Came from Me'—Māori Representation in Ramai Te Miha Hayward's Authorship*. Open Access thesis, Te Herenga Waka-Victoria University of Wellington, 2020, https://doi.org/10.26686/wgtn.17149178.v1, p. 60.

reciting William Cowper's 1788 poem 'The Negro's Complaint' ('Fleecy lo'cks and black complexion. Cannot forfeit nature's claim') to an elderly white man (so not a poet himself, as I mistakenly wrote in the shotlist); and a scene in a hospital operating theatre in which a Black surgeon saves the life of the elderly white man from the club.

It is a peculiar mix, suggesting no guiding intelligence behind the filmmakers' idealism. Only in the musical sequences does the film spring into life. In its online form it opens with an unidentified Black woman at a piano, looking lost in her thoughts before the clapperboard sounds and she launches into fine renditions of 'The Old Music Master' and 'Stormy Weather.'

But the film belongs to Adelaide Hall (1901-1993). She is seen in the sequence filmed in June 1948 at London's Nightingale Club, joyously singing 'Gospel Train,' accompanied by the Felix King Orchestra, members of which are clearly relishing the occasion as they sing the chorus, and at a piano with her pianist Stan, singing 'Swing Low Sweet Chariot' (in several takes). Just for having Hall at her peak, the film is a treasure.

I remember seeing the film for the first time in a cubicle in the BFI basement, just willing it to be better than it was. It was meant to be a seven-reeler, but they would have struggled to get a decent two-reeler out of what was filmed.

So maybe it was not just Emile Norman's ill-health that put paid to the production (it is Emile that Ivy Norman, his wife, refers to in her note cited on the shotlist), but the reels themselves. There was not a releasable film there, and they must have known it.

The People newspaper opened its article by stating that the film 'will either bring fame to the two men behind it—or land them near the bankruptcy court.'[8] Neither happened, it seems. The rushes stayed in the vaults of Norman's Film Service, maybe used as stock footage from time to time. The company carried on into the 1970s—notably Norman Film Productions' offices at 76 Old Compton Street in London's Soho was where the Beatles edited their *Magical Mystery Tour* television film in 1967. When Norman's ceased trading its film library came to the National Film Archive, with *A World is Turning* acquired under the supplied title *(Night Club Band and Singer)*, meaning that a temporary title was given because the correct, original title was not known at the time of acquisition. It was two decades later that I looked at it, possibly

---

[8] 'Challenge Colour Bar for a Film.'

the first person to do so since it was shot, and started peering at those camera slates. *A World is Turning*? What sort of a title is that? Who made this film, and why can I not find anything about it?

The film is now on the *BFI Player* and *YouTube*. It has been acclaimed as a lost treasure, viewed sympathetically for what might have been. The blurb on the *BFI Player* calls it 'extraordinary.' Well, technically it is not, but the idea of it is. That was the intention of Norman and Maingot (and the Haywards), to make an audience believe that here were extraordinary people, with their own voice. The power lay in its remarkable title, thrilling to the idea of inevitable change. In aspiration, if not in execution, that is what makes what we have of *A World is Turning (Towards the Coloured People)*, revolutionary.

Originally published as '*A World is Turning*,' 20 May 2021, https://lukem-ckernan.com/2021/05/20/a-world-is-turning, and reproduced here with small emendations. *A World is Turning* can be seen *BFI Player* at https://player.bfi.org.uk/free/film/watch-a-world-is-turning-1948-online and on *YouTube* at https://www.youtube.com/watch?v=Jv-rXtJ4j30. The online version of the film is in a different order to the shotlist description, which can be read at https://collections-search.bfi.org.uk/web/Details/Choice-FilmWorks/150467874 and on the *Colonial Film* website at http://www.colonialfilm.org.uk/node/1457.

49

Film is a River

Navigating William Raban's Thames Film

It is good to explore a river. One can proceed upstream, in search of a source whose precise location might never be determined. Or one can follow the river downstream until it widens out upon reaching the sea, the exact point on the map at which the one turns into the other being equally beyond determining. Of course, one may stroll along only part of a river, not caring for one's direction at all, but that is not exploration. If you go on a quest, it must be for the elusive, not the obvious.

I have been walking parts of the Thames and Medway estuaries recently, following the rivers until they disappear into the North Sea. It was while walking along the former from the Thames Barrier down to Dartford that I was reminded of a film that made a huge impression on me when I first saw it, at the National Film Theatre, over thirty years ago. It was *Thames Film* (UK 1987), made by the artist filmmaker William Raban.

Thames Film is a meditative documentary that follows the Thames on a slow-moving boat from central London out to the North Sea, reflecting on history and time through a combination of narration and quotations (read by John Hurt), archival images and film clips. On first seeing it I was struck by the way it turned the journey of a river into a journey through time, drawing lessons from history as the film offered a successions of haunting images that found a particular poetry in the drab industrial reaches of the estuary, a stretch of water out of sight and out of mind. Raban himself says this about the film's method and intentions:

> By filming from the low freeboard of a small boat, the film attempts to capture the point of view of the river itself, tracing the 50 mile journey from the heart of London to the open sea. This contemporary view is set in an historical context through use of archive images and

the words of the travel writer Thomas Pennant, who followed exactly the same route in 1787.[1]

I watched *Thames Film* again recently and saw all that so
impressed me the first time around. I know more of the history,
and the geography, than I did thirty-two years ago, when the film's
reflections on that which had been forgotten—the wrecks, the
prison hulks, the gibbets, the abandoned industries, all metaphors
for a waning imperial power—felt like a revelation. There were
some jarring breaks from the steady filmic progression, which
cannot have bothered me first time around, as though the filmmaker had temporarily lost patience with the style that he had
imposed upon himself. But overall the film's slow passage down
the river, with Hurt's mournful delivery and the Whistler-like
images of wharfs, jetties, refuse dumps, cranes and power stations,
is as extraordinarily evocative as ever it was.

Yet there was something that bothered me about the film. It
took a while to work out what was wrong. The film starts early
in the morning, with the mists hanging thick upon the river as the
City starts to rise. The sense is that we are on a single journey, travelling down the river as we travel down through time, an unfolding
experience that must end with the fading evening light as we reach
the sea. But the light kept changing. This journey down river was
not in sequence, and if filmed at different times of the day it was
presumably filmed over more than one boat journey. The reverie
had been tarnished.

Worse still, the film was not entirely honest about the direction
in which it was travelling. We passed by landmarks I recognised
that could not be on the left or right-hand side of the estuary if
we were progressing in the one direction out to sea. At first I was
unsure of what was going on (one abandoned wharf can look much
like another), but by the time we got to Canvey Island, near the
end of the journey, it was obvious that the boat had sailed both
up and downstream as the petrochemical site appeared on either
side of the frame in different shots. The promised illusion had been
broken. I wanted, I needed, *Thames Film*, to flow just the one way,
from city to sea, like time.

---

[1] 'Thames Film,' LUXONLINE, https://www.luxonline.org.uk/artists/wil-
liam_raban/thames_film.html. Thomas Pennant was a Welsh naturalist, collec-
tor and traveller, who wrote about a journey taken from London to the Isle of
Wight, via Dover.

Has anyone written about rivers and film? There are some great river films in which the journey of the characters up or down stream becomes a journey of discovery profoundly analogous with film itself: *Apocalypse Now* (USA 1979), *L'Atalante* (France 1934), *Deliverance* (USA 1972), *The African Queen* (UK/USA 1951), *Fitzcarraldo* (West Germany/Peru 1982), *Une Partie de Campagne* (France 1946), *Louisiana Story* (USA 1948), *Aguirre, der Zorn Gottes* (Mexico/Peru/West Germany 1972), *The River* (USA 1938 and France/India/USA 1951). The river is not just an obstacle to be negotiated, but reflects the inescapability of time. It determines the direction and the pace at which the character must travel, whatever the effort they may make. They are in a story, but not of their own making.

Film, as a physical object, is (or was) so like a river. All narrative forms take us on a progression through time, in the story told and in the time we devote to absorbing that story, but only film showed us this in its literal physical form; that is, as a long strip of plastic bearing a succession of images. Yes, there are panoramas (but they present time frozen), friezes (have you tried following the story on Trajan's Column?), cartoon strips (too brief) and graphic novels (they are extended sequences of images but have been turned into book form). Only film gave us an extended journey through time, like a river, that we could see unspooling before our eyes.

Of course, it is necessary to use the past tense. In all but exceptional circumstances, film is shown digitally, while its physical carriers are tape, disc or solid state. What, then, has been lost? It is something to do with a loss of uniqueness, of film as a recognisable entity as opposed to just another digital configuration of ones and zeroes. It is something to do with a loss of the sense of our relationship to narrative and unfolding time—a reel of film tells us more about the precious quality of time than do the duration figures on a DVD.

It is also something to do with that riverine quality, in which the reel of film (a feature film came in several reels, but let us imagine them assembled together on a platter) shows us a source, a journey, and an ending. Though the story those reels hold may have its variations in tempo, its recapitulations and complications, underpinning such surface eddies is the steady flow, twenty-four frames a second (the standard film speed for sound film): unvarying, proceeding unstoppably, until the river reaches its conclusion, and time runs out.

Thames Film.

So film does not have to have a river as its subject to be like a river, but it does bring the metaphor into clear focus. The frustration that I feel with *Thames Film*, on seeing it anew, is that it comes so close to an ideal, only to compromise. That ideal is pure film of some kind, which does not deviate or row back, but takes us on a single journey, in a single direction, surrendering to the only direction in which time and the river ultimately can take us.

By that measure, the only pure films are single-shot films—those early actualities of the Lumière brothers that capture without interruption an action in seventeen metres of film, the 'animated photograph,' as they were known at the time. To cut is to be creative, but it also cheats time.

I wanted *Thames Film* to be a single journey. I wanted it to be true to the river, from (city) source to sea, from early dawn to evening. Though it fails to achieve this without some dissimulation, it is nevertheless a singularly thoughtful and beautiful film. The thought lies in its psychogeographical approach to the river and its submerged history. The beauty lies not only in the haunting images Raban conjures out of a part of the country dismissed by most as ugly (if they are aware of it at all), but in the hypnotic pace, the camera sailing up to each forgotten landmark with a steady, questing spirit, coming face to face with the elusive.

Thames Film is a revered film. Michael Chanan writes admiringly about its relationship to both film and London history:

> The whole film is [...] permeated by the sense of death, which comes in many ways, overtakes every generation, and undoes empires. While the river runs on. And when the empire is finally undone, then the port itself dies. What Thames Film shows us is the river returned to a placid existence, because the port has gone and most of the trade moved elsewhere, but the river still flows between its banks as a sign of the city's history.[2]

Peter Ackroyd writes of the film's visionary qualities:

> There are moments of light and colour that lift the spirit with exaltation. There are giant shapes and structure that fill the mind with awe. There are passages of mist and turbulence that recall the primaeval Thames of swamps and marshes. The multifold images of the river run through this film like the currents and tides of the water itself. It is a film, in every sense, of great fluency.[3]

This pinpoints the film's riverlike qualities, and by extension the riverlike nature of film itself. It rests on that singularly resonant word 'fluency.' In every sense, film goes with the flow.

Originally published as 'Film is a River,' 10 September 2019, https://lukemckernan.com/2019/09/10/film-is-a-river, and reproduced here with small emendations and some additions. William Raban, in a comment made on the online version of this text, writes: 'The 60 mile subject was too extensive to cover in a single day which is why [...] it is a succession of journeys made over 18 months. I settled on filming from starboard side of the boat to comply with shipping regulations and to get close to the banks so the scan is from right to left, running counter to the way we read (in the West).'

---

[2] Michael Chanan, 'On William Raban's Thames Film,' *Literary London: Interdisciplinary Studies in the Representation of London*, Volume 5 Number 1 (March 2007).

[3] Peter Ackroyd, 'Peter Ackroyd on William Raban,' LUXONLINE, https://www.luxonline.org.uk/articles/peter_ackroyd_on_william_raban(1).html. This essay was originally published in the booklet companying the DVD release *William Raban: British Artists' Films*, BFIVD646, British Film Institute, 2004.

50.

A Perfect Light

Poet Derek Mahon and filmmaker Robert Flaherty

> The relief to be out of the sun,
> To have come north once more
> To my islands of dark ore
> Where winter is so long
> Only a little light
> Gets through, and that perfect.

I think this is my favourite film poem. It is not immediately obvious that it is about film; for that you need its title and subtitle: 'Epitaph for Robert Flaherty (after reading *The Innocent Eye*, by Arthur Calder-Marshall, in Montreal, Canada).' It was written by the Irish poet Derek Mahon and first published in 1968 in his collection *Night-Crossing* (the long subtitle appeared later).[1] *The Innocent Eye* is a biography of the American filmmaker Robert J. Flaherty.[2] It is the last two lines that are so acute: 'Only a little light/Gets through, and that perfect.' Is there a better, more poetically concise summation of photographic art?

Though the poem is called an epitaph, it gives the impression of being the thoughts of Robert Flaherty, while at the same time Derek Mahon himself. The location is similarly ambiguous. Mahon references Canada in the subtitle, and with the mention of the north, 'dark ore' and the long winter it seems he is thinking of the Arctic wastes where Flaherty first filmed in 1913 (on the Belcher Islands of Hudson Bay). Although Flaherty had gone out there as a prospector, for iron ore, he became fascinated by the Inuit people and was encouraged to operate a motion picture camera by

---

[1] Derek Mahon, *Night-Crossing* (London: Oxford University Press, 1968), p. 29. The subtitle was added for *Derek Mahon: Poems 1962-1978* (Oxford: Oxford University Press, 1979), p. 25.
[2] Arthur Calder-Marshall, *The Innocent Eye: The Life of Robert J. Flaherty* (London: W. H. Allen 1963).

the railroad entrepreneur William Mackenzie, who had sponsored the prospecting work. He was dissatisfied with the results, and lost much of what he had filmed in a fire, returning in 1920 to northern Quebec to film what became *Nanook of the North* (USA 1922), a study of the lives of the Inuit and what is generally held to be the founding statement of the art of documentary.

But Mahon the Irishman and Flaherty the Irish-American are just as much thinking of Aran, the island location of Flaherty's 1934 documentary, *Man of Aran* (UK 1934). The Aran Islands, in Ireland's Galway Bay, contain no dark ore, but Mahon is thinking of that deep vein of timeless culture, or an idea of that culture, that has drawn so many artists, Flaherty among them. His film notoriously documents a romantic idea of Aran, with the islanders being encouraged to recreate cultural practices, such as the shark hunt, which they had not followed for decades. For Flaherty, literal truth is less important than elemental truth.

So, is the island of the poem in Hudson Bay or Galway Bay? The volume in which 'Epitaph for Robert Flaherty' appears, *Night-Crossing*, contains a second poem, 'Recalling Aran,' while the two poems are book-ended by 'Canadian Pacific' and 'April on Toronto Island,' showing how the poet has purposefully mixed up thoughts of home and abroad. But the poem is an epitaph, and consequently about death ('out of the sun'), the island therefore being not so much an actual place as an idea of death as Ultima Thule—'death as the terminal island... with the island as ultimate art,' as Edna Longley describes it in an essay on Irish and Scottish island poems;[3] the place at the edge of the world, to give the title of another film made about remote lives.[4]

The dilemma for the ethnographic filmmaker has always been that the camera they take with them—the symbol of modern civilisation—helps bring about the destruction of that which it seeks to record ('Each man kills the thing he loves,' as another Irishman put it). Flaherty's solution was to record the dream rather than the actuality—the idea of a pure, remote culture, rather than the compromised reality. He filmed with a poet's eye. Derek Mahon responds with a poet's appreciation of the filmmaker's quest, equating the

---

[3] Edna Longley, 'Irish and Scottish "Island Poems,"' in *Northern Lights, Northern Words. Selected Papers from the FRLSU Conference, Kirkwall 2009* (Aberdeen: Forum for Research on the Languages of Scotland and Ulster, 2010), p. 155, https://tinyurl.com/mswmk7ym.

[4] *The Edge of the World* (UK 1937), directed by Michael Powell, a dramatic film inspired by the evacuation of the Scottish island of St. Kilda.

Inuk drawing of Robert Flaherty filming Nanook,
from *The Innocent Eye.*

escape from the remorseless advance of the modern with the
capture, out of the dark, of that elusive, perfect light.

Robert Flaherty is the subject of a new feature-length documentary, *A Boatload of Wild Irishmen* (Ireland 2010), directed by
Mac Dara O'Curraidhin and written by Brian Winston. It should
encourage anyone to see Flaherty's films, again or for the first
time—*Louisiana Story* (USA 1948), such a beautiful film—and to
learn more about a filmmaker whose vision must inspire anyone
seeking out the dark ore of why it is we want to film the world at
all.

Originally published as 'A Perfect Light,' 1 December 2010, http://the-
bioscope.net/2010/12/01/a-perfect-light, and reproduced here with small
emendations. 'Epitaph for Robert Flaherty,' 'Recalling Aran' (later retitled
'Thinking of Inishere in Cambridge, Massachusetts'), 'Canadian Pacific'
and 'April in Toronto Island' can all be found in Derek Mahon, *Collected
Poems* (Oldcastle: The Gallery Press, 1999).

51.

Travelling Hopefully

Slow TV and phantom rides

In December 2012 the Norwegian broadcaster NRK put on a ten-hour transmission of a train journey. Filmed from the front of a train cab travelling along the *Nordlandsbanen* line between Trondheim and Bodø, a distance of 438 miles, the programme gained one million viewers, or a fifth of the Norwegian population. What was shown was actually a composite of four journeys, filmed over each of the four seasons. The full journey was then made available on NRK's special Nordlandbanen page, which offered the original transmission, each of the four journeys from spring, summer, autumn and winter, and a version which showed the four seasons in parallel on four quarters of the screen.[1]

NRK has enjoyed a succession of hits with such journey programmes, or 'slow TV.' The first was a rail journey along the Bergensbanen between Bergen and Oslo broadcast in 2009, with its real-time transmission of a 2011 Hurtigruten coastal boat journey made between Bergen to Kirkenes over six days—probably the world's longest documentary—being a particular success.[2] 2.6 million people watched it on television and online along the way.

Such events are arguably film in its purest form. You turn on the camera, and let the world go by. No editing, no cheating with the flow of time, no imposition of narrative, the machine entirely subservient to reality. It is a little disappointing, therefore, to see that the *Nordlandbanen* transmission, as well as being a composite of four train journeys, occasionally features inset interviews with people travelling on the train, and has views not just from the front

---

[1] The dedicated *Nordlandsbanen* site, activehttps://arkiv.nrk.no/nordlands-banen, is no longer active, but the full film can be viewed, in ten parts, at https://tv.nrk.no/serie/nordlandsbanen-minutt-for-minutt. Highlights from the broadcast are at https://tinyurl.com/4a6aczux.

[2] All 134 hours, forty-two minutes and forty-five seconds of the *Hurtigruten* 2011 coastal boat journey can be seen on the dedicated NRK site https://tv.nrk.no/serie/hurtigruten-minutt-for-minutt.

but from the side of the train. This turns what was pure journeying into tourism, into something with a purpose. The ideal is for the camera to be travelling at the front of the vehicle, with interruption, so that you are not aware of the vehicle at all but only of the sensational of travelling through space and time, seemingly endlessly. That is purity.

Such film journeys are almost as old as film itself. In October 1897 the Biograph company in America caused a sensation with a new kind of film when it released *The Haverstraw Tunnel* (USA 1897), which showed a New York train journey filmed from the front of the cab.[3] Its most exhilarating feature for audiences was the point where the train went through the tunnel, the screen going black only to return to the light once again. Travelling shots from the side of trains and other forms of transport had existed before *The Haverstraw Tunnel*, but never before had a film turned the audience member into a disembodied figure in this way, hurtling ever forward through the screen. The film was soon billed as *The Phantom Ride—Haverstraw Tunnel*, and 'phantom rides' rapidly became a popular and regular feature of early film programmes, with most film companies jumping on the bandwagon and producing their own versions. An excitable but illuminating review of such a film journey, alongside other views, is provided by this 1898 *Punch* review of the 'American Biograph' at the Palace Theatre, London:

> It is a night-mare! There's a rattling, and a shattering, and there are sparks, and there are showers of quivering snow-flakes always falling, and amidst these appear children fighting in bed, a house on fire, with inmates saved by the arrival of fire engines, which, at some interval, are followed by warships pitching about at sea, sailors running up riggings and disappearing into space, train at full speed coming directly at you, and never getting there, but jumping out of the picture into outer darkness where the audience is, and the, the train having vanished, all the country round takes it into its head to follow as hard as ever it can, rocks, mountains, trees, towns, gateways, castles, rivers, landscapes, bridges, platforms, telegraph-poles, all whirling and squirling and racing against one another, as if to

---

[3] *The Haverstraw Tunnel* can be viewed at https://archive.org/details/haverstraw_tunnel.

see which will get to the audience first, and then, suddenly… all disappear into space!! Phew! We breathe again!![4]

Whether every early audience member's experience of
watching phantom rides was quite so phantasmagorical is open
to question, though the appellation 'phantom' does suggest that
they had an otherworldly, unsettling effect for some. What is
now calming for a Norwegian audience was more energising for
the audience of the 1890s, for whom such a visual experience was
wholly new.

The strange relationship between spectator and screen, particularly at that point where you are sitting still but your mind is
being propelled forward, became a major part of early cinema's
profound appeal, and its commercial success. Some of the first
'cinemas' were Hale's Tours—so named after their founder, George
Hale—which placed audiences inside a mock-up rail carriage, at
the front of which would be projected a film taken from the front
of a travelling train (or other vehicle), while the whole carriage
would rock to and fro to further the session of motion. Hales'
Tours (which originated in the USA and came to the UK in 1906)
offered a variety of such film views for the ten to fifteen minutes
such a show would last, emphasising the touristic experience. But
deeper than the wish to see far-off places was the wish to escape
into travel, and to be forever travelling. The affinity phantom rides
and Hale's Tours have with the virtual reality concepts and amusement offering of today has been much commented on, but simu-
lated roller-coaster rides and other such '4-D' audiences attractions subvert the journey to a particular purpose. The pure film
has no such purpose—it must simply take us on an uninterrupted
journey, without cuts or deviations, seemingly travelling forever.

It is commonly argued that the phantom ride had disappeared
as a film attraction by the late 1900s, to be subsumed as an attraction into larger film narratives, such as the opening titles sequence
of *Get Carter* (UK 1971), or the prolonged car journey in Andrei
Tarkovsky's *Solaris* (USSR 1972). But the phantom ride did not die,
it simply transferred to forms outside the cinema. Amateur filmmakers took up the opportunity, particularly train enthusiasts, who
have created what a variously known as cab rides or train cab videos.
There are numerous companies selling DVDs and Blu-rays of train
journeys from around the world, each generally filmed from the
front of a train and showing the journey from start to finish. Such

---

[4] 'At the Palace,' *Punch*, 6 August 1898, p. 57.

Interior of a Hale's Tour show in London, c.1906.

ventures have certainly been going since the 1980s and probably have an older history than that.

In the age of ubiquitous video equipment, such videos have moved online. There are hundreds of thousands of them, documenting every train journey imaginable from around the world. They are all over *YouTube*, plus numerous dedicated websites, as well as the individual train videos to be found on travel and train company websites (railway companies were the sponsors of train films from the earliest years, as they were seem as an easy form of free advertising).

Nor are such videos limited to trains. The several videos of a meteorite that struck Russia in February 2013 were taken from the front of cars travelling along a road. The reason these video cameras were in place was not out of any desire to record the otherworldly beauty of travel on Russia's roads, or indeed in the hope of recording a passing meteorite, but rather because of the reported corruption of some of Russia's traffic police. Russian car drivers have taken to videoing their journeys to produce an objective record of what they were doing on the road, just in case they are stopped by the police and have a false accusation planted on them. There are, nevertheless, plenty of videos of car journeys that record the journey alone, often employing time-lapse—something probably introduced by the BBC's famous 'interlude' *London to Brighton in Four Minutes* (UK 1953), which in form and intent seems very close to, if very much quicker than, the NRK broadcasts.[5] There are motorbike and bicycle videos filmed from the front of the vehicle, and the whole sub-genre of commuter videos.

Train cab videos are made by train enthusiasts with a passion for the rail experience rather than a desire for creating pure film. The NRK broadcasts are significant therefore, because their primary appeal is not train travel *per se*. It is not even touristic, or a patriotic sentimentality for familiar scenery, though both are obviously part of the local appeal. What seems to make the broadcasts work so effectively is how they gently take people out of themselves. We are disembodied. We float freely through the landscape at an even speed, and though we are on a journey that began somewhere and will end somewhere else, to all intents and purposes we are travelling endlessly.

This seems to be what lies at the heart of the success of the NRK broadcasts. They are are so profoundly peaceful because they find that ideal space between stasis and motion. We are still, and yet we are propelled forward. We are guided by safe hands. We are travelling hopefully, oblivious for a time at least to the fact that all our journeys must, inevitably, one day come to an end.

Originally published as 'Travelling Hopefully,' 9 March 2013, https://lukemckernan.com/2013/03/09/travelling-hopefully, and reproduced here with small emendations.

---

[5] Available on the Alexander Palace Television Society *YouTube* channel, https://tinyurl.com/34ue2cfv.

52.

Football Considered As One of the Arts

Watching Association Football

I have watched a lot of football in my time. I have not been to
that many live professional games—four in total. But despite such
apparent apathy I have seen hundreds, if not thousands, of football
matches. I have seen them on television screens (from black-and-
white era to Smart TVs), I have seen them on computers, tablets,
mobile phones, public screens, cinema screens, videotapes, DVDs
and on Steenbecks. I have seen full games, fragments of games,
highlights, summaries. I have seen football matches as actuality,
drama, animation and computer game. I have listened to games.
I have read descriptions of games.

And every time I have experienced a football match, it has been
the same game, and the same performance. It takes place on the
same stage with roughly the same dimensions wherever it is played.
It takes place over the same period of time (extra time notwith-
standing). Eleven players from one team meet eleven players from
another team, and each side attempts to propel a round ball into a
net positioned behind the opposing team, and to do this more than
the other side, while they mutually abide by an agreed set of rules.
It is the same story every time, with just two outcomes (unless a
game is abandoned)—a win for one side, or a draw.

On the face of it, this is absurd. What entertainment value is
there in seeing the same limited story played out over and over
again? A team wins or loses, it goes up a league table or down it
again, it gets so far in a knockout tournament before being knocked
out of it. It has no inherent meaning, there is nothing to be learned
from it. It simply goes on and on.

Yet billions watch the game, mostly on a screen of some kind.
Why is this so? They must do so because it satisfies as drama. Of
course partisanship is an important part of the appeal, because it is
what drives the narrative. There must be heroes and villains for a
drama to succeed. However, such partisanship is a means to under-

stand the drama, not the end in itself. Football supplies our need for stories; for this reason it qualifies as one of the arts.

If so, then what are the arts? This usually supposes a creative work presented before a public; that is, something produced by an artist and then offered to an audience in a recognised form, such a book, play, song, painting or whatever (one of the reasons conceptual art is such a challenge for the public is because it increasingly rejects any form that might capture it, thereby negating its status as art). Football has no such creator. A manager may organise a team to play in a particular fashion, and there may be individual examples of artistry displayed within a team—which are an important, if supplementary, part of the game's appeal—but what we see is not the playing out of the work of another's imagination, as in a film or an opera. In this respect its art is purely mechanical, a following out of patterns within strict parameters.

But we can look at this differently and say that the artist is incidental to art, or simply another form of mechanics, an agent by which the art form comes to be understood by its public. What matters is not that a work has a creator—or at least, as in an individual footballer's skill, it is of supplementary importance—but that it is understood by an audience. A book or a painting or a song can be enjoyed without the recipient being aware of who its creator is. It is not of fundamental importance to the fulfilment of the audience's need. We, the audience, need experiences which crystallise our understanding of life, be this in the form of a story, or picture. All art ultimately boils down to being a story or a picture, expressing experience in time and space. (Music and song in this argument fit under story).

Football therefore qualifies as one of the arts because it fulfils the need for stories, and to a degree supplies a pictorial pleasure as well. But the problem still remains of the repetitive nature of such art. It is always the same story, with little in the way of character or detail to alleviate the spectator from the unremitting inevitability of it all. This can only be a vital part of its appeal, and not the problem it might seem to be. It is the comforting familiarity. It is the endless variation on a theme. It is the intimation of immortality, the sense that all else may live or die, but a game of football is always being watched somewhere in the world and always will be, and always the same. Football therefore qualifies further as art by the reassurance that it provides. It is the story we can always turn to.

Watching football on a cruise ship.

Yet there is more to football as art than the playing out of eternal tropes. Football is a reflection of social, cultural and aesthetic understanding. Watching England play at the World Cup in Brazil tells us more about the country's place in a post-imperial world with globalised economics than one might ever gain from, say, a David Hare play. It is all there in the harsh clash between sentimental hopes based on a narrow nostalgia and the hard realities of action played out in the present day. There are the individual players, elevated by public expectation and too often brought down by physical inevitability. Football plays out as spectacle, thriller, tragedy and farce.

Football also holds a special place in the arts, because of the relationship between the game seen live, and the game as it is most often experienced, on a screen. The latter must recreate the former. A football game is meaningless without the crowd, through which we understand the drama's import and the narrative is propelled forward. Live cinema screenings of theatre plays rather awkwardly encompass the audience as part of the entertainment. For football, the crowd makes us realise what we are seeing. It reminds us that we are the ultimate creators of this drama.

All of this is true for other sports, of course. Football has primacy only because it is so globally popular, though it has a special status through the way it works so well on the screen. There are the opposing sides, arrayed left and right, each seeking to invade the other's territory. There is the size of the ball, ideally proportioned—roughly the size of a human head—to gain the attention of the casual eye. There is the patterning of formations (4-3-3, 4-4-2, 5-3-2) for those who want to look more deeply into how eleven intersects with eleven in space. There is the particular combination of long, medium and close shots, with restrained camera movement and rhythmic editing, that determines how football is best displayed upon a screen. And there is the game's duration—ninety minutes, with interval, the ideal length for the unfolding of drama, as centuries of theatre and decades of cinema have taught us.

Football must be considered as one of the arts. Why else have I put my book down and decided to watch Argentina versus Bosnia-Herzegovina?

Originally published as 'Football Considered As One of the Arts,' 15 June 2014, https://lukemckernan.com/2014/06/15/football-considered-as-one-of-the-arts, and reproduced here with small emendations. The essay was written during the 2014 FIFA Men's World Cup football tournament. Argentina beat Bosnia-Herzegovina 2-1 in the group stage.

53.

Memory and Migration

John Akomfrah's Mnemosyne

Memory is an entirely personal thing. What we call our memories are constructions of the brain which alter according to time and circumstance. They are not objective, and they do not correlate exactly with reality, as any court of law can demonstrate. One person's memories will never be precisely the memories of another person. Notions of collective or cultural memory are therefore nebulous concepts, more socio-philosophical than anything neural, yet they are powerful notions for all that, because they demonstrate to us how we are connected to other people. They trigger a collective feeling, even while those who share in such memories will each see that which is recalled a little differently, in their own personal way.

This tension between the personal and the collective seems to lie at the heart of John Akomfrah's remarkable film-essay *Mnemosyne* (UK 2010), which is on show at the BFI Southbank. Originally presented at The Public in West Bromwich, the film gained such acclaim, from writers as varied as Ken Russell and Sukhdev Sandhu, that it has been brought to London. Anyone interested in the unique power of film to conjure up more than words can say should try and get there.

John Akomfrah is a co-founder of the Black Audio Film Collective, whose best-known work is the seminal *Handsworth Songs* (UK 1986). Like that film, *Mnemosyne* explores Black experience in a real and an imagined British Midlands territory. In Ancient Greek mythology Mnemosyne was the personification of memory, as well as the mother of the nine muses, and the film is divided up into nine sections, one per muse: Melpomene (tragedy), Clio (history), Euterpe (music), Polyhymnia (sacred song), Urania (astronomy), Thalia (comedy), Erato (love), Terpsichore (dance) and Calliope (poetry). Its visual style is extraordinary. It features startlingly beautiful images of an unnamed far northern territory dominated by ice and snow, in which solitary figures in yellow, blue

Archive film image from *Mnemosyne/The Nine Muses.*

or black coats, with hoods raised, stand with their backs to the camera or else walking in long shot, identity always hidden. They are like mythological figures, seeing beyond what mere mortals see. This is combined with black-and-white and colour archive film of the Black community in the Midlands taken from the archives of the BBC, the Media Archive of Central England and Birmingham Central Library.

What is especially haunting about the film is the way in which it takes archive film originally produced for documentaries, news pieces, promotional films and such like, and turns it into something mysterious, real and quite unreal at the same time. The many images of snowbound streets and cars take on an extraordinary contemplative quality. Faces from the past ask of us that we understand their hopes and sorrows. Whatever the original purpose was in taking such films, they have taken on their own lives. The images do not speak alone, however. Akomfrah overlays his melange of present and past film with quotations from Milton, Beckett, Nietzsche, Sophocles, Shakespeare, Pound, Cummings, Tagore and others, with Homer's *Odyssey* predominant. Sometimes these touch on themes of migration, or exile; often they are more elusive, and more personal to the filmmaker. Sometimes there is an obvious connection with the muse in question, such as the disco dancing for Terpsichore or the haunting use of Leontyne Price singing 'Motherless Child' for Polyhymnia, muse of sacred poetry. At other times it is bitterly ironic, as in its use of Midlands MP Enoch Powell's notorious anti-immigration 'rivers of blood' speech (delivered in Birmingham in 1968), placed under Thalia, the muse of comedy.[1]

Mnemosyne is clearly 'about' the immigration of Black and Asian communities to Britain and the hostile and alienating reception so many received on settling in this country. It is filled with great sorrow. But it also seems to be about the shifting nature of archive film itself, which signifies different things from those elements it originally meant to record, such as the film's factory scenes, snowbound traffic, canal journeys and interviews with little Englanders, as time moves on and perceptions alter. *Mnemosyne* shows that film, like our memories, is ever-changing, recording some sort of a historical reality but at the same time capturing something altogether more mysterious, forever open to interpretation. Film itself must always be migrating, leaving the past behind, but unable to forget it.

Originally published as 'Memory and Migration,' 3 August 2010, http://britishlibrary.typepad.co.uk/movingimage/2010/08/memory-and-migration.html, and reproduced here with some additional text. The film released theatrically and later on disc under the title *The Nine Muses* (UK 2010).

---

[1] No footage exists of that part of the speech in which Powell refers to the 'River Tiber foaming with much blood,' which gave the speech its familiar name.

54

On Not Liking David Attenborough

The pursuit of astonishment in natural history films

The latest natural history series narrated by Sir David Attenborough, *Blue Planet II* (UK 2017), is being broadcast in the UK. As with so much else of the work associated with him, it has been given a rapturous reception by viewers and reviewers alike. This, they say, is the best of television. This is why we do not complain as much as we might otherwise do about paying for a television licence. This is astonishing.

But I beg to differ.

The first thing to say is that David Attenborough is a great man. In a mean and difficult age he has stood out for decades as a beacon of decency, reason and intelligence. He is a figure who has graced the age because he is a product of the age, being a broadcaster (in every sense) whose understanding of the television medium has given him a voice that could not have existed at any other time.

Attenborough has been making natural history films since the 1950s, alongside writing, lecturing and occasionally running parts of the BBC. The turning point in his career was the series *Life on Earth* (UK 1979). This outstanding work was the *On the Origin of Species* for our times. It traced the varieties of life, broadly arranged in order of evolutionary history, from sea-living invertebrates, to insects, fish, land creatures, birds, mammals and finally humans, 'the compulsive communicators,' as the thirteenth and final episode put it.

The series gained acclaim for the quality of its cinematography, the boldness of its ideas (most famously the sequence in which Attenborough communed with gorillas), its innovative music (by Edward Williams) and the cohesiveness of its ideas. It was one of several grand television series made at that time, in which a wise Western figure gave a view of history and achievement over multiple episodes, including Kenneth Clark's *Civilisation* (UK 1969), Jacob Bronowski's *The Ascent of Man* (UK 1973) and Carl

Sagan's *Cosmos* (USA 1980-1981).[1] But *Life on Earth* trumped all of these through its modesty. It was not a pronouncement on how things should be seen; it was observation of a world in which we were significant only in that we were the observers.

Life on Earth was accompanied by an eponymous book that was its equal. Indeed it may be one of the great books of the twentieth century. Divided into thirteen chapters that follow the thirteen episodes of the series, with the two frequently sharing the same language, it is nevertheless an exceptional work in its own right. It has the mission of explaining the world of understanding opened up by Darwin, after 120 years of corroborative investigation. Its exceptionalism lies in the clarity of its argument and the facility of its writing style. Here is one paragraph, selected at random, as illustration:

> When the first amphibians appeared, there was, of course, one comparatively safe place for their eggs and young—the land. At that time no other vertebrates were there to steal eggs and gulp the larvae, no risks comparable to those threatened in the water by shoals of hungry fish. If the amphibians could manage to deposit their eggs out of water, their young would certainly have greatly increased chances of survival. But there were problems. How could the eggs be prevented from drying out and how could tadpoles develop out of water? Whether ancient amphibians overcame these difficulties we do not know. Had they done so they would certainly have greatly accelerated the rate at which they colonised the land. Today the attraction of the land for breeding is not so great, for the amphibians no longer have it to themselves. There are reptiles, birds and even mammals that relish amphibians eggs and tadpoles. Nonetheless, many frogs and toads still find it advantageous to follow this strategy.[2]

This is a model of good style. It is clear, unpretentious, precise in its choice of word and phrasing, using words with particular resonance (gulp, relish) sparingly but effectively. It is a pleasure to read, equally to listen to—it is impossible to read Attenborough's

---

[1] As Controller of the BBC2 television channel at the time, Attenborough was responsible for the commissioning of *Civilisation* and *The Ascent of Man*.

[2] David Attenborough, *Life on Earth: A Natural History* (London: Collins/ British Broadcasting Corporation, 1979), p. 146.

prose without imagining his melodious voice narrating it. But more than this, there is the propulsion of the argument, based around the strategies for survival that are fundamental to Darwin's theory. The paragraph leads us in the space of a few lines from ancient to present times. It is also compellingly visual, each sentence a cut from one view to a complementary view.

Life on Earth was followed in by a sequel *The Living Planet* (UK 1984), which if anything was the greater work, televisually. Arranged geographically rather than through time, it surveyed the ways in which living organisms adapted to the conditions of their surroundings, from ice caps, to jungles, to deserts. Perhaps the most memorable sequence, in which Attenborough winched himself up the different levels of a tropical rainforest, was also one which exemplified how visual style married argument. This was a series that foregrounded visual evidence, and made the television medium the tool for discovery.

Both series pushed back the boundaries of how natural history was filmed. Cameras were placed where cameras had never previously been placed, and again and again we were shown sequences where we were told that such scenes had never been seen before. The pursuit of evidence led to a thirst for astonishment. And so the seeds of doubt were sown.

It is unlikely that anyone considered *Life on Earth* to be the first in a trilogy, but overseas sales of the programmes demanded more of the same, and if *The Living Planet* served as a natural complement to the first series, *The Trials of Life* (UK 1990) was a follow-up very likely to have been encouraged by the marketing department of BBC Worldwide, the broadcaster's commercial subsidiary. The theme of the series was the different ways in which animal species live, tracing their trials from birth to death. It was here that sensation began to take over. Maybe it was the sequence in which orcas attacked sea lions on the shore that marked the turning point. This was sensation for sensation's sake, a televisual thrill that existed of itself, irrespective of, and indeed ultimately irrelevant to, the argument that ostensibly it illustrated.

In film studies terms, *The Trials of Life* is a series of attractions. They are spectacles designed to excite the viewer's curiosity. They exist in isolation. They defeat, and are the antithesis of argument. As Tom Gunning argues, in a famous 1986 essay on 'The Cinema of Attractions' as a defining feature of early cinema, it is 'a conception that sees cinema less as a way of telling stories than as a

An orca attacking sea lions, from
The Trials of Life, 'Hunting and Escaping.'

way of presenting a series of views to an audience, fascinating because of their illusory power [...] and exoticism.'[3]

And so it has been with the successor series *Life in the Freezer* (UK 1993), *The Blue Planet* (UK 2001), *Planet Earth* (UK 2006) and their sequels: that we are presented with a sequence of exotic thrills—usually bloody thrills, exploiting tension and terror—that say nothing beyond themselves.

It is not that these later series are totally devoid of an argument. Each stresses the essentials of survival that underpinned the first two series, while environmental concerns are repeatedly expressed. But as Attenborough has aged, and now serves chiefly as figurehead and voice, so such messages have become homilies, additional to rather than integral to what we are being shown. Attenborough writes in *Life on Earth*:

> The fact is that no species has ever had such wholesale control over everything on earth, living or dead, as we now have. That lays upon us, whether we like it or not, an awesome responsibility. In our hands now lies not only

---

[3] Tom Gunning, 'The Cinema of Attractions: Early Film, Its Spectator and the Avant-Garde,' *Wide Angle*, vol. 8 no. 3/4, Fall 1986, pp. 63-70.

our own future, but that of all other living creatures with whom we share the earth.[4]

This has been the governing theme of all his best work. It is how he has taken on the baton from Darwin, developing the argument from understanding to responsibility. And undoubtedly the later 'Planet' series communicate a combination of awe and urgency that speak powerfully to millions of us. But I look on *Blue Planet II*, and I do not recognise any of it. It is not the world in which I live. It is some other world, impossibly beautiful, riven through by the remarkable, that exists on HD screens but at a profound remove from the reality to which I feel I belong.

Life on Earth and *The Living Planet* opened our eyes to our place in time and space. They were evolutionary in intent, and revolutionary in effect. Now ingenuity of camera technique, combined with a desire for shock—the shock of astonishment, not just the shock of violence—has produced memorable television but increasingly poor argument. And the life exists in the argument.

Originally published as 'On Not Liking David Attenborough,' 5 November 2017, https://lukemckernan.com/2017/11/05/on-not-liking-david-attenborough, and reproduced here with small emendations.

---

[4] Attenborough, *Life on Earth*, p. 308.

55.

Coming To You Live

Live and almost live television at the 2016 Olympic Games

There was an interesting moment in the heat of the Rio Olympic Games coverage on the BBC when the presenter Clare Balding told us to look at some sport in progress—I think it was the golf—saying 'let's see what he does next,' or words to that effect, as some crucial putt was made. However, having just switched over channels, I had seen that self-same clip five minutes ago. On one channel it had been live; on the other it was being presented as live when it no longer was. Had I not switched channels, would I ever have known, or been bothered about it?

The liveness of the broadcast Games has become a hot issue. *The Times* had an excellent piece which documented a night's channel-hopping of the Games, showing how much was live and how much delayed, the liveness often being calculated with reference to reports on social media.[1] In the USA, the broadcast rights-holder NBC has come in for a great deal of criticism for showing the Olympic events on a delay, to coincide with optimum scheduling times, forcing those who want to know that what they are seeing is definitely live to seek out web streams.

The simulation of liveness for sports broadcasting is a complex business. Golf, in particular, is seldom wholly live. Programme editors cut to and fro between players playing shots at just the right time, giving the sense of a continuous stream of successive actions, which suits the television viewer but is not an accurate reflection of the muddled reality. It is a liveness of the imagination, conjured up on the fly in the mixing suite.

But what the NBC case shows, along with instances of people complaining about the combination of live and repeat in the BBC's juggling of multiple sports across assorted channels, is the audience's belief and trust in the live nature of television. Live televi-

---

[1] James Ghreerbant, "'And now it's time to cross over to the live archery,'" *The Times* [London], 10 August 2016, p. 64.

sion means two different things. Actual live television, in which we see what is happening at the moment that it happens, is a rarity. Once it was the mainstay of television; now it is confined largely to news and sports (and so much of 24-hour news is repeated content, either filler documentaries or repeated interviews and the like). An event such as the Olympics stands out because it brings so much unaccustomed liveness to our screens (unless you are in the USA, of course).

But live television also means an anticipation of liveness, of all broadcast content being live in effect, because television works through audience expectation of something fresh continually replacing what we are witnessing at any one point. This is what cultural studies academic Raymond Williams called 'flow'— the collection of disparate broadcast elements that just keep on coming, one after the other.[2] It is what television immerses us in, and which is the secret of television's success, namely that it is so like the experience of life—not just in what we see but in how we experience what we see, with always something new to look forward to (which must always be something predictable).

This is not just an aspect of television; it *is* television. Television is defined by the illusion of being live, in every sense. As we all know, this is being chipped away at by the encroachment of catch-up TV and video streaming services such as Netflix or Amazon. Video on demand is a different proposition to the endless flow of traditional television. What had been a passing stream has turned into a lake.

There are other differences between traditional television and video on demand, such as the breakdown of modes of domestic consumption, but it is the change in the sense of liveness that is changing television into something else. My Smart TV is a hybrid invention: it offers me both television and post-television. I can watch television as it is broadcast, or I catch up on whatever I want to catch up on, whether I let the BBC's schedulers do this for me, or by selecting programmes or streams for myself.

Despite all the choice, I still thirst for what is live. I still value above all other small-screen experiences the privilege of being there, as it happens. An on-demand world is one that has become out of touch.

---

[2] *See* Raymond Williams, *Television. Technology and Cultural Form* (London: Fontana, 1974).

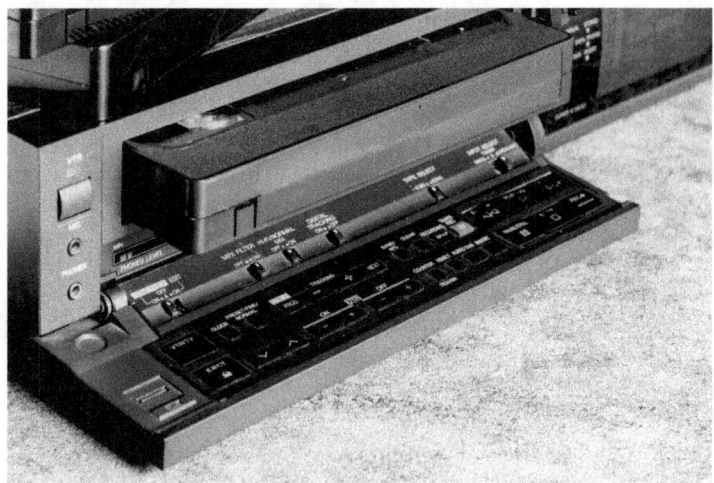

VHS tape in a VCR player.

The news last month that the last VHS-tape video cassette recorder (VCR) had been produced generated a number of interesting obituaries for the medium.[3] Most picked up on the crucial aspect of time-shifting, that power of intervention which video recording gave to the user, and which first started to interrupt the flow. Yet time shifting and on demand are not quite the same thing. Time shifting gives us control over that which is live. On demand does the shifting for us.

Of course this is all liberating, freeing the user from the dictates of the programmers, and overwhelming us with choice. But the diminution of liveness may have a cultural impact which needs exploring. Television, so often criticised for being a medium that lulled us into a state of apathy, may have been quite the opposite. We can watch television apathetically, but that is not the same thing as what it offers of itself. It offers us the immediacy of the moment, a moment that we share with all others watching at the same time. On demand separates us; television unites us.

Television has obvious social benefits for the lonely or the elderly, while being a means of instruction for the young, but we all gain from its mirroring of the idea of life. That is why news and sport are so important, because they are what is keeping television as television. Take them away, and we may be left in some strange

---

[3] For example, Ian Bogost, 'Rest in Peace, VCR,' *The Atlantic*, July 2016, https://www.theatlantic.com/technology/archive/2016/07/vrc-is-dead/492992.

limbo, the repercussions of which we do not know as yet. Social media, it can be argued, are filling the gap, connecting us to one another and to the moment in ways that go far beyond television's simple one-to-many model. But social media demand that you join in; television asks only that you switch on. It is the kinder medium.

There is such excitement in seeing a live sports event. I can follow Laura Trott's progress in the Omnium on Twitter and have instant information through a multiplicity of connections. Seeing it, however, makes me really there. One is reporting, the other is witnessing. It is possible to follow live video streams, of course—that is what those disappointed by NBC are being encouraged to do. However, that is not something new—that is television continued by other means. Whether it strengthens television by combining video with other social media streams, or whether it dissipates its better nature, only time will tell.

Originally published as 'Coming To You Live,' 16 August 2016, https://lukemckernan.com/2016/08/16/coming-to-you-live, and reproduced here with small emendations. The 2016 Olympic Games took place in Rio, Brazil, 5-21 August.

56

Broadcasting on the Beach

Improvisatory television at the 2016 Olympic Games

Following on from the previous essay about the value of sport and live television in helping to define what television is, I saw something else to note about the BBC's coverage of the Rio Olympic Games. The BBC used three terrestrial channels to broadcast Olympic video, plus its website and app—BBC One and BBC Two with other programmes interspersed, and BBC Four continuously from early afternoon to early morning. The main anchor for the BBC Four coverage was Dan Walker. I thought that what he and the production team broadcast was quite exceptional in its way—even a new kind of television.

The set-up was that BBC built a leaf-fringed cabin on Copacabana beach and broadcast from there. The greater part of the broadcasts was, of course, coverage of the assorted live—or near live—Olympic sports, with an emphasis on the so-called minor sports. It was also the case that the moment that any such sport became interesting—which meant that a British competitor looked like they might win a medal—then the coverage switched over to the greater audience on BBC One, and Four left us with Australia v Serbia at basketball, or some such niche attraction. It was broadcasting for those who wanted to see any sort of sport, and were not that inclined to start waving flags.

In between the sport came Walker. Rather than do the usual sort of links between clips, with background puffery and athlete interviews, Walker made his location the star attraction. Behind the cabin you could see the waves crashing on the beach, and the ordinary Brazilians, in all shapes and sizes, drifting by. Much of it was broadcast at night, which added to the hypnotic mundanity of the scene. Walker interviewed the locals, made running jokes of some of the regulars—a team of bin-men, a tubby jogger who looked like the chef Anthony Worrall Thompson—and then befriended them. Most notably, and bravely, he spotted a passing hen party and interviewed the bride, Maria de Cezar, the video of which

Dan Walker and Maria de Cezar.

swiftly went viral and made her an international celebrity.[1] Meanwhile Walker read out from Tweets and emails, as the audience reacted to, and by extension became a part of, the broadcast as it spread out from the screen across social media. It was funny, engaging and illuminating.

What was striking was the bold, improvisatory nature of this kind of broadcasting. It had some connection with radio broadcasting, in which a DJ might riff on comic ideas and the enthusiasm of his audience in between the songs. It had something of the vox pops you get on breakfast television (Walker's day job), with all the riskiness of combining the passing public with live television. It had qualities of musical improvisation, the performer turning up on stage with no idea of what they are to play until they start playing. But never before have I seen something which took such elements and sustained them for so long a period, a tightrope walk maintained for two weeks and not just a few hours.

Above all it was a celebration of liveness on television. It broke through the predictable elements, the procession of units that make up television's flow, to create an environment where anything might happen, and be allowed to happen. It found adventure in the ordinary and the accidental. Of course the elements of risk were minimised as much as possible, and the programmes were forever cutting back to the sports, but the potential for rude reality to intrude on television's dream world was always there. It made television look vulnerable, but also quite special.

---

[1] 'Moment Bride-to-be Crashes Olympic Coverage,' *BBC News*, 13 August 2016, https://www.youtube.com/watch?v=2-sXO5GjgJk.

The balancing act between the controlled and the unscripted only worked so well because of Walker's skillful bonhomie and awareness of three different audiences all at once—those around him, those watching television, and those online—plus a smart production team. But it was not just good anchoring; it demonstrated what television can do so well, which is to reveal the possibilities of the immediate moment. Television is defined by the qualities it has of immediacy and intimacy, yet so much of broadcasting tries to neutralise these effects, through predictability and the manufacturing of emotion. Television, generally so timorous, rarely lets itself go, as a medium for discovering the here and now. That is what these broadcasts did so well. There should be more of them.

Originally published as 'Broadcasting on the Beach,' 23 August 2016, https://lukemckernan.com/2016/08/23/broadcasting-on-the-beach, and reproduced here with small emendations. The 2016 Olympic Games took place in Rio, Brazil, 5-21 August.

57.

Lost in an Instant

The liveness of television and archiving the live

In the Rio 2016 gold medal bout of the 80kg taekwondo between Lutalo Muhammad of Great Britain and Cheick Sallah Cissé of Ivory Coast, Muhammad was ahead on points with one second to go. In one second he would win the gold. The clock had been stopped while the athletes got once more into position. It started up again, and literally in a split second Cissé aimed a blow at Muhammad's head and was victorious. The whole story of the contest, the balance between victory and defeat, took place in a second, in an instant. And then was lost.

I have written two essays inspired by the live coverage of the Rio Olympic Games: one on live television versus on-demand, one on the particular example of BBC Four's inventive reporting of the Games. This third essay is about what happens when live stops being live and becomes recovered live, or archive.

BBC historian David Hendy asked of the second of this series whether I had read *Television and the Meaning of 'Live'* by Paddy Scannell.[1] I had not, but I am engrossed in it now. *Television and the Meaning of 'Live'* is about the meaning of life, through the prism and metaphor of television. Scannell takes as his guide the German philosopher Martin Heidegger (1889-1976) and his enquiry into the nature of phenomena (phenomenology). I had not previously read the man, and all I knew of him is that he got rather too involved in National Socialism, only proving the fact that the brightest minds can still make the biggest fools. His great work is *Being and Time* (1927), which as Scannell explains is an investigation into the meaning of existence focussed on the nature of the everyday, and the position of we humans within that environment. The elementary components of this are place, people and time, those points which fix us in the everyday. This Scannell then

---

[1] Paddy Scannell, *Television and the Meaning of 'Live': An Enquiry into the Human Situation* (Cambridge: Polity, 2014).

applies to television (and radio), in particular the notion of live television and what it means when we switch on a television and we say that it 'comes to life.' Television, like life, lives in a constant state of now.

It is deep stuff: some of it obvious, much of it extraordinarily stimulating. The element of the book that I want to pick up on here is its thoughts about the broadcast archive. In a section on the passing living moment, he writes:

> For thousands of years writing, in its many transformations, has been the sovereign way in which the past has been preserved and the words and deeds of the dead generations have been renewed in the life and times of the present. In the last century, two revolutionary technologies of record—the audio- and videotape and then digital recorders—have transformed the relationship between the living and the dead, past and present, as they put on record (for the record), words and deeds—speech-act-events—in their living enunciatory moment. Both technologies were developed in response to the exigencies of live broadcasting; first on radio and then, a generation later, on television. Through these technologies history is transformed. Technologies of writing produce history in the present as the past—the past as moving away from the present. The new audio-visual technologies record history in the making: the future as it comes to presence; history in the making of the immediate unfolding now of concern, realized as such in the enunciatory speech-act-event. The past is no longer preserved indirectly in the trace of the written. It is preserved directly (*en direct*, as the French say) in its own living immediacy in audio-visual recordings.[2]

For Scannell the special quality of audiovisual technologies is that they can capture the liveness of events, 'as they unfold in the immediate now of their coming into being.' Such technologies conquer time, enabling the scholar (Scannell's particular interest) to stop time, work it back and forth. 'The dialectics of immediacy become available to scrutiny and analysis. I can begin to figure out the workings of time.'[3]

---

[2] Scannell, *Television and the Meaning of 'Live,'* p. 95.
[3] Scannell, *Television and the Meaning of 'Live,'* p. 97.

Lutalo Muhammad, losing the gold.

The dream of capturing time encouraged the invention of motion pictures in the first place. The French medical investigator and pre-cinema pioneer, Etienne-Jules Marey, in the early 1880s, developed a camera capable of capturing motion as a series of images on a single plate, later on a strip of sensitised paper. He called such work 'chronophotography,' literally 'photographing time.' Marey was able to capture a precise moment in time, to study the nature of movement but also (as the name of his science indicates) to study time itself.

But he did not capture time at all. His work does not portray time itself but rather the idea of time.[4] The movement is lost as the moment is past, and what is captured of it is only an illusion—held on a glass plate, a strip of plastic, a magnetic tape, a digital signal—and nothing of the true nature of the moment at all. We can only lose time, never hold on to it.

Scannell stresses the practical value (to the scholar) of being able to replay this illusion of time, the unfolding now forever recoverable, turning time present into history. But nevertheless the replaying of live is not live. It has lost its nature, and with that a great deal of its interest. The focus of these three essays has been on sports, something of great interest to Scannell (who focusses on football—Heidegger loathed television but made an exception whenever the football was on) and to Marey, whose assistants made chronophotographic records of Olympic athletes at the Paris Games in 1900. Who wants to see archived sports films? Only

---

[4] Luke McKernan, 'Motion and Time,' Viewfinder, no. 57, December 2004, pp. 8-9, https://lukemckernan.com/2024/03/11/motion-and-time.

Pole vaulter captured on a single photographic plate,
from Marey's book *Le Mouvement* (1894).

the specialists. You do not get repeated football matches.[5] The millions who watched the Olympic Games live will be replaced by a few thousand who will bother to look up the dwindling number of online videos from the Games while they still remain on news sites. The moment is past. The story is over. We know who won.

The live recording, of a sports event or whatever, tries to persuade us that what it represents is still live, that it still matters. It never succeeds. Even if we do not know who won, we may tell from changes in film or video quality that what we are seeing is a record from the past, or simply because it is no longer being shown in a live context. It is no longer what it thought it was; instead it is a reminder of lost time, of the irrecoverableness of the past.

The International Olympic Committee has this week launched the Olympic Channel, a combination of online live television channel, video showcase and archive.[6] Setting aside the television channel, the site is a monument to dead video. It is a collection of short video packages that seek to encapsulate moments of past Olympic greatness, bound up with the usual messages about the spirit of the Games. It is hard to say who the audience would be for such fare, except maybe physical education coaches looking for something to inspire their charges. The majority of us do not care, because we know who won, and we only watched when this footage was live because we did not know at that point who would win. The point of live is that it leave us in a state of anticipation, full of questions. The recording nullifies these.

Scannell asserts that writing technologies produce history in the present as the past, while audiovisual technologies record

[5] As the essay 'Another Time' in this book demonstrates, this is not always the case.
[6] The channel site continues at https://www.olympics.com/en/olympic-channel.

history in the making. The one shows the past receding away from us; the other shows the future as it became now. They view time from opposite directions.[7] This is a beautiful observation, but I am not sure that it stands up in reality. Our point of interest, our point of view, change when what is live becomes what was live. Of course we can apply our imaginations to reinvigorate the moment. We can forever watch Lutalo Muhammad with one second to go until glory, and try and identify that precise instant when hope and expectation died. Its contemplation turns a second into an infinity. But live cannot be recreated as live. We can imagine it as live, but it will be the idea of live. Our archives do not record the moment, but something that has changed because it has joined our archive. However much we may look at it for what it once was, the moment when the future became now is forever lost.

Originally published as 'Lost in an Instant,' 8 September 2016, https://lukemckernan.com/2016/09/08/lost-in-an-instant, and reproduced here with small emendations. The 2016 Olympic Games took place in Rio, Brazil, 5-21 August.

---

[7] Scannell, *Television and the Meaning of 'Live,'* pp. 211-212.

58.

Well, Here We Are In Front of the Elephants

The birth of YouTube

YouTube is five years old. On 23 April 2005, Jawed Karim stood before a video camera wielded by Yakov Lapitsky in front of the elephant enclosure at San Diego Zoo. Karim gave the anxious look at the camera we all give when we sense that filming has started and we ought to have to say something, and then uttered the immortal words, 'Well, here we are in front of the elephants.' There was not much else he could say—there were the elephants, it was a self-evidently true statement. Nevertheless he added that 'these guys have really, really, really long trunks,' a statement that could be challenged both for its irrelevance and for the fact that very few animals other than elephants have trunks, so theirs are not so much long as just about the right size. 'And that's pretty much all there is to say' were his concluding words, and the video was over—all nineteen seconds of it.

And that was the first video to be uploaded onto *YouTube*, entitled *Me at the Zoo* (USA 2025).[1] It is not, on first sight, the most notable of starts for a revolution in how we communicate, but Jawed Karim and his colleagues were not then aware of what they were going to unleash upon the world. But *Me at the Zoo* is a revolutionary film in its way. It is a film without purpose, a passing statement, a shrug of the shoulders expressed in video. It does not entertain, instruct, make a point, debate or have any kind of structure to it. Because of the platform, the cheapness of the camera equipment, the ease of uploading, and the available bandwidth, here is something which we had not seen in moving images beforehand—video as non-event. This is part of what makes *YouTube* so special. It is a home to much creativity, but although that is marvellous in itself, it is not fundamentally new. But film made simply for the purpose of filling space, film that shows us off-guard, not performing—that is something that commercial film and television

---

[1] https://www.youtube.com/watch?v=jNQXAC9IVRw.

Jawed Karim at the zoo

have seldom allowed space for, if ever. The home movie has to a degree performed this function historically, but home movies are — as a rule — purposeful. Economics has also decided their content, since film and processing cost money and what you shot on your cinefilm has to represent best value. The avant garde has tried to do away with film's habitual structures, and plays with time and space in a way that seems close to what *YouTube* encourages, but ultimately the avant garde is every bit as studied in form and technique as conventional film.

Me at the Zoo, and the countless videos that have followed it, have been created because there was a space to be filled. People have filled that space with all manner of videos, many of which have a clear purpose (to entertain, to instruct, to insult, to argue, to show off, and so on), but just as many have no more purpose than to say, here I am, or I have nothing much to say today, or I have just seen this so I videoed it. And then even those videos which do have some sort of purpose — often those of people saying hello to friends, sharing information, or responding to someone else's personal video — often these are most fascinating for the moments beyond the main action. We see people preparing to film, or thinking what to say next, just being themselves. Film traditionally has never found space for such moments. It has always been so studied, so concerned to be an art form, worried about cutting out waste. *YouTube* reveals us at points when we are arguably at our most interesting, when we are still thinking, when we are not yet sure what we want to say. It has put the private into a public space, and changed our ideas of both utterly.

Originally published as 'Well, Here We Are in Front of the Elephants,' 22 April 2010, http://britishlibrary.typepad.co.uk/movingimage/2010/04/well-here-we-are-in-front-of-the-elephants.html, and reproduced here with small emendations.

59.

Films Beget Films

The art of the footage researcher

Watching a BBC television programme on the history of the UK and the European Union, *Europe: Them or Us* (UK 2016), I noted the great amount of archive footage used and how skilfully it had been woven into the argument.[1] I looked, as I always do on such occasions, at the credits, to see from where the footage had been taken, and who had been the researcher. Happily all of the archive sources were named and likewise the researcher, Alex Cowan. Now I can remember him when he was just starting out in the business, probably in the late 1980s, and it got me to thinking about the overlooked art of the footage researcher, and how much they as a profession have contributed to history and culture.

For a good part of my own professional life, I have been lucky to have known many great footage researchers, some still in the business, some now working in other fields, and a few sadly no longer with us: Elly Beintema, Lisa Pontecorvo, James Barker, Jane Mercer, Aileen McAllister, Gerry Healy, Liz Heasman, Rosalind Bentley, Jack Amos, Judy Patterson, Declan Smith, Stuart McKay, Cy Young, Maggi Cook, Alex Cowan, Kathy Manners, Tony Dalton, Victoria Stable, Christine Whittaker, and many more. Some have crossed the barrier between footage research and production, such as Jerry Kuehl (*The World at War*), Lutz Becker (producer of documentaries on the rise of Hitler), Steve Humphries (oral and social historian turned filmmaker), Jonathan Lewis (*The First World War*), Taylor Downing (*Flashback*) or Adrian Wood (*The British Empire in Colour* and other 'colour' series). All have contributed greatly to some of the most intelligent and memorable programming of the past few decades.

Film is a time machine, or so it appears to be. It records the scenes and the sounds of the points in time in which it was created,

---

[1] *Europe: Them Or Us* was a two-part series, broadcast in the UK on BBC Two, 12 April and 19 April 2016.

and when played back it shows us those times. However, what we see is always coloured by our own times, so that what appears to be a fixed archive of the past is in fact ever-changing, because we the viewers must always change. This elusive history is what makes archive film so magnetic, though equally so frustrating—the vision of a receding truth. It is what has drawn a distinguished if largely unheralded band of people to devote their professional lives to uncovering its mysteries. We should do much more to praise them, and to learn from them.

The footage researcher's role in life lies somewhere between a poet and a drudge. Their job is to find films in archives that will illustrate the theme of the film or programme for which they have been commissioned to work. They have to find clips that either match what the producer has in mind, or that the script dictates, or they can find material that help shape the programme in a particular direction. They have to negotiate prices for the footage, to arrange the necessary rights agreements, and to deliver the purchased footage and paperwork to the production team. They have to know both history and film history, appreciating the importance of release dates, issue numbers, context, provenance.

Their role as part of that team varies from production to production. Some researchers—the most fortunate ones—are included at the start of the process and play a key role in shaping the look and feel of the finished programme. Others—which tend to form the majority—are there on short contracts with a brief to provide just so much archive wallpaper, say three minutes for inclusion in a thirty-minute programme, and make sure what you get is cheap, with worldwide rights in perpetuity, in colour, and we must have something that no one else has seen before. And you have got two days in which to get it.

The latter is what helps destroy the soul of the researcher, though such commissions do at least help to pay the mortgage. Because each footage researcher is on a quest for the truth, and the greater the opportunity they are given, and the greater the trust the producer has in their skills, the more rewarding the quest will be.

For it is not simply a case of finding a piece of film that matches a line in the script. Anyone can be handed a script where the Battle of the Somme is mentioned, and put in a phone call to Imperial War Museums for that going over-the-top trench footage that we have all seen so many times. The thrill lies in matching image to mood, historical truth to visual truth. This is where the art, and the poetry lies. Film is not reality; it is a reflection of reality. I used to think, in my early days as a film archivist, that the most important thing for an archive film programme was to have clips that showed exactly the events that they described; and the greatest crime was for a film to be shown that claimed to depict an event that it did not. The classic example is the battle of Jutland, the great naval confrontation of 1916 and so an important subject for many programmes about the First World War. But there were no film cameras at Jutland, so how can any programme about Jutland that uses archive film be in any way truthful?

At a basic level, it is not possible. Stills can be used, or maybe fiction film clips, but should you make it clear that they are fictional? And if you use footage from another naval battle, should you tell the viewer? Does the viewer care? Quite possibly not—they just want to have the story well told. They are interested in another kind of truth, to which images and sounds are mere servants.

I have come to realise that insisting the clips must portray what they originally portrayed is a form of pedantry, and that poetic licence is not only a necessity but frequently a virtue. Films have useful meanings outside their original historical contexts, and it is this richness that makes them such useful tools for the researcher. Of course, we will prefer it if archive film clips are what it is said that they are—the power of knowing that what we are seeing actually happened and that the camera recorded it for us is considerable. But there are other forces at play, and managing these is where the great art of footage research lies.

The assembling of pre-existing actuality film to create a new reality is nearly as old as film itself. Compilations at the start of the First World War, such as Charles Urban's *With the Fighting Forces of Europe* (UK 1914), demonstrated what could be done with a footage library. Newsreel companies started to create literal compilations around such obvious topics as war, royalty and aviation, but such works merely collated the obvious. The person who demonstrated that here was a new art form was the Soviet film editor Esfir Shub, creator of such compilation films as *Padenie dinastii Romanovykh* (*The Fall of the Romanov Dynasty*) (USSR 1927) and *Rossiya Nikolaya II I Lev Tolstoy* (*The Russia of Nicholas II and Lev Tolstoi*) (USSR 1928). Shub created both art form and method. She sought out every possible footage source, uncovering collections no longer thought to exist, rescued film stored in damp conditions where the emulsion was already peeling away from the base, assembled her material before making her selection, catalogued it all, then chose precisely according to her theme—while letting the quality of the footage help determine the final form. The task, and the principles involved, have remained the same ever since.

Compilation films grew in number as an awareness of the potential of a history told through film grew, along with the burgeoning of the newsreel archives over time. Notable examples between Shub and the rise of television include *The March of Time* news magazine series (1935-1951), notable for its contentious combination of actuality, archive and re-created actuality; Frank Capra's *Why We Fight* series (USA 1942-1945), made for the US War Department; Nicole Védrès' *Paris 1900* (France 1947); Alain Resnais' *Nuit et Brouillard* (*Night and Fog*) (France 1956), on the Nazi concentration camps; George Morrison's *Mise Éire* (Ireland 1959), on Irish nationalism; and Erwin Leiser's *Den Blodiga Tiden*, or *Mein Kampf* (Sweden 1959), on the Third Reich.

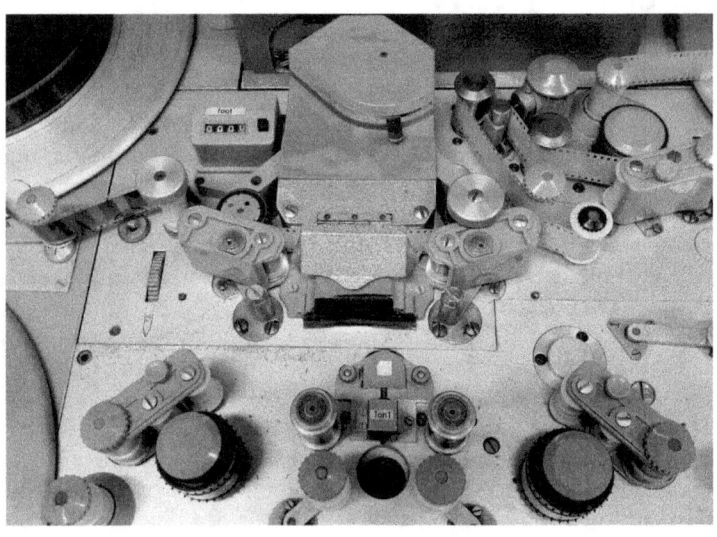

Steenbeck flatbed film editor.

It was television, however, which brought the archive compilation film to the fore. It was able to widen the range of subjects, broaden the audience, and allow for extended treatment of a theme through multiple episodes. Epic series such as the BBC's *The Great War* (UK 1964) and ITV's *The World at War* (UK 1973-1974) used archive film to overpowering effect. However the reaching for effect brought controversy. *The Great War*'s use of fiction film clips mixed in with actuality, and its notorious choice to flip some film so that the Allies were always fighting from the left and the Germans from the right, helped encourage a new school of academic and film historians—Nicholas Pronay, Anthony Aldgate, Paul Smith, Arthur Marwick—who became fascinated by the 'arranged reality' of such films, to use a phrase suggested by Jay Leyda in his great book *Films Beget Films*, published in 1964 and I think still unique in taking the compilation film as its subject.[2]

Audiences did not care about how the film had been manipulated—unless they could tell it had been manipulated. But those who did care were the academics who wanted to know what sort of evidence film offered, and with them a new breed of film professional, the footage researcher, whose task it became to find film that would tell honestly the story that had to be told. They absorbed themselves in histories; got to know every archive, public, commercial and private, in many countries; scoured catalogue cards and shotlists for what they revealed and what they had left out; spent hour after hour hunched over Steenbeck table viewers, poring over films forwards and backwards; papered up sections ready for telecine transfer; and gradually built up a vast knowledge of how the twentieth century had been recorded and preserved on film, with the understanding of how such footage could be re-arranged to be made meaningful again. From this knowledge came such great series as *Out of the Doll's House* (UK 1988), *Forbidden Britain* (UK 1994), *People's Century* (UK/USA 1995-1997) and *The First World War* (UK 2003)—and further afield the work of America's Ken Burns and France's Serge Viallet.

People's Century represented perhaps the peak of the archive compilation series, with its thrilling coup of showing archive film of an ordinary person in extraordinary times, then cutting to that person speaking today, located by some ingenious researcher. It brought home the reality behind the arranged reality. But audience tastes were changing. Producers turned to recreations with actors, colourisation of monochrome footage, and the use of star presenters who just had to stand in a battlefield and conjure up pictures for you with words. Who needs archive film of Jutland when you can just stick historian Dan Snow on a boat in the North Sea and get him to point to where the two fleets were arrayed?[3]

---

[2] Jay Leyda, *Films Beget Films* (London: George Allen & Unwin, 1964).

[3] In *Battle of Jutland: The Navy's Bloodiest Day*, tx. 29 May 2016 (BBC Two), broadcast not long after this essay was originally written, Dan Snow does exactly that—while using archive film supposedly of Jutland as well.

At the same time, online footage libraries started popping up everywhere, and locating footage no longer seemed like a job requiring time, skill or taste. Anyone could do it. Archive producer Jerry Kuehl writes a column in the footage business journal *Archive Zones* on the misuse of archive film by unthinking producers—it is call 'The Office Cat,' because who else do you need to track down footage?[4] The Office Cat loves to point out footage howlers—military hardware in use years before it was invented, films purporting to show events where it is known no film was taken, indeed films showing events before film was invented. I do not always agree with such complaints—as I have tried to argue, there are truths that lie beyond historical truths, but there is a general slovenliness in the use of archive film by some that would never be tolerated for textual sources.

Happily colourisation and re-enactments seem to have been a passing phase, and while presenter-led history television remains common, there has been a modest resurgence of the responsible use of archive footage in programmes.[5] This has been encouraged in the UK by the social history programming nurtured by specialist channel BBC Four, which has demonstrated that audiences prefer archive film when it draws attention to itself. The days of the epic historical series with hours of archive film meticulously researched and contextualised seem over, but new footage continues to be unearthed, such as the opening up of Russian archives, or the spectacular discovery of collections such as the Mitchell & Kenyon archive of Edwardian working-class life, and archive compilation films are looking fresher than ever. There is a growing taste for archive films arranged for art's rather than history's sake, from the haunting reveries of John Akomfrah, such as *Mnemosyne* (UK 2010), to Penny Woolcock's collaboration with the band British Sea Power, *From the Sea to the Land Beyond* (UK 2012).

So one hopes there is still work out there for the footage researcher, even in the era of *YouTube*. But more should be done to appreciate the work that they do. There should be serious study made of the role of the footage researcher. The complex relationship between the original meanings a film had, and the meanings

---

[4] Jerry Kuehl diez in 2018; *Archives Zones* ceased publication in the same year. His video series *Kuehl's Reels*, which investigates the misuse of archive footage, remains on *YouTube* via the *Intelligent Channel*, https://tinyurl.com/mry6hc9j.
[5] Colourisation has enjoyed a resurgence since the production of Peter Jackson's First World War documentary *They Shall Not Grow Old* (New Zealand/UK 2018). See the essay 'The Colours of War' in this book.

it accrues through being shown again in a new context, and the footage researcher's role in negotiating this transference, demands a deeper appreciation. It is not just the re-arrangement of reality; it is the poetics of the profession that intrigue me.

Of course they are working on behalf of producers, and it is the latter who determine what the finished programme will say and how it will say it. But only the footage researcher knows the secret history of the films they have found, bridging the world between the vault and the screen. They know the meanings lost in the transference, as much as the meanings gained. Above all they know that their work creates a kind of history like no other—impressionistic, emotional, elusive but persuasive. We should be understanding it better.

Originally published as 'Films Beget Films,' 26 April 2016, https://lukemckernan.com/2016/04/26/films-beget-films, and reproduced here with small emendations.

60.

Back to Life

Turning portrait photographs into life

I have a family photograph. I know who the woman on the left is, but not the woman on the right, and I long to know more. If only she could tell me something about herself. If only she could talk.

Well, one day maybe not so far away, she will.

I have written about colourisation in its various forms, bemoaning its use in documentaries using archive film, while recognising the fascination that applying colour to photographic records of the past has for many. Most recently this has involved trying the Colourise app, which has enabled many to use basic colourisation to convert black-and-white photographs into colour, of a sort.[1] I mocked the idea by trying out the software on stills from modern feature films shot in monochrome, but it is all too tempting to upload that old photograph from black-and-white days, and see family or friends past given some extra semblance of convincing life, a twitch to the corpse.[2]

But colour will not be enough — we will want movement, and speech. On the former, things are advancing at a significant rate. Deepfake software has caused much alarm over its potential to fool people into believing a public figure is saying something that they have never said, as demonstrated by the viral video of Jordan Peele impersonating the voice of Barack Obama over a video of Obama apparently mouthing those very words.[3] Such fears have

---

[1] Colourise.sg is no longer available (2025), but has been succeeded by a plethora of similar colourisation apps.

[2] The essay on colourisation and archive film, 'The Colours of War,' is reproduced in this book. Other colourisation essays are 'Monochrome,' https://lukemckernan.com/2018/08/11/monochrome (on Dan Jones and Marina Amaral's *The Colour of Time: A New History of the World 1850-1960*) and 'Hidden Colours,' https://lukemckernan.com/2019/04/27/hidden-colours (on converting images from modern monochrome films into colour).

[3] *You Won't Believe What Obama Says in This Video!*, https://www.youtube.com/watch?v=cQ54GDm1eL0.

yet to be translated into the actual world of news, though last year there was worry about a fake video of Donald Trump mocking climate change, produced by a Belgian political party.[4] What was interesting about this was not that it was a convincing recreation of Trump, designed to fool, but that it was not. The Trump figure was an obvious piece of fakery, and the video's commentary admitted as much ('we all know that climate change is fake, just like this video,' 'Trump' tells us). Yet some people still fell for it, complaining bitterly about the American president's prejudice. The story shows that visual authenticity is a complex business. We can be fooled by the palpable fake as much as the plausible fake, if we are so minded.

More convincing, and more indicative of what comes next, is a video released the other day in which Salvador Dalí asks you to take a selfie with him.[5] The video has been created by superimposing a synthesis of Dalí's facial expressions over an actor the same size as the artist, with texts taken from interviews and letters voiced by another actor (in English, French and Spanish). It has been created for the Dalí Museum in St. Petersburg, Florida, which is hosting an exhibition entitle *Dalí Lives*. It is guaranteed that much more of this sort of thing will follow, as the cost of it falls. Imagine visiting a stately home or historical site in the near future, and instead of being greeted by an actor in costume you have Henry VIII telling you his side of the story, then each wife telling you theirs. Add extra dollops of A.I., and you will be holding conversations with them.

Such videos can be created because there is a substantial bank of images of the subject, from which the software can derive convincing verisimilitude in motion. Famous people from modern times have been photographed countless times, but nowadays we are all photographed countless times and could be similarly reanimated, except that we are still here and we video ourselves constantly as well. What would be the point?

But what of those for whom only a few images exist, or even a single image? And what if that image were not even a photograph, but a painting? Can they be brought back to life?

---

[4] Jane Lytvynenko, 'A Belgian Political Party Is Circulating A Trump Deepfake Video,' *BuzzFeed News*, 20 May 2018, https://www.buzzfeednews.com/article/janelytvynenko/a-belgian-political-party-just-published-a-deepfake-video.
[5] Dami Lee, 'Deepfake Salvador Dalí takes selfies with museum visitors,' *The Verge*, 10 May 2019, https://www.theverge.com/2019/5/10/18540953/salvador-dali-lives-deepfake-museum.

A family photograph.

This week there have been reports of an algorithm developed in Russia which pretty much does this. Created by the Samsung A.I. Centre in Moscow and the Skolkovo Institute of Science and Technology, the technology takes a few images of a subject and fuses them into a credible speaking version by training it via the VoxCeleb dataset of human speech amassed by the Visual Geometry Group at Oxford University.[6]

The Realistic Neural Talking Head Models, as they call them, have been mostly created using eight or so images, but it is possible to work with fewer. The most startling outcome of the project is what can be done with a single image. They have made fleeting talking models from single famous photographs of Marilyn Monroe, Albert Einstein, Fyodor Dostoyevsky—and Salvador Dalí. Then they go further. In their demonstration video's most astonishing coup, we see the subject of two paintings, Ivan Kramskoi's 'Portrait of an Unknown Woman' and Leonardo da

---

[6] The paper behind the project is Egor Zakharov, Aliaksandra Shysheya, Egor Burkov, Victor Lempitsky, 'Few-Shot Adversarial Learning of Realistic Neural Talking Head Models,' 20 May 2019, https://arxiv.org/abs/1905.08233v1. The VoxCeleb dataset is at https://www.robots.ox.ac.uk/~vgg/data/voxceleb.

Vinci's 'Mona Lisa,' each turned into three 'talking' versions of themselves.[7]

They are not actually talking, as there is no sound, though they must have been given words to mouth at least, but you can see how this could be developed. For a famous dead person, you could imagine them speaking words they once wrote. Anne Frank could read us her diary; Jane Austen could trigger a publishing explosion with a new kind of audio-visual e-book; William Shakespeare would welcome us to Stratford in David Mitchell's voice.

Living portraits

Realistic Neural Talking Head Model of the Mona Lisa, from
Few-Shot Adversarial Learning of Realistic Neural Talking Head Models.

But even the obscure could be given words to say. There might be diaries or letters that they wrote, and if nothing survives then they could be given words appropriate to their time, locality, class and preoccupations. Their avatars could be fed some basic facts about their lives, and then the algorithms would do the rest, creating the semblance of a life much as colourisation is now doing. It would be as fundamentally meaningless as colourisation is, but how we would love to be deluded. If it is not them, then it *could* be them. It is more than a black-and-white photograph, trapped in its moment of time, which tells me so little. It has a life.

Scary as the implications are, such things will come to pass, we can have no doubt. Aside from the obvious ethical and legal

---

[7] *Few-Shot Adversarial Learning of Realistic Neural Talking Head Models,* https://www.youtube.com/watch?v=p1b5aiTrGzY.

conundrums (what happens when someone makes a video of you saying something you never said?), all sorts of issues must be raised about the archival status of images, whether still or moving. The idea that an archival image should be understood as the output of a particular time and technology, to be comprehended best in its primary state, could be changing. While one still needs an *ur*-image from which to create a digital derivative, it is what is derived that may end up supplying that which is meaningful to us.

The archival digital image may come to mean that which can be inferred from it—you could call it the inferred image. Through deep learning techniques, the image will relay all that previously we imagined it might do when we stared at it and wished that it could tell us more. This could profoundly alter our sense of what we collect, what it signifies, and how it should be understood. It is where the future may take us, but it is also something that lies at the very roots of the moving image. Eadweard Muybridge's sequence photographs of humans and animals, taken in the 1870s and 1880s before photographic moving images existed, nevertheless anticipate motion pictures through the implication of their creation. The images are willing themselves into life.[8]

Of course, the digital image's inherent ability to be manipulated, with all that that means for the understanding of truth and significance, has been long understood, from William J. Mitchell's *The Reconfigured Eye: Visual Truth in the Post-photographic Era* (1992) onwards.[9] The digital image has profoundly changed our sense of what an image means, simply because it is not an end point but a starting point, a row of numbers understood through code, inviting us to tease out its implications.

The question that arises is who owns these inferred meanings? Our audiovisual archives, by which is meant still and moving images, and sound, are filled with objects whose digital lives may be about to alter dramatically. We are already seeing several television programmes riding on the back of the colourisation coup of Peter Jackson's *They Shall Not Grow Old* (New Zealand/UK 2018), which made soldiers of the First World War seem to live anew in colour and speech. The business is bound to expand. There has long been manipulation of images by producers once they have got their hands on the object from the archive. The change comes when it is the archive that does the manipulation, or is at least

---

[8] See 'The Running Man' in this book.
[9] William J. Mitchell, *The Reconfigured Eye: Visual Truth In The Post–photographic Era* (Cambridge, Mass./MIT Press, 1992).

complicit in such activity. Such archives could be on the verge of a new stage in their existence, caring no longer simply for passive objects but for active ones. That which they hold has the potential to mushroom into multiple lives, feeding our demand for an ever more tangible connection with the past. It could end up being an obligation, to unlock the potential in the digitised image, as standard. The audiovisual archive of the future may be an unbounded virtual world.

The woman on the right of the photograph on page 381 could be my great-grandmother, Susanna. We just do not know. There are no other pictures of her, and no clues within the photograph, except that it would be her sister on the left. If she could talk, what would I have her say? If she said, 'Yes, that is who I am,' would I believe her? After a time, perhaps I would.

Originally published as 'Back to Life,' 27 May 2019, https://lukemcker-nan.com/2019/05/27/back-to-life, and reproduced here with small emendations. In 2021 the genealogy site *MyHeritage* launched an animation app, Deep Nostalgia, https://www.myheritage.com/deep-nostalgia.. This converts still images of people, uploaded by the user, into animated portraits. It works best if the subject is looking directly at the camera. It is noticeable that the app makes your ancestor smile.

By the same author

Topical Budget: The Great British News Film
(British Film Institute, 1992)

*Walking Shadows: Shakespeare in the National Film and
Television Archive* (British Film Institute, 1994)
(with Olwen Terris)

Who's Who of Victorian Cinema: A Worldwide Survey
(British Film Institute, 1996) (with Stephen Herbert)

A Yank in Britain: The Lost Memoirs of Charles Urban
(The Projection Box, 1999)

Yesterday's News: The British Cinema Newsreel Reader
(British Universities Film & Video Council, 2002)

Moving Image Knowledge and Access: The BUFVC Handbook
(British Universities Film & Video Council, 2007)
(with Cathy Grant)

*Shakespeare on Film, Television and Radio: The Researcher's
Guide* (British Universities Film & Video Council, 2009)
(with Eve-Marie Oesterlen and Olwen Terris)

*Charles Urban: Pioneering the Non-Fiction Film in Britain and
America, 1897-1925* (University of Exeter Press, 2013)

Breaking the News: 500 Years of News in Britain
(British Library, 2022) (with Jackie Harrison)

Picturegoers: A Critical Anthology of Eyewitness Experiences
(University of Exeter Press, 2022)

Index